LET'S ST

Let's Study

MARK

Sinclair B. Ferguson

THE BANNER OF TRUTH TRUST

THE BANNER OF TRUTH TRUST
3 Murrayfiel Road, Edinburgh EH12 6EL
P.O. Box 621, Carlisle, Pennsylvania 17013, USA

*

© Sinclair B. Ferguson 1999
First Published 1999
Reprinted 2002
ISBN 0 85151 755 2

*

Typeset in 11/12pt Ehrhardt MT
at the Banner of Truth Trust, Edinburgh
Printed and bound in Finland by
WS Bookwell

*

FOR

ANNE FLAVELLE

IN MEMORY OF
ALAN
WHO FOLLOWED JESUS CHRIST
AND ENCOURAGED OTHERS
TO COME WITH HIM

Contents

Contents

Preface

Let's Study Mark is the second volume in a projected series of
books which explain and apply the message of the New Testament.
The series is designed to meet a specific need in the church. While
not technical commentaries, each volume will comment on the text
of a biblical book; and while not merely lists of practical
applications, they are concerned with the ways in which the
teaching of Scripture can affect and transform our lives today.
Understanding the Bible's message and applying its teaching are
the aims.

Like other volumes in the series, *Let's Study Mark* seeks to
combine explanation and application. Its concern is to be helpful
to ordinary Christian people by encouraging them to understand
the message of the Bible and apply it to their own lives. The reader
in view is not the person who is interested in all the detailed
questions which fascinate the scholar, although behind the writing
of each study lies an appreciation for careful and detailed scholarship. The aim is exposition of Scripture written in the language of
a friend, seated alongside you with an open Bible.

Let's Study Mark is designed to be used in various contexts. It
can be used simply as an aid for individual Bible study. Some may
find it helpful to use in their devotions with husband or wife, or to
read in the context of the whole family.

In order to make these studies more useful, not only for
individual use but also for group study in Sunday School classes
and home, church or college, study guide material will be found on
pp. 277–303. Sometimes we come away frustrated rather than
helped by group discussions. Frequently that is because we have
been encouraged to discuss a passage of Scripture which we do not

[xi]

understand very well in the first place. Understanding must always be the foundation for enriching discussion and thoughtful, practical application. Thus, in addition to the exposition of Mark, the additional material provides questions to encourage personal thought and study, or to be used as discussion starters. The Group Study Guide divides the material into thirteen sections and provides direction for leading and participating in group study and discussion.

The text which forms the basis of the studies is *The New International Version.*

The Gospel of Mark is one of the keys to the New Testament, indeed to the whole Bible. The most compact of the Bible's four accounts of the life and ministry of Jesus, it is an ideal starting place for anyone asking the question, 'Who is Jesus?'. It is safe to say, in addition, that every Christian should have a working knowledge of its contents.

Ten years ago an earlier version of these studies appeared under the title *Understanding the Gospel* (Eastbourne: Kingsway, 1989). That book had not been very long in print when the stock was destroyed in a warehouse fire! Since the earlier version was written with the same goal as the volumes in the *Let's Study* series, I am delighted that, phoenix-like, the material which it contained is now arising from the ashes.

In working again through Mark's narrative of the life and ministry of Jesus, I have found it more thrilling than ever to have the privilege of reading and studying this Gospel. It is my hope and prayer that something of that thrilling privilege will be shared by everyone who reads these pages.

SINCLAIR B. FERGUSON
St George's-Tron Church
Glasgow, Scotland

The Gospel According to Mark

When John Mark wrote out his 'good news' about Jesus two thousand years ago, his Gospel was a completely new kind of book. No one had ever written one before. In fact, no one would have known what a Gospel was!

Of course, books about great men and the records of their lives had been composed. What made the Gospel of Mark unique was this: it was not written merely as the memoir of Jesus as a great man, not even of the greatest man who had ever lived. Rather, it was meant to persuade its readers that Jesus was the Son of God. Mark says as much in the first words of his book: 'The beginning of the gospel about Jesus Christ, the Son of God.'

This theme – the identity of Jesus of Nazareth – is one which reappears in the course of the story of his life and work. Mark records how, later, Jesus himself raised the question: 'Who do people say I am?' (*Mark* 8:27). At the climax of the Gospel, the same question appears. This time it is found on the lips of the high priest: 'Are you the Christ, the Son of the Blessed One?' (*Mark* 14:61). It is the central question in the entire book. It keeps appearing, in different ways, to remind us that this is the question we are being invited to ask, and to answer, for ourselves.

Who is Jesus of Nazareth? What is the good news (gospel) about him?

We all have our own answer to that question. This book presents us with Mark's answer. It is full of important information which will help us to understand what Jesus said and did, what his life was really like, and who he claimed to be. It is the earliest reliable record we have about him. For that reason, understanding Mark's Gospel is a major step in coming to know, understand and believe in Jesus himself.

THE AUTHOR OF THE GOSPEL

Although we call this book 'Mark's Gospel', it was actually written anonymously. But there is an unbroken tradition in the Christian church, dating back to the second century, that it was indeed written by John Mark.

Around the year A.D. 140, Papias, who was the bishop of the church at Hierapolis, recorded something he had heard from an older contemporary: 'The elder said this also: "Mark, having become the interpreter of Peter, wrote down accurately whatever he remembered of the things said and done by the Lord, but not however in order."'

Within another forty years, two further testimonies tell the same story. An anonymous preface to the Gospel of Mark, written sometime after A.D. 160, records:

> Mark . . . who is called 'stump-fingered', because he had rather small fingers in comparison with the stature of his body. He was the interpreter of Peter. After the death of Peter himself he wrote down this same gospel in the region of Italy.

A similar testimony is found among the writings of a leading early Christian writer, Irenaeus of Lyons: 'After the death of [Peter and Paul] Mark, the disciple of Peter, also transmitted to us in writing the things preached by Peter.'

These statements tell us a number of things about this Gospel. It was written by John Mark who was the friend and disciple of Simon Peter. In fact, the Gospel Mark wrote was in a sense Peter's; Irenaeus even suggests that Mark's Gospel contains the kind of account of Jesus which Simon Peter himself used to give in his preaching.

You will notice this as you read through the Gospel. Parts of it breathe the air of an eye-witness account, others even express Peter's own personality. In Mark's Gospel, everything seems to happen 'immediately' or 'without delay'. That sounds just like Simon Peter!

In this connection, it is interesting to notice the similarity between the sermon Peter preached to the household of Cornelius and the structure of Mark's Gospel:

You know the message God sent to the people of Israel, telling the good news of peace through Jesus Christ, who is Lord of all. You know what has happened throughout Judea, beginning in Galilee after the baptism that John preached – how God anointed Jesus of Nazareth with the Holy Spirit and power, and how he went around doing good and healing all who were under the power of the devil, because God was with him.

We are witnesses of everything he did in the country of the Jews and in Jerusalem. They killed him by hanging him on a tree, but God raised him from the dead on the third day and caused him to be seen. He was not seen by all the people, but by witnesses whom God had already chosen – by us who ate and drank with him after he rose from the dead. He commanded us to preach to the people and to testify that he is the one whom God appointed as judge of the living and the dead. All the prophets testify about him that everyone who believes in him receives forgiveness of sins through his name (*Acts* 10:36–43).

Like the Gospel, the sermon begins with the baptism by John in Jordan, the anointing of Jesus with the Spirit, and the ministry of Jesus commencing in Galilee and ending in Jerusalem. It then records the eye-witness account of what Jesus did in Jerusalem, his crucifixion and resurrection. The Gospel follows the outline of Peter's sermon very closely. Both convey the sense of commitment to Jesus Christ which we know Peter had, and which Mark himself was eventually to show.

JOHN WHO?

We know relatively little about John Mark (to give him his full name). It is almost certain that he was a native of Jerusalem. His mother, Mary, owned a house there large enough for many Christians to gather in it for prayer (*Acts* 12:12). The family were closely related to Barnabas, one of the leading early Christians, and also a man of considerable wealth (*Acts* 4:36–37).

It has been suggested that Mark actually identifies himself in the course of writing his Gospel. Two anonymous figures appear towards the end of the narrative. Mark 14:14 refers to a householder in Jerusalem in whose home the disciples and Jesus celebrated the Passover. Mark 14:51 refers to a young man who fled naked from the scene of Jesus' arrest. It is certainly not impossible that these are references to Mark – rather like the appearance of an artist in some minor role in a scene he had painted himself. More important, and certain, is the fact that Mark joined the mission of Paul and Barnabas (*Acts* 12:25). Later, however, he left and returned to Jerusalem under something of a cloud. When Barnabas suggested that Mark should accompany them again, Paul refused. So considerable was the difference over him that Paul and Barnabas thereafter engaged on separate missions (*Acts* 15:36–41).

It is encouraging to discover that Mark reappears in the New Testament in three of Paul's letters. In Colossians 4:10 Paul writes: 'My fellow-prisoner Aristarchus sends you his greetings, as does Mark, the cousin of Barnabas. (You have received instructions about him; if he comes to you, welcome him.)' Obviously Paul and Mark were united again, the past had been forgiven, and Paul was making certain that none of the churches belittled Mark because of what had happened.

In Philemon verse 24, Paul mentions Mark as one of his 'fellow-workers'.

In Paul's last recorded letter, he urged Timothy: 'Get Mark and bring him with you, because he is helpful to me in my ministry' (*2 Tim.* 4:11). No more eloquent testimony to John Mark's value as a Christian could be expected.

Later in the New Testament records, we find Mark alongside Simon Peter as his 'son' in the faith (*1 Pet.* 5:13). Peter and his little group of fellow-workers are in 'Babylon' at this time, probably a reference to Rome. If this is so it confirms the early traditions in the Christian church that Mark originally wrote the Gospel in Italy and for the use of the church at Rome.

As you read through the Gospel, this background may bring its contents to life, from time to time. Here is someone writing about Jesus who was probably on the fringes of the early disciple band; his relatives included those who had known him; his friends and perhaps even his parents were those who had known him well. Here is a man who has had first-hand knowledge of the Apostles Peter and Paul. Not only so, but he has experienced failure as well as success in the service of Christ. Perhaps it was this that first drew him so close to Peter. It was certainly this that would have helped him to understand how Peter must sometimes have felt during the ministry of Jesus. Now Mark is in Rome and writing for a church which the Roman emperor is persecuting. Paul has been martyred and Peter too; the infant church is like a ship tossed on the waves of an uncontrollable storm as it had been during Jesus' ministry (*Mark* 4:35–41). Will it survive? Where will it find strength? This Gospel provides the answers to these questions – and not only for the early church – for the church today as well. It was good news for the first century; it is good news for our own, too!

The Pattern of Mark's Gospel

Mark's Gospel develops the story of Jesus' ministry in a very straightforward and simple way.

INTRODUCTION
1:1–13. Jesus' ministry is set in the context of the ministry of his forerunner, John the Baptist.

MINISTRY IN GALILEE
1:14–6:13. Jesus' early public ministry in Galilee. Already in this section, Mark introduces us to the beginnings of the conflict between the religious leaders and Jesus which we shall see runs through the whole of the Gospel.

Jesus is described as the Lord of men and nature, and teaches some of the great principles which govern life in his kingdom. This section includes the rejection he experienced in his home town of Nazareth, and his sending out of his disciples to preach and teach the message he had brought concerning the kingdom of God.

WITHDRAWN FROM CONFLICT
6:14–8:30. A period of withdrawal which comes to a climax with Simon Peter confessing his faith in Jesus as the promised Messiah of God.

TOWARDS JERUSALEM
8:31-10:52. Jesus explains that he is a suffering Messiah, and will die in Jerusalem. The section ends with Jesus passing through Jericho on his way to Jerusalem for the last time in his life.

THE CONFLICT HEIGHTENS

11:1–13:37. Jesus ministers in Jerusalem, preaching and teaching in a context in which the scheming and opposition of the religious leaders grows almost daily, leading to its climax.

THE PASSION

14:1–15:47. Jesus spends his last hours with his disciples before he is betrayed by one of them, arrested, and tried by Jewish and Roman leaders alike. In a 'rigged' trial his opponents cannot produce evidence from their witnesses sufficient to condemn him. But he is condemned nevertheless, taken out and executed by crucifixion. He is buried in a borrowed tomb in front of which a large gravestone is rolled.

THE RESURRECTION

16:1–end. The Gospel comes to an end with the story of the resurrection of Jesus. Jesus is risen and is alive for evermore!

I

In the Beginning

The beginning of the gospel about Jesus Christ, the Son of
God. It is written in Isaiah the prophet: 'I will send my
messenger ahead of you, who will prepare your way' – 'a voice
of one calling in the desert, "Prepare the way for the Lord,
make straight paths for him."' And so John came, baptising
in the desert region and preaching a baptism of repentance for
the forgiveness of sins. The whole Judean countryside and all
the people of Jerusalem went out to him. Confessing their sins,
they were baptised by him in the Jordan River. John wore
clothing made of camel's hair, with a leather belt round his
waist, and he ate locusts and wild honey. And this was his
message: 'After me will come one more powerful than I, the
thongs of whose sandals I am not worthy to stoop down and
untie. I baptise you with water, but he will baptise you with
the Holy Spirit' (Mark 1:1–8).

How did the gospel begin? Each of the four Gospels gives us
a slightly different perspective on that question. Matthew
traces the story back through the family tree of Jesus to the
patriarch Abraham, to whom God had given his wonderful
promises (*Matt.* 1:1–17).

Luke traces it even further back. He wanted to emphasise the
universal appeal of Jesus, and so he set his life and ministry in
the context of the whole of human history, from its beginning in
Adam and Eve (*Luke* 3:21–37).

In a sense, John traces the gospel back even further. He calls
Jesus 'the Word' of God, and tells us that his origin lies in eternity.
He was with God in the beginning (*John* 1:1–14).

Mark begins his Gospel by telling us two simple things. First, the gospel is about Jesus Christ. It is not good advice about how to live, but good news about a person. Then secondly, Mark sets the scene for Jesus by telling us about John the Baptist and the significance of his life and ministry.

SCRIPTURE FULFILLED

In Malachi 3:1, God had promised that he would send a messenger to the people before the coming of his Messiah, whose task would be to prepare his way. Isaiah 40:3 gave a further description of this messenger. He would be a 'voice in the desert'. His message would be: 'Prepare for the coming of the Lord.'

The coming of Jesus was not an afterthought on God's part. It was something for which he had planned and prepared during the long years of the Old Testament. Now the time had come for God to work. He sent John as the messenger he had promised so long before. After centuries of silence, many recognised that God was speaking to his people once again. Now he was saying something new: God was about to speak for the last time.

Mark runs together two quotations here. He introduces them with the words: 'It is written in Isaiah the prophet.' Yet it is only the second quotation which comes from Isaiah. Why should they both have the same introduction? Did Mark make a mistake? Could it be that he did not know his Bible very well? Is this – right at the beginning of the earliest Gospel – an indication that it is far from being an error-free description of Jesus?

It stretches credibility to think that Mark would make such an elementary mistake. Perhaps he was quoting these words from an already existing summary of Old Testament texts which had been gathered together to bear witness to Jesus. The probable explanation is that it is only when Malachi 3:1 is quoted alongside the passage from Isaiah that the full significance of what Isaiah says is clear. The voice which cries out in the desert is actually the herald who immediately precedes his Master's visitation. Together the two passages explain John's significance and his relationship to Jesus. They indicate not only that the Lord's way was to be prepared, but that he was coming very soon.

PREACHING REPENTANCE

The burden of John's preaching was repentance (v. 4). He exposed his hearers' sins and called on them to turn from them, washing them away symbolically in the River Jordan by being baptised. Only in this way would they enjoy forgiveness and a new life.

John was the last of the Old Testament prophets. He made a tremendous impression on his contemporaries. Huge numbers came to hear him speak. There was what we would call a revival. People even came from Jerusalem to hear him. Think of going to the Yorkshire Dales from London because you had heard there was a man there who preached as though he really knew God and understood men's hearts too! Even some of those who attended Jerusalem's temple services were noticed among the listeners.

Everything about John told people he was a prophet. He was in the mould of Elijah. His clothing was 'desert wear'; his diet was desert food. He stood out from his contemporaries as clearly and recognisably as his great predecessor (see *2 Kings* 1:8).

John's message was also similar to Elijah's. The people had broken the covenant with God. They were under his judgment. Only by turning away from their sins and turning back to the Lord and his ways would they be ready when the long-promised Messiah came.

POINTING TO JESUS

In the Old Testament, the task of the prophet was twofold. He spoke God's word about the present, and he showed God's word about the future. We find John doing both of these things. He forth-told and fore-told the message of the Lord. He explained to the people the significance of the Messiah's coming: he would be more powerful than John. So much greater would his dignity be that John was scarcely worthy to untie the thongs of his sandals (v. 7). John also prophesied what this Messiah would do. In contrast with John's baptism with water, the One who came after him would baptise people with the Spirit of God himself.

John preached that the turning point of human history was about to take place. The Messiah was about to come. Only one adequate response was open to the people: repentance.

The style and content of John's ministry have a great deal to teach us today. His preaching was Spirit-directed in a special way. Like the Spirit, he did not seek glory for himself (see *John* 16:13–14). Instead he pointed people to Jesus. There is no clearer mark that we are filled with the Spirit of God. For the fullness of the Spirit does not primarily show itself in signs and wonders, but in the way we say (with John): '[Christ] must become greater; I must become less' (*John* 3:30).

Have you ever said that?

2

The Messiah

At that time Jesus came from Nazareth in Galilee and was baptised by John in the Jordan. As Jesus was coming up out of the water, he saw heaven being torn open and the Spirit descending on him like a dove. And a voice came from heaven: 'You are my Son, whom I love; with you I am well pleased.' At once the Spirit sent him out into the desert, and he was in the desert for forty days, being tempted by Satan. He was with the wild animals, and angels attended him (Mark 1:9–13).

One of the outstanding features of Mark's Gospel is its fast-moving style. He conveys a sense of constant activity in several interesting ways. For example, Mark constructs many of his sentences simply by joining one statement to another by the use of 'and'. He frequently uses the Greek word 'immediately', although this is not always clear in the NIV. In these simple ways he makes us feel the energy of the events he is describing.

He produces the same effect by describing very briefly what other Gospel writers spend a good deal of time on. The baptism and temptation of Jesus illustrate this. Matthew and Luke describe them in considerable detail (see *Matt.* 4 and *Luke* 4), while Mark devotes only a handful of verses to this strategic event in Jesus' life.

This does not mean that Mark wanted to play down these events. In fact, the brevity of his description underlines the starkness of what took place: Jesus the Saviour, the Son of God, stood with sinners in the River Jordan and was baptised by John. Jesus, the Lord of Creation (as Mark will later explain), went hungry and thirsty in the wilderness and was tempted by the devil. Mark did not feel that the contrast between Jesus' personal identity and Jesus' experience as Saviour needed to be underlined. It was enough simply to state the facts: he was the Son of God, yet he entered into the arena of flesh and blood, shared his life with sinful men and women, and experienced to the full the fiercest of onslaughts from the Tempter.

Mark identifies three elements in these verses.

INAUGURATION

The baptism of Jesus marked his public inauguration as the Messiah. He came into the world to be the Saviour of sinners. Now, for the first time, he engages in an activity which shows this. He has not come in pomp and circumstance to lord it over men; but in lowliness and humility, to save them. Here already he indicates how he will become our Saviour: by standing in the river in whose waters penitent Jews had symbolically washed away their sins, and allowing that water, polluted by those sins, to be poured over his perfect being.

Unlike the other Gospel writers, it did not serve Mark's purposes to tell his readers how John actually argued with Jesus about his being baptised. John knew that Jesus did not need to be baptised as a symbol of repentance – he had no sins from which he needed to repent. He was the spotless Lamb of God, who needed no offer of forgiveness. But Mark allows the inherent 'contradiction' to stand, because it leads us directly to the heart of Jesus' ministry. His baptism inaugurates him publicly into his role as the priest who bears away the sins of men in order to bring them forgiveness and salvation.

Jesus' water baptism inaugurated him into a ministry which reached its fulfilment later in his baptism in blood upon the cross (see *Luke* 12:50). What we have here is Jesus' public acknowledgement that he had come to stand where sinners should stand, receive what they should deserve, and in return give to them his gift of grace and fellowship with God.

IDENTIFICATION

As Jesus was coming out of the water, he saw heaven being torn open and the Spirit descending on him like a dove. It was an assurance to him of God's approval of his actions. Furthermore, now that he had publicly committed himself to his task of salvation, he was being 'sealed' by the Holy Spirit (*John* 6:27).

The *visual* part of God's seal came in the presence of the dove-Spirit. It is a reminder of the way in which God's judgment came to an end when the dove which Noah sent from the ark found a place to rest. It symbolises the beginning of God's new creation. It was as though he were saying: Jesus is the One in whom I will begin again.

But there was also a *verbal* part to God's seal of approval on Jesus. A voice spoke from heaven to identify him. It explained Jesus' identity by means of the Old Testament promises. Jesus is God's beloved Son; the One whom God loves; Jesus is the One with whom the Father is well pleased. Three Old Testament passages are used here. There is an echo of the voice which Abraham heard when he was challenged to sacrifice his only, much-loved son (*Gen.* 22:2); then of the proclamation of the Son as King (*Psa.* 2:7); lastly there is an echo of the words which introduce the Suffering Servant (*Isa.* 42:1).

The voice from heaven bears witness to Jesus' identity. He is the Son of God, the King in God's kingdom; he is much-loved and enjoys a unique relationship with his Father. He is also the One who has come to suffer for the sins of the people, the servant who would be wounded, bruised and chastised for others (*Isa.* 53:4–6).

The whole of Jesus' own understanding of his task and ministry is summarised in these three statements.

TEMPTATION

Mark's record now takes an unexpected turn. The Spirit of God has just descended on Jesus; now the same Spirit sends him out into the desert to face an onslaught of temptation from the hands of the devil.

Why should Mark (alone) specifically mention that Jesus was with 'wild animals' (v. 13)? Jesus Christ came to be what Paul called the last Adam and the second man (*1 Cor.* 15:45, 47). He came to undo what Adam had done by his sin and fall. But if he was to reverse what Adam had done, he needed to enter into the world not as Adam found it but as Adam had left it. So when he was tempted, he was not in a garden, like Adam. He was not, like Adam, surrounded by the animals over which he exercised dominion (*Gen.* 1:28). He was in a desert, surrounded by wild beasts. It was in a fallen, broken, sinful, disintegrating world that Jesus faced temptation and the powers of darkness, in order to win for his people a way back to the Tree of Life.

3

The Reign of God

After John was put in prison, Jesus went into Galilee,
proclaiming the good news of God. 'The time has come,' he
said. 'The kingdom of God is near. Repent and believe the
good news!' As Jesus walked beside the Sea of Galilee, he
saw Simon and his brother Andrew casting a net into the lake,
for they were fishermen. 'Come, follow me,' Jesus said, 'and
I will make you fishers of men.' At once they left their nets
and followed him. When he had gone a little farther, he saw
James son of Zebedee and his brother John in a boat, pre-
paring their nets. Without delay he called them, and they left
their father Zebedee in the boat with the hired men and
followed him (Mark 1:14–20).

The stage has now been set by Mark for the ministry of Jesus.
John has been the herald of his coming. His Father and his
Spirit had also heralded his identity as the long-promised Messiah.
He had faced his inaugural conflict with the kingdom of darkness.
Now John the Baptist had been imprisoned. It was time for Jesus
to begin his ministry in word and action. These verses record a
summary of the message Jesus preached, and the impact he made
upon people as he summoned them to respond to it.

THE MESSAGE

Jesus' message is outlined in verses fourteen to fifteen. It is, first
of all, 'good news'. Interestingly, the passage which Mark had
cited from Isaiah 40 (in verse three) had also spoken about the
proclamation of good news. In fact the subject matter was the same:

'See, the Sovereign Lord comes with power, and his arm rules for him' (*Isa.* 40:9–10). Isaiah had spoken about the 'gospel' of the reign of God in a world of darkness and disintegration. Now Jesus was saying that the message which Isaiah had prophesied was being fulfilled: 'The kingdom of God is near' (v. 15).

THE KINGDOM

What did Jesus mean? We tend to associate a kingdom with a geographical area over which a monarch reigns. But in Scripture 'the kingdom of God' describes an activity: God's reign over his people and his world. That rule was exercised wherever God was present. The Old Testament revelation had led people to believe that one day God would establish that reign personally. This was the 'good news' which Isaiah had brought. Jesus' words meant: the time has come; God's reign is beginning to be seen. But how? In Jesus himself. That was the meaning of the word from Psalm 2 spoken at his baptism. God was publicly installing his Son as King in his kingdom. From now on Jesus would speak and act publicly with authority and majesty.

The stories which follow are meant to illustrate the reign of God, now present among men in Jesus himself. He calls men into his kingdom; he subdues the forces of the kingdom of darkness; he restores those who are sick, and banishes the effects of sinfulness as well as forgiving the sins themselves. This is good news indeed!

REACTIONS

This message demands a response. If the kingdom of God has come near, and the King himself is already present, life must change. The old lifestyle of indifference to God and his will must be abandoned. Loyalty to the King must be the order of the day. There must be a personal application of the herald's summons: 'Prepare the way for the Lord, make straight paths before him' (v. 3). Your life must become consistent with the fact that a King is present.

But how? Jesus gives a straightforward answer: *Repent!* That is, turn away from your sinful lifestyle, and in the light of my presence live in a way that will please God. Abandon your old self-centred manner of life, and live the new life of a royal subject.

Was Jesus' message, then, no more than the best possible advice men could hear? By no means! Repentance can never exist on its own. It must always be accompanied by faith. Only through receiving the good news of the King – his proclamation of forgiveness and new power – can we ever turn our backs on sin and live in a way that pleases God. We abandon all our efforts to rule our own lives and establish our own kingdoms, but we succeed in doing that only when Jesus exercises his royal power over us through our trust in him and the message he brings us from God.

DISCIPLESHIP

The King has come to gather people into his kingdom. Almost casually, Mark tells us of the impact Jesus made on people's lives. In doing so, he illustrates what it means to 'repent and believe the good news'.

Simon and Andrew, James and John were invited to follow Jesus (v. 17). Probably the first readers of this Gospel had known Peter well enough, and listened to his sermons frequently enough to know that this was not the first encounter these men had had with Jesus (see *John* 1:35ff). Mark neither ignored nor deliberately hid that fact. But he wanted to show the challenge to discipleship in its simplest and starkest terms. It means hearing Jesus calling you, and leaving everything for him. For these men that entailed leaving their previous lifestyles and becoming the 'fishers of men' Jesus promised to make them (v. 17).

In principle the challenge is exactly the same for us. It may not necessarily involve such a dramatic change in our everyday occupations (although that is by no means infrequent); but Christ's call and his kingly reign over our lives does mean that from then on they are no longer at our own disposal. My family (v. 19), my occupation (v. 17), even my profitable business partnership – James and John shared a fishing business large enough to employ others (v. 20) – all must now be at the disposal of Jesus Christ.

These men were called to be 'fishers of men'. When the picture of 'fishing' is used to describe the activity of God in the Old

Testament, it always has an ominous ring to it. God's 'fishing' takes place in the context of judgment (for example, Jeremiah 16:16–18). Jesus did not hide that fact from his new disciples. Their mission was to rescue men from the judgment of God. The fact that his reign was already on the horizon lent an air of urgency to the work of those who were to be 'fishers of men'.

Being a disciple of Jesus involves a radical commitment to him and the urgent task of serving him. That is no less true today than it was for Peter and Andrew, James and John.

4

A Startled Congregation

They went to Capernaum, and when the Sabbath came, Jesus went into the synagogue and began to teach. The people were amazed at his teaching, because he taught them as one who had authority, not as the teachers of the law. Just then a man in their synagogue who was possessed by an evil spirit cried out, 'What do you want with us, Jesus of Nazareth? Have you come to destroy us? I know who you are – the Holy One of God!' 'Be quiet!' said Jesus sternly. 'Come out of him!' The evil spirit shook the man violently and came out of him with a shriek. The people were all so amazed that they asked each other, "What is this? A new teaching – and with authority! He even gives orders to evil spirits and they obey him." News about him spread quickly over the whole region of Galilee (Mark 1:21–28).

We traditionally associate Jesus with Nazareth. That was certainly his 'home town'. But there are some indications in the Gospels that, at least for a period of time, he made the city of Capernaum his base. Matthew called it 'his own town' (*Matt.* 9:1).

Capernaum was situated on the north-west shore of Galilee. It was a place of some importance – a tax-office was there; a Roman centurion lived there, indicating that it was probably a military post of some kind. It was there, apparently, that Peter and Andrew and probably James and John also lived (see 1:29).

On the Sabbath (Saturday), Jesus went with his friends to the local synagogue for the service, where he was invited to teach. The congregation immediately recognised that there was something completely 'different' about him. Everyone who had been present that morning spoke about his 'authority' (vv. 22, 27). It had been no ordinary service. They had seen things and heard things which profoundly impressed them.

WHAT THE CONGREGATION SAW

While he was speaking, a man called out to Jesus from the congregation. If you have ever been present at a church service which has been loudly interrupted by someone shouting, you will remember what the atmosphere is like on such occasions. This man was demon-possessed, says Mark, and his attitude was menacing: 'What do you want with us?' he bawled at Jesus.

That kind of language appears in a number of places in the Old Testament. It is that of combat, and it immediately produced a situation of confrontation (see 2 Sam. 16:10; 19:22).

You can imagine what thoughts raced through the people's heads: What would Jesus do? How would he handle this situation? The demon-possessed man continued to shout: 'Have you come to destroy us? I know who you are – the Holy One of God' (v. 24). In exposing Jesus' identity, the demon hoped to subdue him in order to maintain his own influence in this poor man's life.

Notice the sense of fear which grips this demon. It seems to know that the presence of Jesus marks the end of the road. The coming of the King and the inauguration of his kingdom implied the destruction and end of the kingdom of darkness. In its guilt, the demon is terror-struck by what Jesus might do.

We do not know whether or not this kind of outburst had ever happened before in the synagogue at Capernaum. In any case, the situation was an indictment of the spiritual condition of the people. Was that congregation so spiritually dead that it had been possible for a demon-possessed man to attend without being disturbed by what was sung or prayed or taught? Or could it be that this was simply another in a whole series of outbursts against God which the elders lacked the power to withstand?

In the event, Jesus spoke with tremendous vigour and feeling to the demon and commanded him to leave the man. The man shook visibly, and with an ear-piercing shriek the demon left him. Never had the people seen the power of God demonstrated so clearly as this. The tragedy was that they saw Jesus do such mighty works and remained spiritually unchanged. No wonder Jesus later spoke so strongly about the fate of Capernaum (*Matt.* 11:23–24).

WHAT THEY HEARD

We have no details of the message Jesus preached that day. We only know that the combination of his words and deeds had an immediate effect. The people were especially conscious of the 'new' teaching he gave. It was not that he added to Scripture – after all, he had been expounding it. It was the way in which he taught from Scripture, with freshness and directness – the people called it 'authority' (v. 27) – which made the lasting impression. It was so different from the usual teaching they heard from the teachers of the law, which seemed second-hand by comparison.

Jewish teaching in the time of Jesus was heavily dependent on what the 'authorities' from the past had to say. Just as a preacher today who quotes constantly from others may eventually give the impression he cannot speak with any authority himself, so it was in Jesus' time. The teaching which depended on the authorities rather than on God's word ceased to have any sense of authority about it. What God had to proclaim had been hidden by what men had said about it.

Some of these people had been listening to such lack-lustre teaching for years. In all likelihood they did not realise that they were being spiritually starved. No one had been disturbed in that synagogue for a long, long time. But suddenly everything was different when Jesus arrived. They knew now that something had been missing.

It is not too difficult to see the similarities between the spiritual condition of the Capernaum synagogue and that of many of our own congregations. What effect would it have if Jesus were to preach in your church? The tragedy of Capernaum was that they did not listen. Our tragedy is that Jesus continues to speak to us through the New Testament, and far too often we do not listen either.

5

At Home

As soon as they left the synagogue, they went with James and John to the home of Simon and Andrew. Simon's mother-in-law was in bed with a fever, and they told Jesus about her. So he went to her, took her hand and helped her up. The fever left her and she began to wait on them. That evening after sunset the people brought to Jesus all the sick and demon-possessed. The whole town gathered at the door, and Jesus healed many who had various diseases. He also drove out many demons, but he would not let the demons speak because they knew who he was.

Very early in the morning, while it was still dark, Jesus got up, left the house and went off to a solitary place, where he prayed. Simon and his companions went to look for him, and when they found him, they exclaimed: 'Everyone is looking for you!' Jesus replied, 'Let us go somewhere else – to the nearby villages – so that I can preach there also. That is why I have come.' So he travelled throughout Galilee, preaching in their synagogues and driving out demons (Mark 1:29–39).

Jesus preached about the kingdom of God. In his presence it had come near. He called men and women to turn away from their sinful lifestyle (repent) and to trust and serve him (believe).

The rest of this chapter illustrates, in different ways, Jesus' claim that the reign of God was now being exercised in his ministry.

First of all, Jesus had exercised his royal prerogative to summon men to leave everything in order to enlist in his service. Then he had preached with the authority of God himself, and shown his power over the kingdom of darkness. Now, in this section, he continues to establish his kingdom by deeds of mercy and grace.

A MOTHER-IN-LAW

After the synagogue service that Saturday, Jesus went with James and John to the home of Simon Peter and Andrew. It was then that Jesus learned that Peter's mother-in-law had been taken ill with a fever.

Here, for the first time, we encounter Jesus in one of those run-of-the-mill situations which take place daily around us, and yet for those who are involved in them may be major crises in their lives. Jesus responded by showing his Lordship in this domestic situation. He went to where Peter's wife's mother lay in bed, took her hand firmly, and helped her to her feet. Immediately she regained strength and the fever disappeared. In fact, far from needing a period of convalescence, she ministered to the disciples and even made a meal for them!

This miraculous healing was an act of wonderful compassion on the part of Jesus. But, like all the miracles, it is a clue to the identity of Jesus and the significance of his coming. Think of what happened to Peter's mother-in-law. She was sick and debilitated; her life, however momentarily, had become useless. What Jesus did was to restore her to what she was meant to be, a whole and healthy woman. Thus restored, she served Jesus and his disciples. Jesus restored God's order and purpose to her life. In doing so he gave his disciples a miniature reproduction of the exercise of his kingly rule.

This miracle is a brief glimpse for us of what will happen when the kingdom of God comes in its final form when Christ returns. He will come and restore his world under his authority.

Of course, we do not see this yet. But in Jesus we see that this great reversal has already begun (*Heb.* 2:5–9).

AFTER SUNSET

How much this little group of people must have enjoyed lingering over the meal which Peter's mother-in-law served! What light spirits they must have had, now that their burden had been lifted. But they were not left alone for long. As soon as the sun set, they began to hear voices around the house – crowds of needy people had gathered to seek Jesus' help.

Mark makes a point of mentioning that this did not take place until after sunset (the Jewish day was measured from sunset to sunset). It was now the day after the Sabbath. The townspeople were, apparently, anxious not to break the Sabbath regulations they had been taught. According to these traditions, helping someone to seek healing might be regarded as 'work' and so it was avoided. In this, Mark gives us a vivid insight into the spiritual plight of the people. Their religious leaders and teachers could not heal and restore them. All they could do was condemn them for 'working' on the Sabbath. By contrast, Jesus taught his disciples the blessings of the Sabbath (and what a blessing they had found this particular Sabbath to be!). He brought healing where the religious leaders could not bring any.

Notice, in passing, that Mark is careful to distinguish in his list of the needy between those who were sick and those who were demon-possessed. It is not true to say that in the Gospels sickness is confused with demon-possession. Clearly Mark knew that not all sickness is demonic in nature. It requires healing, not exorcism. Jesus distinguished these two things and dealt with them in different ways. He healed those who were sick, and he drove out the demons. He also silenced the demons lest they revealed who he was. Their purpose, of course, was to create conflict for him before his time to die had really come. So he exercised his royal power and commanded them to be silent.

BEFORE SUNRISE

The verses which follow (vv. 35–39) bring us into the early hours of the next day, but they are intimately related to the events of the Sabbath in Capernaum. Humanly speaking it must have been an exhausting day for Jesus. But before anyone else in the house had stirred, he had gone to a quiet place in order to pray and spend time in deliberate communion with his Father. He needed to pray that his first day of public ministry in Capernaum would bear fruit, and he wanted to pray over the actions which he was about to take.

How little Peter and the others understood about this. When they eventually found the Lord, they said, with a hint of reproach in their voices, 'Everyone is looking for you!' (v. 37). They did not seem to realise that he did not set the course of his life by the whims of the popularity polls in Capernaum. Rather than return to popular acclaim, he shared with his disciples another plan. They must leave the town, for the moment, and go throughout Galilee preaching about the kingdom of God and demonstrating its power. 'That', said Jesus, 'is why I have come' (v. 38). Did he mean 'come from Capernaum' or 'come from God'? Perhaps he meant both. Certainly, both were true. And so, for a time, the little band of disciples went with their Master as he began to announce the kingdom of God wherever they went. He knew why he had come; but it would be some time before his disciples understood it very clearly.

Sometimes when we read passages like this we are too anxious to ask the question: How does this apply to me? What must I do? It is a good thing for us to pause to admire Jesus first. Then we can ask ourselves: Do I share his sense of the need for prayer and prolonged communion with the Father? If I know why he came, am I committed without reserve to the service of his kingdom?

6

A Leper Cured

*A man with leprosy came to him and begged him on his knees,
'If you are willing, you can make me clean.' Filled with
compassion, Jesus reached out his hand and touched the man.
'I am willing,' he said. 'Be clean!' Immediately the leprosy
left him and he was cured. Jesus sent him away at once with a
strong warning: 'See that you don't tell this to anyone. But
go, show yourself to the priest and offer the sacrifices that
Moses commanded for your cleansing, as a testimony to them.'
Instead he went out and began to talk freely, spreading the
news. As a result, Jesus could no longer enter a town openly
but stayed outside in lonely places. Yet the people still came to
him from everywhere* (Mark 1:40–45).

Leprosy was one of the commonest and most feared of all
diseases in the world of the New Testament. The Old
Testament law gave detailed regulations about it (e.g., *Lev.* 13–14).
These have led medical experts to conclude that the term 'leprosy'
covered a wide variety of skin diseases, including what we today
call leprosy. Not only did the leper suffer from the ravages of the
disease itself, but he became 'unclean' and was regarded as unfit for
society. He was separated from home and family and consigned to
a living death, apart from all the blessings of common life. There
were few more terrible words to the Jewish ear than to be
pronounced 'unclean'. By the same token, to hear the priest pro-
nounce the word 'clean' must have brought relief almost beyond
description. That is why the leper in this story asks to be cleansed
as well as healed. He wanted to be free from the disease. But
perhaps even more, he longed to be free from the stigma, isolation
and rejection which belonged to it.

LEPERS 'CLEANSED'

There is something especially appropriate in the fact that when the kingdom of God came in Jesus Christ, lepers were healed and cleansed. Few things more powerfully illustrate what Paul later said about Jesus:

> What the law was powerless to do in that it was weakened by the sinful nature, God did by sending his own Son in the likeness of sinful man . . . in order that the righteous requirements of the law might be fully met in us, who do not live according to the sinful nature but according to the Spirit (*Rom.* 8:3–4).

The law was powerless to help the leper. If a man were clean, it would not condemn him; if unclean it could not save him. But it was unable to change him. But what the law was powerless to do, Jesus did. Yet, like the entire Gospel which Mark was writing, this story is intended to teach us more about Jesus than about leprosy. There are several things we should notice.

COMPASSION

First, this story underlines the tender compassion of Jesus (v. 41). When this poor man came pleading for help, Jesus was so moved with compassion that he reached out and touched him. Since, according to the rabbis, to touch a leper was to become unclean (even a chance encounter with a leper could render one unclean), voluntarily to touch a leper was almost an incredible thing to do. But Jesus did it deliberately. He wanted to heal the man, of course; but he could have done that without touching him. By touching him, he was really saying: 'I am prepared to become, by choice, what you are by nature – a man under the judgment of the law – in order to share with you what I have – freedom and life.'

As in all miracles, so in this one, Jesus is showing his grace and salvation. He is demonstrating the power of his kingdom. But he is also demonstrating the way in which his kingdom comes: through identifying himself with us in our sin, and bearing the judgment of the law of God against it. He became sin for us, although he was himself sinless, so that we might receive his righteousness in the presence of God (see *2 Cor.* 5:21; *Gal.* 3:13).

[21]

STRONG WARNING

Notice the 'strong warning' which Jesus gave to this man (v. 43). He was to keep silent about what had happened. At first sight there may seem to be something almost out of character about this. Why should Jesus speak with such energy and force? The reason he did not want the man to speak was because he knew how easily his miracles would be misunderstood; they would gather a crowd of followers who were interested in him exclusively because he could do signs and wonders. Jesus wanted people to see that his miracles were signs of the kingdom of God, and that it was submitting to the reign of God, not being a spectator of wonders, which really mattered.

Perhaps there is another reason why Jesus spoke so forcefully to this man in particular. Did Jesus see that, despite his faith (v. 40), there was something unstable and immature about him ? Did Jesus sense that he was just the kind of man who would blurt out every last detail of what had happened? In the event, the stern language proved to be all too appropriate, for the man did exactly what Jesus had urged him not to do. He was the epitome of the person who comes to Jesus for salvation, but then refuses to submit to Jesus because he believes he really knows best how to live his own life (and, alas, often thinks that he knows better than Jesus how to organise the kingdom of God!).

OBEDIENCE

Jesus told this man to fulfil the regulations of the law 'as a testimony' to the priests. It may be that the 'testimony' to which Jesus refers was intended to be a witness against these religious leaders. If they recognised the healing, why did they not recognise the Healer? It is also an illustration of the fact that the followers of Jesus do not overthrow the law; they keep the law (see *Rom.* 3:31). But they do not keep the law in the law's strength, for it has power only to condemn, not to change and energise them. They keep the law because the healing and saving touch of Jesus has been on their lives.

How sad it is to record that this man whom Jesus had so

wonderfully helped and restored – to whom he had given nothing less than new life instead of the living death he knew before – actually became an obstacle to Jesus. In fact, he became an obstacle to Jesus because of the way he witnessed to him! His life underlines a basic lesson of discipleship: the Lord's work should be done only in the Lord's way, according to the Lord's word. There is no better principle by which to serve him than the one which Mary learned and taught: 'Do whatever he tells you' (*John* 2:5).

7

Only God Can Forgive Sins

A few days later, when Jesus again entered Capernaum, the people heard that he had come home. So many gathered that there was no room left, not even outside the door, and he preached the word to them. Some men came, bringing to him a paralytic, carried by four of them. Since they could not get him to Jesus because of the crowd, they made an opening in the roof above Jesus and, after digging through it, lowered the mat the paralysed man was lying on. When Jesus saw their faith, he said to the paralytic, 'Son, your sins are forgiven.' Now some teachers of the law were sitting there, thinking to themselves, 'Why does this fellow talk like that? He's blaspheming! Who can forgive sins but God alone?' Immediately Jesus knew in his spirit that this was what they were thinking in their hearts, and he said to them, 'Why are you thinking these things? Which is easier: to say to the paralytic, "Your sins are forgiven," or to say "Get up, take your mat and walk"? But that you may know that the Son of Man has authority on earth to forgive sins . . .' He said to the paralytic. 'I tell you, get up, take your mat and go home.' He got up, took his mat and walked out in full view of them all. This amazed everyone and they praised God, saying, 'We have never seen anything like this!' (Mark 2:1–12).

Following the disobedience of the leper whom he had healed, Jesus was forced to remain outside the centres of population. But some days later he returned to Capernaum, which was now his 'home' (v. 1). A large crowd gathered at his house there and listened to his preaching. But now, for the first time in the Gospel,

Mark introduces a more sinister element. This story, and the four which follow, all have an element of controversy attached to them. They are paralleled by a further five stories of controversy which occur towards the end of the Gospel (11:27–12:37).

The account of the healing of the paralytic introduces us to this hostility to Jesus and crystallises the reason for it.

BRINGING THE ROOF DOWN

While Jesus was preaching a group of men brought one of their friends in the hope that Jesus would heal him. Finding the house jammed with people, they had carried him up the outside stairs to the flat roof. They then began to remove a section of the roofing (a less drastic action than it appears to a twentieth-century westerner!). Determined that Jesus should help their friend, and convinced that he could heal him, they lowered him right down to where Jesus was.

CONTROVERSY

Jesus 'saw' something in these men and their friend – the one thing for which he invariably looked: faith. Immediately he responded, and said to the man, 'Son, your sins are forgiven' (v. 5).

That was remarkable for several reasons. In the first place, Jesus obviously spoke to this needy man with exceptional concern and tenderness. By contrast with the teachers of the law who were 'sitting there' (as Mark vividly puts it), Jesus was concerned for people. But, more important, he saw that this man's chief need was to receive forgiveness.

Perhaps his friends were immediately disappointed. They had brought him for visible help, not invisible encouragement! Little did they realise that they were witnessing an event which would eventually lead to Jesus' crucifixion. Nor did they sense that, in fact, Jesus had put his finger on this man's (and everyone's) greatest need: to be cleansed from the guilt of sin.

No doubt Jesus could sense what they were thinking. But he was immediately confronted by the thoughts of another group of men. Written all over their faces were the words: 'This is blasphemy!

Who does this carpenter from Nazareth think he is? God alone can forgive sins!' There was nothing wrong with their theology.

But there was something wrong in their logic. They reasoned: since only God can forgive sins, and this man claims to forgive sins, then he must be blaspheming. There was, however, an alternative conclusion: perhaps he did have the authority to forgive sins, in which case he must be . . . God! But that was impossible!

This was really the heart of the conflict between Jesus and the religious leaders of his time. At one level it became a debate about the application of God's law (for example, the use of the Sabbath, see vv. 23ff). But to see it only on that level would be to miss the point. The crux of the controversy was theological, not merely moral. It was about the character of God. The religious leaders were saying: 'God cannot come to us like this and do these things so humbly and graciously. Therefore this man cannot be the Son of God.' The reason they eventually crucified Jesus was because they would not tolerate what his words and works revealed about the character of God – that he saves sinners.

EASIER SAID THAN DONE?

They were inwardly accusing Jesus of blasphemy. But Jesus had an answer. He presented them with a challenge: Which course of action do you think is easier – (i) saying to this man, 'Your sins are forgiven,' or (ii) saying to him, 'Get up and walk'?

The answer is, of course, that it is easier to say, 'Your sins are forgiven.' That is a statement whose truth is difficult to prove or disprove. To say to someone who is paralysed, 'Get up and walk' is to make a statement whose effects can readily be seen. It is the more difficult thing to *say*.

Notice Jesus' logic. He has just said 'the easy thing'. Now to prove that he has the power actually to forgive sins, he says the difficult thing (in the eyes of the religious leaders): 'Get up and walk.' To the amazement of the whole assembly, the man did just that. Jesus had healed him with a word. His action argued for only one conclusion. If his word of healing has been effective, surely his word of forgiveness must have been effective too!

Jesus saw their thoughts; he saw their logic; he demonstrated his divine authority. He was the Son of Man who had the right to forgive sins. 'Isn't Jesus tremendous?' the people said as they went home that day (v. 12). The authority of the Son of Man to forgive sins seemed to be exercised so easily. They could not yet have understood that it was an authority given to him because he had come to sacrifice himself, and to die on the cross to bring men forgiveness.

Here Mark unveils what lies at the heart of the gospel: men need forgiveness; Jesus gives it. The degree to which you see your own need of that forgiveness is the measure of how clearly you understand the gospel.

8

Legalism or Holiness

*Once again Jesus went out beside the lake. A large crowd
came to him, and he began to teach them. As he walked along,
he saw Levi son of Alphaeus sitting at the tax collector's
booth. 'Follow me,' Jesus told him, and Levi got up and
followed him. While Jesus was having dinner at Levi's house,
many tax collectors and 'sinners' were eating with him and
his disciples, for there were many who followed him. When
the teachers of the law who were Pharisees saw him eating
with the 'sinners' and tax collectors, they asked his disciples:
'Why does he eat with tax collectors and "sinners"?' On
hearing this, Jesus said to them, 'It is not the healthy who
need a doctor, but the sick. I have not come to call the righteous, but sinners.'* (Mark 2:13–17).

In the story of the restoration of the paralysed man, Mark
introduced us to one of the underlying themes in his Gospel:
the conflict between the religious leaders and Jesus over the
character of God and the offer of forgiveness through Jesus. The
four stories which follow continue this theme and, inevitably, share
a similar structure: first, the scene is set, then an accusation is laid
against Jesus in various ways, and finally, Jesus resolves the issue by
an authoritative statement.

LEVI

Following a further teaching session, Jesus walked along the lake
shore. He saw Levi (Matthew) sitting at the tax collector's booth.
He was collecting taxes for the Roman government, probably
on goods which were *en route* between Syria and Egypt. Tax

collectors in general were regarded as 'sharks' and even traitors, since their profession implicated them with the occupying Roman forces. But Jesus called this man to be his disciple. He responded by leaving everything (see *Luke* 5:28). Mark provides no more details. It seems likely, however, that Levi had already been exposed to the work and words of Jesus. This call was probably the climax of his pilgrimage rather than its beginning.

It is what follows which particularly interests Mark. Levi invited Jesus and a number of others for dinner. Many of them belonged to the same stratum of society as Levi himself. It seems he threw a 'conversion party' to which other tax collectors and 'sinners' were invited. In all likelihood there was a mixture of disciples and 'interested parties'. One would give a good deal to know what the theme of the table conversation was!

THE PHARISEES

The occasion was not hidden from 'the teachers of the law who were Pharisees' (v. 16), and Mark records their reaction. This is the first reference to the Pharisees in Mark's Gospel. They were the spiritual descendants of a group known as the Hasidim (an expression used often in the Psalms for the faithful). They had stood for devotion to the law, especially when, two centuries before Christ, Greek philosophical and religious ideas had begun to influence contemporary life greatly.

Always a minority group, they held that keeping the law was a primary religious duty. They also believed that the law could be adapted to every situation. Their 'scribes' sought to show in what way the law was binding on each human situation. Eventually they determined that the law contained 613 commandments (248 positive and 365 negative ones!).

In order to make sure that these commands were fulfilled, the scribes set a 'hedge' around them – adding to them other laws which would protect the faithful from falling into sin. To be a Pharisee, therefore, was to commit oneself to a life of radical separation, and to live in accordance with an enormous list of do's and don'ts.

Among those don'ts was the Pharisees' refusal to buy food from, or to eat food in, the homes of those who were not Pharisees, in case the food they ate had not been tithed, and they should thus break a fundamental principle of the law.

Jesus was doing exactly what these Pharisees refrained from doing. For all we know this particular group of Pharisees may have asked their question out of real concern for Jesus. They may even have admired many of the things he had said and done. All the more reason for him to break the traditions so flagrantly. Did he not understand them? In any event, it is perhaps significant that they asked (or accused?) Jesus' disciples first, 'Why does [Jesus] eat with tax collectors and "sinners"?' (v. 16).

DEVASTATING REPLY

Our Lord's answer is simple, brilliant and devastating. Had the Pharisees grasped its significance and followed it through, their lives would have been completely revolutionised. Doctors do not visit those who are well, but those who are sick (v. 17).

Jesus was teaching these men important lessons:

(i) *He was rebuking their misdirected zeal.* They were concerned for the glory of God and for moral purity, which was commendable. But God's concern for his glory and for purity among men had led him down through history to visit his sin-diseased people to heal them. If the Pharisees were really anxious to see men and women become holy, then their separation to God should have led them to a loving commitment to the people, to show them God's way.

(ii) *He was also exposing their false holiness.* If their so-called 'holiness' expressed itself only in criticism of sinners and not in caring for them, it was not the kind which God wanted, nor the type that Jesus exhibited.

Think of the modern-day surgeon. He 'scrubs up' before his operation. Why is he so careful to be clean? In order to help those who are diseased or physically deformed. True holiness is like that, replied Jesus. My holiness is like that. It is not contaminated by my eating with these sinners. Rather, it seeks to make them whole and holy too.

9

Conflict Continued

Now John's disciples and the Pharisees were fasting. Some people came and asked Jesus, 'How is it that John's disciples and the disciples of the Pharisees are fasting, but yours are not?' Jesus answered, 'How can the guests of the bridegroom fast while he is with them? They cannot, so long as they have him with them. But the time will come when the bridegroom will be taken from them, and on that day they will fast.

No-one sews a patch of unshrunk cloth on an old garment. If he does, the new piece will pull away from the old, making the tear worse. And no-one pours new wine into old wineskins. If he does, the wine will burst the skins, and both the wine and the wineskins will be ruined. No, he pours new wine into new wineskins.' (Mark 2:18–22).

So far in this chapter, Mark has recorded conflicts between the religious leaders and Jesus over (i) the issue of granting forgiveness and (ii) the question of eating with those who disregarded the 'traditions'. Now a third controversy arises, this time over the matter of fasting.

FASTING

The Pharisees fasted – twice a week according to Luke 18:12. They were not slow to point out that the disciples of John also fasted. In view of this, was it not strange that Jesus' disciples did not do so? It is just possible that the question was asked sincerely. But the pattern of opposition to Jesus is too clearly marked in this chapter for that to be likely.

No doubt the questioners were anxious to convey the impression of sincerity. It is not difficult to imagine the scene as they ask Jesus (with all due deference!) why it is that his disciples are not fasting. The words contain a thinly veiled criticism of him: how can he be a truly godly leader of this growing band of people when they come third in the spirituality league table, points behind the Pharisees and even the disciples of John? Clearly John's name could be used approvingly when it suited the situation to do so!

Mark does not stress the exact timing of this incident. In this chapter his order is topical rather than necessarily chronological – these various incidents are probably drawn from different periods in Jesus' ministry.

It is possible that John's disciples were fasting because their leader had been imprisoned. That was no time for eating and drinking! It is equally possible that fasting was a prominent part of the lifestyle which characterised those who gathered round John. He himself was a man of great austerity, and his message was intended to produce similar austerity in others. While John's disciples did fast, their reasons for doing so were very different from those of the Pharisees.

But the real issue in such matters is always: what does God command us to do? While the Old Testament recorded various seasons of fasting, God had established only one fast day each year – on the Day of Atonement (*Lev.* 16:29–34). Men might fast for many good reasons on other occasions. Jesus himself did – for forty days on one occasion. But to insist on such fasting, as the Pharisees did, was to go beyond the law of God. And to insist on what God has not insisted on is to seek to outdo God with man-made traditions. If Paul could tell Timothy that Scripture provided all he would need to be a true man of God (*2 Tim.* 3:15–17), adding to that Scripture (as the sects invariably do) is to develop the mentality of the Pharisees and with similar repercussions.

PATCHES AND WINESKINS

Jesus would have been perfectly justified in resting his case on the straightforward teaching of the Old Testament. But he took the matter further, and defended his disciples' actions: it would be inappropriate for them to fast. The illustrations which follow explain why.

Jesus' disciples are like a bridegroom's friends. Imagine them fasting when they would normally be feasting in their joy at being with their friend just before his wedding! It would be inappropriate. The time would come for the disciples to fast, when the 'bridegroom' (Jesus) was 'taken from them'. Mark uses a strong word here, reminiscent of what had been said of the Suffering Servant in Isaiah 53:8: 'By oppression and judgment, he was taken away.' He is pointing, in a veiled way – for those who have ears to hear – to his coming death. Then, when he had been seized, the disciples would indeed mourn.

For Jesus' disciples to fast would be like someone sewing unshrunk cloth on an old garment, or someone pouring new wine into old wineskins. When the cloth is washed and the patch shrinks, the garment will be in a worse state. As the new wine continues to ferment, it will burst the wineskins – both wine and wineskins will be lost.

What does Jesus mean? In these final illustrations, he not only emphasises that fasting is inappropriate for his disciples, but that the way of the Pharisees with their legalism and their man-made traditions, and the way of the gospel of grace cannot be harmonised. They are mutually incompatible. Jesus' teaching on godly grace and forgiveness for sinners destroys the old cloth of the Pharisees; it bursts open the old wineskins of their religion.

The religion of the Pharisees was that God would keep covenant with them if they kept the law and did so by keeping within the 'hedge' which their man-made traditions had built around it. It was a religion which depended, ultimately, on the contribution man is able to make to his own salvation.

By contrast, Jesus preached grace, unmerited favour (indeed, de-merited favour!) and free forgiveness. His gospel began with God; the salvation he preached depended entirely on God. He underlined the difference between this and the teaching of the Pharisees. Now they must choose: God's way or man's way. Which was it to be?

The choice remains the same.

10

Lord of the Sabbath

One Sabbath Jesus was going through the cornfields, and as his disciples walked along, they began to pick some ears of corn. The Pharisees said to him, 'Look, why are they doing what is unlawful on the Sabbath?' He answered, 'Have you never read what David did when he and his companions were hungry and in need? In the days of Abiathar the high priest, he entered the house of God and ate the consecrated bread, which is lawful only for priests to eat. And he also gave some to his companions.' Then he said to them, 'The Sabbath was made for man, not man for the Sabbath. So the Son of Man is Lord even of the Sabbath.'

Another time he went into the synagogue, and a man with a shrivelled hand was there. Some of them were looking for a reason to accuse Jesus, so they watched him closely to see if he would heal him on the Sabbath. Jesus said to the man with the shrivelled hand, 'Stand up in front of everyone.' Then Jesus asked them, 'Which is lawful on the Sabbath: to do good or to do evil, to save life or to kill?' But they remained silent. He looked round at them in anger and, deeply distressed at their stubborn hearts, said to the man, 'Stretch out your hand.' He stretched it out and his hand was completely restored. Then the Pharisees went out and began to plot with the Herodians how they might kill Jesus (Mark 2:23–3:6).

The series of conflict stories at the beginning of the Gospel draws to a close with two incidents which took place on the Sabbath day. The weekly Sabbath was simply part of the way of life for the orthodox Jew. It was a day which God had instituted from the beginning of history (*Gen.* 2:2–3). It also stood as a reminder to the people that he was the God of salvation as well as creation (*Deut.* 5:12–15). To abandon the Sabbath day was to turn one's back upon the God of the covenant.

But when the theologians of the Pharisees examined the Sabbath law, they noticed that it forbade working (*Exod.* 20:8–11; *Deut.* 5:12–15). They therefore asked the question: What exactly is involved in 'working' and how can we make sure that we avoid such 'work'?

Characteristically, their answer involved a lengthy list of regulations which would surround the individual with a 'hedge' to make sure that he was never in danger of breaking the commandment. In actual practice, the breach of these man-made regulations was equated with disobedience to God's law.

Mark gives us the impression that the Pharisees took every opportunity to observe Jesus and his disciples in order to 'score' them against their list of do's and don'ts. Here he gives us two illustrations of their scrutiny.

BACK TO SCRIPTURE!

As the disciples walked through the grainfields one Sabbath, they instinctively picked some heads of grain (v. 23). This, to the Pharisees, was a form of reaping. Since reaping was working, it was obviously unlawful on the Sabbath.

Jesus could have answered this accusation in different ways. He could have accused the Pharisees of being ludicrously petty. But they would have then charged him with indifference to the law. Instead he answered them with a question of his own. Hadn't David entered the house of God and eaten the bread which was to be eaten only by the priests (*1 Sam.* 21:1–6)?

This incident took place when Ahimelech was the priest. It is difficult to know exactly why Jesus says, therefore, 'in the days of Abiathar the high priest' (v. 26). Possibly the phrase means 'in the part of Scripture about Abiathar the high priest' (the same phrase is used in this way in Mark 12:26). Alternatively, the phrase may simply mean something like someone saying, 'Did you see the film on TV last night in which President Reagan starred?' although it was made many years before he became the President of the United States.

But notice that Jesus is not content to leave the matter here. There is more to this issue than drawing attention to a passage which embarrassed the Pharisees. What lay behind it was a funda-mental biblical principle: the Sabbath was made for man, not man for the Sabbath (v. 27). It was given to man to meet his needs and to bring him special blessing, not to restrict his life and reduce him to a rule-keeping robot.

The Pharisees were like the committee of a golf club which had beautiful fairways on which to play. But in order to preserve the fairways from being cut up with divots, they insisted that golfers always play their shots from the rough grass at the side. But golf-courses, like Sabbaths, are meant to be enjoyed, not preserved as living museums! Tragically, the Pharisees were turning the day of blessing into a burden.

A DAY FOR DOING GOOD

The same principle arises even more clearly in Mark 3:1–6. Here is a man in the synagogue with a shrivelled hand. The Pharisees are there, watching our Lord's every move. Will he try to heal this man on the Sabbath?

In full view of his detractors, Jesus commanded the man to stand. Realising what was at stake, he asked a question before healing him: what does it mean to keep the law of God? Does it mean doing good, or doing evil, saving life, or killing? The point was clear. Jesus was again arguing that God had given man the Sabbath for his blessing. What could be a greater physical blessing to this man than to heal his shrivelled hand? The Pharisees taught that only if the man's life were in danger was healing on the Sabbath permissible – but not otherwise. But observe Jesus' point: why should the Sabbath, of all days, be the one day on which he refrained from bringing blessing to this man? The idea was quite ludicrous!

But there is, perhaps, something yet more profound in what Jesus did. The law concerning the Sabbath permitted this man great joy, but it could not heal him and restore him to the joyful condition for which he had been created. The scribes and Pharisees could not do that – only Jesus could. As a matter of fact, only Jesus could help this man really to enjoy the blessing of the Sabbath day. That was something these Pharisees were powerless to do. Perhaps that was why they immediately began to plot how they could destroy him (v. 6).

Jesus demonstrated beautifully that he alone is able to give the grace we need to enter into the joys of obedience to the commandments of God. It is grace which produces such obedience, not legalism.

11

Hostility Abounds

Jesus withdrew with his disciples to the lake, and a large crowd from Galilee followed. When they heard all he was doing, many people came to him from Judea, Jerusalem, Idumea, and the regions across the Jordan and around Tyre and Sidon. Because of the crowd he told his disciples to have a small boat ready for him, to keep the people from crowding him. For he had healed many, so that those with diseases were pushing forward to touch him. Whenever the evil spirits saw him, they fell down before him and cried out, 'You are the Son of God.' But he gave them strict orders not to tell who he was (Mark 3:7–12).

The antagonism of the Pharisees to Jesus was plain for all to see. No matter how hard they might try to disguise the fact, their questions were deliberate efforts to 'catch him out'. The sequel to their failure to do so is highly significant: they 'began to plot with the Herodians how they might kill Jesus' (3:6). Here were men who were outwardly devoted to honouring and keeping the law of Moses, deliberately planning to commit murder. The reason they needed to 'plot' was in order to do it 'legally'!

The presence of Jesus was showing up some of these Pharisees for what they really were: men who served God with their lips, but whose hearts were far from him (*Isa.* 29:13). Before this Gospel comes to an end, we shall hear Jesus himself quoting these words to them.

TWOFOLD ERROR

The great error of the Pharisees was twofold. They had a wrong view of God, and consequently an inadequate view of sin. Unlike

[38]

the Old Testament prophets and psalmists, they could not see that knowing God meant knowing him in his infinite and heart-searching holiness. It involved knowing one's own heart in its perversity and self-centredness.

Only when we see these two things do we recognise how much we need the grace of God. Anyone who has ever sensed the real nature of God would not imagine that his favour could be earned by external rules and regulations. On the Lord's authority, Isaiah had declared such 'righteousness' to be 'filthy rags' (*Isa.* 64:6) Isaiah himself, perhaps the holiest man of his time, had come to see that he too was a 'man of unclean lips' (*Isa.* 6:5) who needed pardon and cleansing.

The Pharisees underlined their inconsistency by joining forces with the Herodians, the supporters of Herod, who for that reason were also supporters of the Roman occupation (see *Mark* 12:13). How inexpressibly sad that these Pharisees, the 'separated ones', could pride themselves in being 'separated' from rank-and-file sinners, but were prepared to associate with 'upper-class' sinners! No wonder they plotted against Jesus – they could not rest until this thorn in their flesh was removed.

It is against this background that Jesus' withdrawal is to be understood. He knew that the Pharisees were mortally opposed to him. He knew men's hearts well enough to realise they would stop at nothing to be rid of him. But he was not there to march time to the drumbeat of the Pharisees. He was his Father's Son. He followed a heavenly plan and timetable. The time of final confrontation still lay in the future. And so, for the moment, Jesus withdrew (v. 7).

DEMONIC HOSTILITY

In the final analysis, there is something demonic about the way the Pharisees attacked Jesus. Their hostility was aroused to such an extent that eventually they lost control of themselves (see *Mark* 14:65). It is interesting, therefore, that when Jesus withdraws from direct confrontation with them, he finds himself facing a different kind of 'plot' against his ministry.

Crowds flocked round Jesus for healing. Men and women whose

lives were dominated by the presence of evil spirits came in large numbers. Mark records their consistent response: 'They fell down before him and cried out, "You are the Son of God"' (v. 11).

Why did the demons cry out like this? And why did Jesus silence them? Should he not have welcomed their confession? After all, would people not then be able to say, 'Even the demons recognise his deity?' Why, then, did Jesus clamp down on them with such force? (Mark uses a word here which occurs in the Greek Old Testament in divine rebukes.)

The cry of the demons was a cry of despair, not of faith. It was uttered with malevolence and antagonism, not joy and loyalty. It was calculated to destroy Jesus' influence by suggesting that there was an association between him and those who recognised his identity. What Satan could not do through the Pharisees' rejection of Jesus' claims, he would try to do through the demons' recognition of them. But both men and demons are to be judged by their fruits – and the fruits of both were obvious and profoundly evil.

JESUS' RESTRAINT

By contrast with the confession of the demons, it is noticeable that the Lord showed considerable restraint in revealing his identity. On a number of occasions we find him insisting on it being kept relatively secret. The reason emerges very clearly. The Son of God had come to be the Saviour of men by living and dying as the Suffering Servant. He would only properly be understood and trusted when that dark side of his experience was appreciated. If people thought of him as the Son of God, or even as the Redeemer, without learning how he would redeem, they would never really know him. The Pharisees *thought* they knew who he was; so did the demons. But neither understood the real truth of the matter. They saw him only as their Destroyer, not their Saviour.

In fact, there are no other ways to think about Jesus. He is one or the other to you. But which?

12

The Twelve

Jesus went up on a mountainside and called to him those he wanted, and they came to him. He appointed twelve – designating them apostles – that they might be with him and that he might send them out to preach and to have authority to drive out demons. These are the twelve he appointed: Simon (to whom he gave the name Peter); James son of Zebedee and his brother John (to them he gave the name Boanerges, which means Sons of Thunder); Andrew, Philip, Bartholomew. Matthew, Thomas, James, son of Alphaeus, Thaddaeus, Simon the Zealot and Judas Iscariot, who betrayed him (Mark 3:13–19).

M ark's Gospel is characterised by movement and activity. Occasionally, however, he gives the impression of the passage of time by introducing a little section like this one, in which he summarises an important period in Jesus' ministry.

Jesus selected a small group of twelve men to share his life in a special way. He chose twelve as a symbol of the fact that he was building the 'new Israel' out of the old. These men would be the 'brothers' he would use to establish his kingdom throughout the whole earth. As we read Mark's words we should have a sense of thrill in recognising that here Jesus was beginning an 'evangelistic campaign' which would lead ultimately to ourselves and the church in the twentieth century.

Perhaps this is one reason for the extraordinary diversity of the men Jesus chose. There were no 'clones' in this group. By any standard they must have been quite a handful. Who else could have bound together Simon the Zealot (v. 18, presumably a strong nationalist before he had become a follower of the Lord) and Matthew (Levi the tax collector)? It was one thing to choose a Simon Peter, but choosing the 'Sons of Thunder' (v. 17) along with him was quite a step to take! And then, of course, there was Judas Iscariot who already bears the epitaph 'who betrayed him' (v. 19). (He drags it behind him like a ball and chain through the Gospel.)

Mark tells us that there were three reasons why Jesus chose these men.

COMPANIONSHIP

Jesus wanted men to 'be with him' (v. 14). He was a true man himself. It was instinctive in his human nature to desire the companionship of others. He rejoiced in the bonds of their friendship. He loved them, taught them and grieved over their faults. We can even say that Jesus 'needed' them, just because he was truly and fully human – and to be truly and fully human means to be made for friendship. It is never good for man always to be alone (*Gen.* 2:18).

He wanted them to 'be with him' for their sake as well as his own. Only through such intimate contact would they really get to know him and be able to fulfil the task of bearing witness to him. Only in this way would they be fully exposed to the powerful influence of his life and ministry.

Years later people would be astonished at the apostles' power and wisdom, especially by their knowledge of the Scriptures (despite the fact that they had never studied theology!): 'They took note that these men had *been with Jesus*' (*Acts* 4:13, emphasis added). That became the secret of their lives. Through Scripture and by Christ's Spirit, it is still possible to be 'with him'. We should therefore take careful note of the effects of such communion and long for them in our own lives. People thought that the apostles were 'unschooled' (*Acts* 4:13). They could not have been more mistaken. They had been scholars in the best of schools!

APOSTLESHIP

The second reason Jesus chose these men was 'that he might send them out to preach' (v. 14). Later in the Gospel narrative they do precisely that (*Mark* 6:7). But Jesus had a longer-term mission in view. These were the men who would continue the ministry he was beginning, of proclaiming the coming of the kingdom of God through his own life, death and resurrection. They would go into the whole world as preachers of this good news. They were apostles ('sent men').

In some respects, the preaching of the apostles was unique. It was authenticated by 'signs, wonders and various miracles' (*Heb.* 2:4) which were intended to be 'the things that mark an apostle' (*2 Cor.* 12:12). Paul, at least, did not expect that such authentication would mark all preaching down through the ages. These men possessed a unique role in the history of Christ's kingdom which enabled them once and for all to give the word of God (the New Testament) to the church.

But, for all that, there is a pattern in Jesus' dealings with his disciples which he continues to use. He calls us to be with him in order to send us out to others to bring to them the good news of the kingdom of God.

AUTHORITY

The third reason Jesus called them was to give them his authority (v. 15). Just as he was able to cast out demons so, in the same way, they would show that the kingdom of God had arrived. Again this was fulfilled later in the Gospel narrative (see *Mark* 6:7).

Two things should be noted here. One is that even during Jesus' ministry the gift of exorcising demons was not given to all of his followers. As a matter of fact it was exercised by comparatively few of them. It would be a grave mistake, therefore, to assume that 'exorcising demons' was part of the average Christian's experience in New Testament times. Furthermore, we should not ignore the real significance of this exorcism. It marked the permanent hostility between the kingdom of Christ and the kingdom of darkness. The whole of Jesus' ministry focused on his destruction of the works of the devil (*1 John* 3:8). He did not come to wrestle merely with flesh and blood, but with the powers of darkness (*Eph.* 6:10–18). The same was true for the apostles. The same is true for us as well.

13

The Greatest Sin of All

Then Jesus entered a house, and again a crowd gathered, so that he and his disciples were not even able to eat. When his family heard about this, they went to take charge of him, for they said, 'He is out of his mind.' And the teachers of the law who came down from Jerusalem said, 'He is possessed by Beelzebub! By the prince of demons he is driving out demons.' So Jesus called them and spoke to them in parables: 'How can Satan drive out Satan? If a kingdom is divided against itself, that kingdom cannot stand. If a house is divided against itself, that house cannot stand. And if Satan opposes himself and is divided, he cannot stand; his end has come. In fact, no-one can enter a strong man's house and carry off his possessions unless he first ties up the strong man. Then he can rob his house. I tell you the truth, all the sins and blasphemies of men will be forgiven them. But whoever blasphemes against the Holy Spirit will never be forgiven; he is guilty of an eternal sin.' He said this because they were saying, 'He has an evil spirit' (Mark 3:20–30).

Whenever we read the Gospels we need to pay attention both to what is said and also to the way in which it is said. These books are Gospels, not simply biographies. Consequently, the writers select and present their material in order to convey their message in different ways.

SPLIT SCREEN

Here Mark gives us his equivalent of modern television's 'split screen' (as, for example, in a golf tournament, the two leading competitors may be shown playing on different holes at the same time). He introduces scene one, which centres on the concern in Jesus' family circle over the publicity his ministry was receiving. Their instinct was to take him home quietly, because they were convinced he must have lost his senses.

The second scene pictures the Jerusalem theologians again. They had come down to Capernaum in order to declare the city 'seduced' by Jesus. One of their arguments for this was that Jesus was exorcising demons by the power of the prince of demons, Beelzebub (v. 22).

The parallel between these two events is significant for Mark. They present us with the only possible interpretations of Jesus which are open to us: he is either mad (the family's view) or bad (the Pharisaic theologians' view) or he is what he claims to be, divine (Mark's view).

THEOLOGIANS REBUFFED!

Mark's first focus is on the theologians. He notes the vigour of our Lord's response to them.

First of all, Jesus refuted them. Their criticism is logically incoherent. How could Satan drive out Satan? The idea is unthinkable. No kingdom which is at war with itself can possibly stand. If Satan was really opposing himself, 'his end has come' (v. 26). But the one thing which was so obvious from Jesus' confrontation with the powers of darkness was that their end had not come. The devil was alive and kicking.

STRONG MAN BOUND

Secondly, Jesus provides the true explanation of his ministry. He pictures Satan's victims as the possessions of a strong man. How are they to be taken out of his hands and restored to their rightful owner and former dignity? Only if someone enters the house of the strong man, binds him and then takes possession of the goods. This is exactly what Jesus had come to do – destroy the influence of the strong man, Satan, on people's lives and restore them to their family fellowship with God. Jesus had come into the 'house'

[45]

of 'the prince of this world' (cf. 12:31; 14:30; 16:11). In his ministry, and supremely on the cross and through the resurrection, he
would overcome him and liberate his people. That was the true
significance of these exorcisms, if only these official theologians
had the eyes to see it.

UNFORGIVABLE

Thirdly, Jesus followed this teaching with some words of direct
practical application. Notice the serious tone of what he says in
verses 28–29. There is no sin which places a man beyond forgiveness, no matter what blasphemy may be involved – except one sin:
blasphemy against the Holy Spirit.

This statement has sometimes caused readers of the Gospels
great distress, and forced them to ask: 'Have I committed the
unpardonable sin?' There is nothing trivial about that question.
Indeed, Jesus seems to suggest it may be the most important
question we ever ask ourselves. But what is blasphemy against the
Holy Spirit?

Mark gives a partial explanation. The reason Jesus spoke in
these terms was 'because they were saying, "He has an evil spirit" '
(v. 30). Here is the one certain sign that a man is in danger of
committing this sin – a stubborn resistance to Jesus which eventually expresses itself in treating him as the ultimate evil in our
lives.

This sin takes its contemporary forms. It is the sin of regarding
conversion to Christ and obedience to him as Lord as the ultimate
folly. This was precisely the wilful blindness to Christ and
hardness of heart against him which these theologians had begun
to display.

It is often said, with some wisdom, that if you are anxious that
you have committed blasphemy against the Spirit, you need
not fear – for this blasphemy is always accompanied by complete
indifference to such sin. But that advice cannot be treated casually,
for the person who sins against the Lord, and is at first sensitive to
the potential consequences of his sin, may one day be the very
person who becomes indifferent to it. The vital thing is to retain
that sensitivity throughout the whole of our lives. It can be retained

only by keeping close to Christ; and doing so will guard us from such sin.

Mark's Gospel impresses on us that the greatest of sins are often those of the most religious of men. He underlines for us the basic lesson that it is not religion, but Jesus, that saves.

14

Christ's True Family

Then Jesus' mother and brothers arrived. Standing outside, they sent someone in to call him. A crowd was sitting around him, and they told him, 'Your mother and brothers are outside looking for you.' 'Who are my mother and my brothers?' he asked. Then he looked at those seated in a circle around him and said, 'Here are my mother and my brothers! Whoever does God's will is my brother and sister and mother' (Mark 3:31–35).

In the previous section of his Gospel, Mark presented us with a 'split screen'. He introduced one situation and then turned to describe another. In verses 21–22 he allowed us to eavesdrop on the conversation in Jesus' family. But then, as we see them making their way to the crowded house where Jesus was, we find ourselves witnessing a controversy between Jesus and the professional theologians.

But now Jesus' mother and brothers have arrived (v. 31). They cannot get into the house because of the crowd. So they relay a message to Jesus. Imagine the scene as the word is passed from one to another through the crowd: 'Tell him that his family is here and they want him to go home – now!'

A SPIRITUAL FAMILY

Jesus' response to the message was totally unexpected. He turned to the crowd, who had presumably heard the message too, and said: 'Who are my mother and brothers, but those who do the will of God?' (v. 34). His disciples were his true family!

We do not expect to hear Jesus put family loyalties into second place. In fact, his words seem a little harsh and unfeeling. After all, his relations were only concerned that he should not make a spectacle of himself.

But Jesus was not being difficult. We know how deeply sensitive he was to his family bonds (see *Luke* 2:51–52; *John* 19:26–27). Yet he realised that natural ties are not the only bonds in the world, nor are they necessarily the most lasting ones. They are of great importance (as *Exod.* 20:12 makes plain), but they do not have priority over our commitment to God's will and his family. Those bonds are the most basic of all. They were in our Lord's life and they must be in ours too.

Jesus turned this crisis in his own life into an opportunity to teach some important lessons about discipleship.

CHALLENGE

He was, first of all, presenting a challenge to his natural family. Yes, they were bound together by blood, by upbringing, by sharing family experiences of joy and sorrow. But Jesus (as Mary and Joseph had known for many years) possessed a higher loyalty to his Father in heaven and to those who belonged to him (see *Luke* 2:49). No ties of natural affection would ever take precedence over that.

This was an enormous challenge to the disciples because Jesus was saying to them: 'Is your relationship to me "natural" or "spiritual"? Does it depend merely on the "accident" of birth and upbringing, or on your knowledge of who I am and your personal commitment to me?'

The fact that his family feared for his sanity (v. 21) does not encourage us to think they had much spiritual insight at this stage of the Gospel record. Jesus wanted them to think seriously about who he really was and what their relationship to him was going to be.

SACRIFICIAL SERVICE

Jesus was also giving the crowd an insight into the significance and costliness of his obedience. He called them to put the kingdom of

God first in their lives, even before their families (see *Luke* 9:59; 14:26). But he was not inviting them to a pathway of discipleship he had not walked himself. He himself had left home and family for the sake of the gospel. Those were precious things to him; but nothing would be allowed to stand between him and obedience to his Father. His disciples were to follow him.

Later in the Gospel, Mark gives us a further insight into Jesus' own sacrificial service. Describing his burden in the Garden of Gethsemane, Mark uses the word 'troubled' which has as its root meaning, 'to be away from home' (*Mark* 14:33). Jesus bore the weight of an eternal homesickness on the cross, for the sake of the gospel.

ENCOURAGEMENTS

But Jesus was also giving encouragement to those who were prepared to follow him. Those who do the will of God are his brothers and sisters (v. 35). What greater privilege could there be than to be identified with Jesus and his family? We have intimate fellowship with him now; but we are also fellow-heirs with him of the glory of God – provided we suffer with him (*Rom.* 8:17).

Jesus was opposed by the religious leaders. He was also mis-understood by those to whom he instinctively looked for support. His family were not the last to try to silence Jesus. The Pharisees, Sadducees, Herodians and Romans all tried to do the same. That was tragic. But even more tragic were those occasions when his own disciples tried to keep him quiet lest the cost of following him proved to be an embarrassment to them. Simon Peter did that on more than one occasion.

Perhaps you are tempted to do the same. If so, remember his words of encouragement: 'Whoever does God's will is my brother and sister and mother.'

15

Sowing in Different Soils

Again Jesus began to teach by the lake. The crowd that gathered round him was so large that he got into a boat and sat in it out on the lake, while all the people were along the shore at the water's edge. He taught them many things by parables, and in his teaching said: 'Listen! A farmer went out to sow his seed. As he was scattering the seed, some fell along the path, and the birds came and ate it up. Some fell on rocky places, where it did not have much soil. It sprang up quickly, because the soil was shallow. But when the sun came up, the plants were scorched, and they withered because they had no root. Other seed fell among thorns, which grew up and choked the plants, so that they did not bear grain. Still other seed fell on good soil. It came up, grew and produced a crop, multiplying thirty, sixty, or even a hundred times.' Then Jesus said, 'He who has ears to hear, let him hear.'

When he was alone, the Twelve and the others around him asked him about the parables. He told them, 'The secret of the kingdom of God has been given to you. But to those on the outside everything is said in parables so that "they may be ever seeing but never perceiving, and ever hearing but never understanding; otherwise they might turn and be forgiven!"' Then Jesus said to them, 'Don't you understand this parable? How then will you understand any parable? The farmer sows the word. Some people are like seed along the path, where the word is sown. As soon as they hear it, Satan comes and takes away the word that was sown in them. Others, like seed sown on rocky places, hear the word and at once receive it with joy. But since they have no root, they last only a short time. When trouble or persecution comes because of the word, they quickly fall away. Still others, like seed sown among thorns, hear the word; but the worries of this life, the deceitfulness of wealth and the desires for other things come in and choke the word, making it unfruitful. Others, like seed sown on good soil, hear the word, accept it, and produce a crop – thirty , sixty or even a hundred times what was sown' (Mark 4:1–20).

Most preachers have one particular 'style' of preaching. That was not true of Jesus. Admittedly, he does seem to have taught the same material more than once; he also seems to have had a certain 'style' to his speech. But when we examine his preaching as a whole, we immediately recognise different approaches and styles.

There is, for example, the well-ordered, clearly divided Sermon on the Mount (*Matt.* 5:1–7:29). In a different style altogether is his wonderful discourse in the Upper Room (*John* 13:1–16:33).

But whatever style of preaching Jesus used, one element was constant: he always used parables when he spoke to 'outsiders' (cf. v. 34).

PARABLES ARE MIRRORS

What are parables and why did Jesus use them? We sometimes say they are 'earthly stories with a heavenly meaning', but that is only partially true. For the parables are more than pleasant stories or Christian versions of Aesop's fables. They reflect the principles of the kingdom of God, and consequently serve as mirrors of our own lives. They force us to ask the question, 'Where do I stand in relation to the kingdom of God?' They show us our own hearts in the light of God's word.

Jesus explained this to the disciples when they asked him about the meaning of the parable of the farmer who sowed in different kinds of soil. In effect the parables were the word of God in seed form, planted in men's lives through Jesus' preaching. Those seeds could lodge in men's hearts and bear fruit. After hearing Jesus speak, a listener might say: 'I knew he was talking about me. I could see myself in that parable he told.' That was exactly what

Jesus intended. Just like the parable Nathan told King David
(*2 Sam.* 12:1–7), Jesus' parables said to his hearers, 'You are the
man.'

Yet people could listen to Jesus' teaching and spiritually be none
the wiser. They could 'see' and 'hear' what he said, and yet think of
Jesus merely as a story-teller. His stories remained that – stories
and nothing more. They never understood the message they
contained. They did not appreciate that they were not listening to
a fine story-teller, but to the summing-up of a judge. In fact they
were blind and deaf to all God was saying to them (*Mark* 4:11–12).

FOUR RESPONSES

This parable was the key to all of Jesus' teaching in parables, and so
he explained it carefully to the disciples (v. 13ff). The seed is the
message of the kingdom of God; the soils represent the different
conditions of men's hearts (notice that in Palestine, sowing
preceded ploughing, as the parable indicates). Those who hear
God's word respond in four different ways.

Some people hear the message, but it is like 'water off a duck's
back' to them (vv. 4, 15). Their minds are full of other things
which make them impervious to the gospel. The message of the
kingdom simply slides over the surface. Yes, they heard what was
said; but the slightest change in conversation will obliterate any
impression they might have had of God speaking to them. Satan
will see to that. He steals away the seed of God's word.

Others seem to respond much more positively. The message fills
them with joy (vv. 5–6). But as Jesus suggests, this is an inadequate
reaction, because a response of joy untinged with sorrow or shame
for our sin, or the grief of repentance, is a superficial reaction.
Underneath remains the rocky substratum of our hearts which
makes them resist the real and lasting impact of God's word. The
trials of the Christian life will test the true nature of their response
(v. 16).

Yet others are like soil which is in many respects good, but is
infested with weeds (v. 7). No weeding has been done to give an
opportunity for growth. Although a crop begins to grow, it is
choked. So it is, Jesus says, with some people who hear the gospel

(vv. 18–19). They do not allow it to root out sin from their hearts. They hanker after other or better things than they now possess. Eventually their priorities become completely confused. The kingdom of God is crowded out of their lives by the weeds of the world. They did not respond to the so-called 'negative' elements in the gospel (see *Rom.* 8:13; 13:12; *Col.* 3:5–9). They used no weedkiller, and so the spiritual thorns drain away the supply of life.

By contrast there is the good soil (v. 8). Here the seed takes root. Weeding and ploughing is done with a view to the harvest. Sometimes that exceeds all expectation (v. 20).

But how do we become good soil? Only by God's grace, as our hearts are ploughed up to receive his word and as we allow its influence to counteract sin in our lives. That means stubbornly resisting the influence of the desire for 'other things', and seeking first the kingdom of God (*Matt.* 6:33).

If there are only four ways to respond to the word of God, to what category does your response belong? That is the question this parable is designed to make us ask.

16

Lights and Seeds

He said to them, 'Do you bring in a lamp to put it under a bowl or a bed? Instead, don't you put it on its stand? For whatever is hidden is meant to be disclosed, and whatever is concealed is meant to be brought out into the open. If anyone has ears to hear, let him hear.' 'Consider carefully what you hear,' he continued. 'With the measure you use, it will be measured to you – and even more. Whoever has will be given more; whoever does not have, even what he has will be taken from him.'

He also said, 'This is what the kingdom of God is like. A man scatters seed on the ground. Night and day, whether he sleeps or gets up, the seed sprouts and grows, though he does not know how. All by itself the soil produces corn – first the stalk, then the ear, then the full grain in the ear. As soon as the grain is ripe, he puts the sickle to it, because the harvest has come.'

Again he said, 'What shall we say the kingdom of God is like, or what parable shall we use to describe it? It is like a mustard seed, which is the smallest seed you plant in the ground. Yet when planted, it grows and becomes the largest of all garden plants, with such big branches that the birds of the air can perch in its shade.'

With many similar parables Jesus spoke the word to them, as much as they could understand. He did not say anything to them without using a parable. But when he was alone with his own disciples, he explained everything (Mark 4:21–34).

The parables of Jesus were like missiles launched against the kingdom of darkness in men's hearts. They were 'timed' to destroy the self-confidence of men and women, and to overcome all opposition to their conversion to Christ. They were calculated to bring people to a point of decision. That is why their central theme is the way in which the kingdom of God is established in the world.

We have already seen that the parable of the farmer and the soils was a 'key' one. It was a parable about how parables work. But the Hebrew word for 'parable' *(mashal)* has a wide range of meanings. It can refer to a story or illustration (such as the farmer and the soils), or to a word picture, or a wise saying. These different kinds of parable appear in the verses which follow.

THE LIGHT WILL SHINE

'Why do you bring a light into a house?' Jesus asked. 'Do you hide it under a bowl or a bed?' (v. 21).

You can almost see the crowd smiling at the very idea. A light is meant to illuminate what is concealed by darkness (v. 22). So it is put on a stand so that everyone can see.

Jesus challenged his hearers to think through the significance of this parable: 'If anyone has ears to hear, let him hear' (v. 23). He even added another parable 'Whoever has will be given more; whoever does not have, even what he has will be taken from him' (vv. 24–25).

The point of this parable is the contrast between the present concealment of the kingdom of God and its future manifestation. Jesus is among his disciples as a veiled king. But just as a lamp brought into a house is placed where it will shine brightly, so it will be with him. The day will come when Jesus will give light to the whole world (*John* 1:9). He will not remain hidden for ever.

This is why Jesus also stresses the importance of how we hear – now. If we fail to grasp the mystery of the kingdom of God now, and do not respond to it now, we may be increasingly alienated from it in the future. But if we do respond to it, we will grow in our understanding and appreciation and increasingly experience its blessings.

THE POWERFUL SEED

In verses 26 to 29, Jesus tells another of his 'farmer's tale' parables. In the earlier one about the soils, he had emphasised the importance of our response to the message of God's kingdom. This parable shows us that there is another side to the way in which the kingdom is established. It is like the seed which the farmer sows – it possesses its own power to germinate and bear fruit. Whether the farmer sleeps or rises, whether he understands crop growth or not, 'the seed sprouts and grows' and 'all by itself the soil produces corn' (vv. 27–28).

Jesus is not contradicting himself. Rather, he is telling two parables, each of which prevents us from misunderstanding the other. Both are necessary to understand the mystery of God's kingdom. The first one emphasised the need for responsive hearts. The second stresses the power of God's kingdom to overcome opposition and establish itself. What Jesus is saying is that from the outside his preaching and teaching may seem as fruitless an occupation as that of a man throwing seeds about in a field. But it is that activity which eventually produces the crop – because of the power of the seed to germinate in the soil. It may appear to our eyes that nothing is happening. But all the time the seed is at work to produce the harvest.

What an encouragement this must have been for the disciples of Jesus! And what a vital lesson for us, too! We do not always see or understand the ways of Christ; but we can have confidence that he is sowing his powerful seed and that it will bear its own fruit. His word 'will not return . . . empty' (*Isa.* 55:11). There will be a harvest.

SHELTERS GROW FROM SEEDS

The closing verses of this section contain Jesus' famous parable of the mustard seed, which was proverbially the smallest seed the people planted (v. 31). It was so small that the birds could easily swallow it (and often did, much to the frustration of every mustard farmer and his scarecrows!). Yet that mustard seed could grow into a plant so large that the birds which could have swallowed it would later find shade under its branches.

The kingdom of God is like that mustard seed. Saul of Tarsus and many others since, who were once 'birds of the air', tried to swallow it and destroy its influence in the world. But one day they too came to find shelter in its branches. Think what hope that must have given to the Christians in Rome who first read Mark's Gospel in the face of suffering and persecution. The kingdom would not be destroyed. In fact, one day the Roman Empire which sought to destroy it would seek shelter under its branches.

Think what hope this gives us in whatever part of the world we serve Jesus Christ. We are his mustard seeds today!

17

Ruler of All Nature

That day when evening came, he said to his disciples, 'Let us go over to the other side.' Leaving the crowd behind, they took him along, just as he was, in the boat. There were also other boats with him. A furious squall came up, and the waves broke over the boat, so that it was nearly swamped. Jesus was in the stern sleeping on a cushion. The disciples woke him and said to him, 'Teacher, don't you care if we drown?' He got up, rebuked the wind and said to the waves, 'Quiet! Be still!' Then the wind died down and it was completely calm. He said to his disciples, 'Why are you so afraid? Do you still have no faith?' They were terrified and asked each other, 'Who is this? Even the wind and the waves obey him!' (Mark 4:35–41).

The series of parables Jesus had told described the principles and power of the kingdom of God. In the section which Mark now introduces, he shows us how that power was manifested in real-life situations in the ministry of Jesus.

We have seen that one of the recurring themes of Mark's Gospel is: Who is Jesus? Mark constantly draws us into the story of his life so that we ask ourselves that question. Here he tells us how the disciples asked it: 'Who is this? Even the wind and the waves obey him!' (v. 41).

In these three stories, the stilling of the storm (4:35–41), the restoration of the demon-possessed man (5:1–20), and Jesus' victory over disease and death (5:21–43), Mark invites us to draw one conclusion about Jesus: he is the Messiah; he is God's Son; he is the King. He reigns over the forces of nature and chaos; over the powers of darkness; over sickness, disease, sorrow and even death itself. Jesus is Lord!

But when the disciples took Jesus that evening 'just as he was' (v. 36), they had, as yet, little real understanding of him, and no indication of what was about to happen. They were planning just another crossing of the Sea of Galilee. Some of them were fishermen and knew that lake like the backs of their hands. The trip was no more out of the ordinary for them than our daily journey to work. But it was to be interrupted frighteningly by a storm, and ended dramatically with Jesus, the carpenter of Nazareth, demonstrating his lordship when the fishermen of Galilee were helpless.

The disciples of Jesus were clearly diverted from trusting him by the storm. Their mistake was to focus attention on their circumstances rather than on Jesus. Perhaps it is not surprising that we often make the same mistake when we read this story. We become fascinated by the storm, but the real point of the story is to tell us several very important things about the Lord Jesus.

JESUS LEADS INTO STORMS

The plan to cross to the other side of Galilee by boat originated with Jesus himself (v. 35). Crossing over was, for the disciples, simply a matter of fitting in with Jesus' purposes and obeying him.

That underlines one of the most important principles of the Christian life. Sometimes we find ourselves in difficulties because of our own sin and foolishness. But there are times when the Lord himself will lead us into difficulties. Contrary to the picture sometimes painted of the Christian life, Jesus did not solve all the disciples' problems and protect them from trials and perplexities. In actual fact, sometimes he led them quite deliberately into them. This was such an occasion.

It is interesting to think of Simon Peter in this context. Later on he was to write to Christians who were facing persecution: 'Dear friends, do not be surprised at the painful trial you are suffering, *as though something strange were happening to you*' (*1 Pet.* 4:12, emphasis added).

Was he remembering the trial into which they had been led as immature disciples? Had he begun to learn then that the Lord sometimes leads his followers through dark valleys and difficult places? But why? This passage answers that question too.

THE TEST

Mark describes Jesus in words which must have come directly from Peter, the eye-witness: 'Jesus was in the stern, sleeping on a cushion' (v. 38, a fact no other Gospel writer mentions). The squall arose, and the water came over the sides of the boat and threatened to sink it. The disciples panicked, and shouted at him through the wind, 'Teacher, don't you care if we drown?' (v. 38). Notice the reply. Having stilled the storm, Jesus asked his disciples, 'Why are you so afraid? Do you still have no faith?' (v. 40).

Two issues were at stake in this situation. The disciples had been doubting whether Jesus really cared for them. They had lost faith in his love for them. Hence their question: 'Do you not care?' It was the cruellest question they could have asked, because the very reason he was in the boat, indeed in the world, and the reason he was going to die on the cross for them was precisely because he cared for them. Yet they were not persuaded in their hearts that this was so, and as a result they allowed the storm to come between them and the assurance of their Master's devotion to them. We are like them in many ways. When storms arise, we doubt his love. We allow our faith to be diverted from its anchor in the cross, and lose our moorings in the storms of life. We have so little faith!

The second issue was that the disciples had failed to trust Jesus' word. He had spoken about going over to the other side of the lake (v. 35). In the storm, they had forgotten what he said. They had not held on to his word to give themselves the assurance that they would reach the shore safely. They had allowed the voice of the storm to silence the voice of the Lord. Perhaps if they had remembered Isaiah 40:27–31 and 50:10, they would have had stronger faith.

SEEING HIS GLORY

Jesus stilled the storm (v. 39). His words are reminiscent of the strong language he uses elsewhere in this Gospel to rebuke demons

(1:25; 3:12; 9:25). Jesus is subduing the powers of darkness and bringing order out of chaos. But perhaps the most important thing for the disciples was this: for a brief moment they saw the majesty, power and glory of Jesus unveiled. They witnessed his lordship over nature and its forces. Like men in a storm who see the world momentarily illuminated by lightning and are able to get their bearings again, the disciples saw Jesus 'just as he was', in his glory. It made them realise that if they could answer one question they would have their bearings both for time and eternity: 'Who is this? Even the wind and the waves obey him!' (v. 41).

Sometimes we draw from this story the lesson: Jesus stilled the storm in nature, and he can still the storm in our hearts too. That, of course, is true. But it is not the central truth of this passage, for Mark tells us that the stilling of the natural storm raised a spiritual storm in the disciples' hearts: 'They were terrified' (v. 41). They had taken Jesus 'just as he was' (v. 36), and now they were awed to discover who he really was!

Every test and trial, every storm in life is another opportunity for you to see the glory of Jesus Christ and discover his power in your life.

18

Evil's Bondage

*They went across the lake to the region of the Gerasenes.
When Jesus got out of the boat, a man with an evil spirit
came from the tombs to meet him. This man lived in the
tombs, and no-one could bind him any more, not even with a
chain. For he had often been chained hand and foot, but he
tore the chains apart and broke the irons on his feet. No-one
was strong enough to subdue him. Night and day among the
tombs and in the hills he would cry out and cut himself with
stones. When he saw Jesus from a distance, he ran and fell on
his knees in front of him. He shouted at the top of his voice,
'What do you want with me, Jesus, Son of the Most High
God? Swear to God that you won't torture me!' For Jesus
had said to him, 'Come out of this man, you evil spirit!'
Then Jesus asked him, 'What is your name?' 'My name is
Legion,' he replied, 'for we are many.' And he begged Jesus
again and again not to send them out of the area. A large
herd of pigs was feeding on the nearby hillside. The demons
begged Jesus, 'Send us among the pigs; allow us to go into
them.' He gave them permission and the evil spirits came out
and went into the pigs. The herd, about two thousand in
number, rushed down the steep bank into the lake and were
drowned* (Mark 5:1–13).

Jesus had shown himself to the disciples as the Lord of nature by
stilling the storm on the Sea of Galilee. Now he stands before
them as the Lord of men and the Overcomer of the powers of
darkness. But before we look in greater detail at the power and
grace of Jesus, we should focus our attention on the man whose
name was Legion. He was demon-possessed.

Now, not all men are demon-possessed; yet, by nature, all men are ruled by dark and sinister forces (*Eph.* 2:2). In this sense, Legion vividly illustrates the terrible plight of the human condition. It may be that this is the reason the Gospel writers devote a good deal of time to recording the story of his deliverance.

BONDAGE

The first and most obvious thing about Legion was that he was a slave. His life was dominated by an evil, or (as some translations rightly put it) unclean spirit (v. 2). He was the pawn of evil powers, and as a result he was uncontrollable. He did not control himself; and he could not be controlled or subdued by others. People had tried to help him by restraining him with chains (v. 4), but all to no avail. With demonic strength he simply snapped them and carried on his sad life among the tombs. His condition seemed totally incurable. He was destined to belong to a closed world of hopelessness, anguish and despair.

Legion was also utterly alone. He was isolated from the rest of humanity and in a sense alienated from himself as his self-destructive tendencies reveal. He cut himself with stones (v. 5). He loathed others; but he also seemed to hate himself (contrast *Mark* 12:28–31).

DELIVERANCE

When Jesus entered this man's life, two apparently contradictory things took place. On the one hand, he ran to Jesus; on the other, when Jesus began to rebuke the demons, he shrieked at the top of his voice, 'What do you want with me, Jesus, Son of the Most High God?' (v. 7) He seemed to know that Christ could deliver him, and so he was drawn to him, and yet he shook with dread at the possible consequences. He simply could not take any more 'torture' (v. 7).

Would you not think that a man with such profound need would yield readily to Jesus, the deliverer? Theoretically we would. But to think that would suggest we understand the human heart all too superficially. No man yields to Jesus easily by nature. Tragically, like Legion, men often hold on to their bondage in evil rather than yield to the pain of transformation by Christ's power and grace.

This is underlined by the conversation that follows. The man's name, Legion, expresses the fact that he has been used as an outpost of demonic activity in this world. Perhaps, in this military language, we are meant to catch the fact that Satan's opposition to the kingdom of God is not haphazard but ruthlessly well organised. However, not even the gates of hell can prevail against our Lord's onslaught against them.

MORE VALUE THAN PIGS?

Over the centuries many people have been puzzled by the events that followed, and especially the fact that Jesus sent the demons from the man into the huge herd of pigs grazing on the bank of the sea. Two thousand of them were drowned (v. 13). The philosopher, Bertrand Russell, pointed to this story to explain (in the words of his famous essay), 'Why I am not a Christian'. Why this dreadful destruction? No answer is given by Mark, but there were probably several reasons. One was to expose the terrible power of these demons and their ultimate goal of destroying whatever they inhabited. By the same token, this holocaust of pigs as the demons took possession of them underlined the enormous power which Jesus had exercised in his authority over them.

But there is another reason. Here was a man who had been held captive in pain and shame by these evil spirits. How could he be persuaded that they would never again be able to enter and dominate his life? How could he be sure that the salvation Jesus had brought to him would never be lost? There was only one way, and Jesus chose it. It is misplaced sentimentality to weep over the destruction of the pigs. It shows that we do not have our priorities aligned to those of Jesus. (How strange it is that so many people who enjoy bacon and eggs find this scene so distasteful!) Jesus, by contrast, who had taught his disciples that they were of more value than many sparrows, also teaches them that the deliverance of one man is worth two thousand pigs and more!

Legion's story records in capital letters what is true of all men by nature: we are slaves to evil; we are not free; we are bent, ultimately, on self-destruction. Neither we ourselves, nor others, are capable of breaking the powers which have bound us. Christ alone can break the power of sin in our lives and set us free.

Are you still in the position of saying to him about your own sinful habits: Do not send them away (v. 10)? Why will you not yield to the pain of Christ's gracious work of deliverance? Why will you hold on to the sin which is destroying you? Your place is with Legion – your mind submitted to Christ, your life given over to your Lord's disposal.

19

Responses to Jesus

Those tending the pigs ran off and reported this in the town and countryside, and the people went out to see what had happened. When they came to Jesus, they saw the man who had been possessed by the legion of demons, sitting there, dressed and in his right mind; and they were afraid. Those who had seen it told the people what had happened to the demon-possessed man – and told about the pigs as well. Then the people began to plead with Jesus to leave their region. As Jesus was getting into the boat, the man who had been demon-possessed begged to go with him. Jesus did not let him, but said, 'Go home to your family and tell them how much the Lord has done for you, and how he has had mercy on you.' So the man went away and began to tell in the Decapolis how much Jesus had done for him. And all the people were amazed (Mark 5:14–20).

The coming of Jesus to the region of the Gerasenes had brought consternation. No sooner was Jesus on dry land than a demon-possessed man was screaming at him. Within a few minutes, two thousand pigs had gone hurtling to their death, and the herdsmen (whose responsibility they were) had raced back to town to 'explain' to the owners what had happened. In the midst of this confusion, only two people remained calm – Jesus, and Legion. When the townspeople came out, they saw them both – and to their astonishment Legion was sitting beside Jesus, clothed and completely sane. Jesus had made him 'normal' again.

MEN MADE NEW

In a sense, making people 'normal' again was the essence of Jesus' ministry. He came, he said, to save sinners – to restore men's broken lives by his grace and to repair the ruins into which God's image (man) had fallen. Legion is a perfect illustration of what Jesus does in any life which he enters to possess and transform. He makes men new.

But notice that Mark records two completely different responses to what Jesus did.

TRAGIC REQUEST

Think for a moment about the townspeople. What did they see? There was Legion, a man they all knew. It had been many years since they had seen him look the way he did that day. They had been long accustomed to hearing his shrieks as he ran through the graveyard in the middle of the night (v. 5). For years they had warned their children not to play near him. Perhaps they had even used him as a kind of bogy-man to frighten naughty children. There was no greater threat heard by a Gerasene child than 'I'll send you up to old Legion if you don't behave!'

Some of these people were probably related to Legion. Others remembered playing with him in childhood. What kind of response do you think would be appropriate when they saw him gloriously normalised? For years they had not been able to control him, but now he was as biddable as an obedient child. What an occasion for rejoicing!

So we might think. But we would be seriously mistaken. For Legion seems to have been greeted with a stony silence. There was no 'welcome-mat' on the faces of his townsfolk that day. Were they so taken up with gratitude to Jesus that for a moment they forgot Legion? On the contrary. They begged Jesus to leave their shores (v. 17).

What possible explanation can there be for such a response to the power of God? A moment's self-examination should give the answer. Jesus' presence had cost the Gerasenes dearly in terms of this world's goods. What had Legion ever been or done to merit the expenditure of two thousand (of their!) pigs for his salvation?

If these were the thoughts passing through the minds of the people, they were wrong on several counts. In the first place, they did not understand the depths of man's need, or the costliness to Christ of the salvation of men. To 'save' Legion would ultimately cost the Lord Jesus his life. The loss of these pigs was incidental by comparison. But they valued their pigs more than Legion's salvation. In doing so, they revealed that they valued their pigs more than their own salvation, and more than they valued Legion's Saviour.

But there was probably another element in their rejection of Jesus. They could see the radical transformation which Jesus had produced in Legion's life. Did they fear Jesus' continued presence with them because they suspected it might produce a similar transformation in them? Could it be that they would prefer to have Legion demon-possessed and live without Christ themselves? If so, it was they who were ensnared and in bondage to the Evil One.

How tragic that men, both then and now, cling to the sins which will ultimately destroy them, and beg Jesus to leave them rather than change them.

YOUR WILL BE DONE

Legion's response was very different. With all his heart he wanted to follow Jesus and be with him. He longed to have Jesus' protecting presence (v. 18). Yet our Lord had other plans for him, and refused his request (v. 19). He wanted to use him as his permanent apostle to the region of the Decapolis. So he gave him orders to return to his home and family, and to tell them what the Lord had done for him (v. 19)

Legion obeyed. It seems that his life left a lasting impression on his people. For later in the Gospel, when Jesus returned to Decapolis, some people brought him a man who was deaf and almost completely dumb (*Mark* 7:31–37). They believed Jesus could deliver him. Had they learned that from Legion?

Mark presents us here with a contrast which may seem puzzling at first sight. Jesus refused the request of the man who trusted him, but granted the request of those who rejected him. We need to learn that Jesus' refusals to his followers are always because he has some better purpose for us than that which we request. But our refusals of Jesus, when granted, lead to hardness of heart and judgment.

Like the parables, the miracles of Jesus bring us a profound challenge. The challenge of this one is simple: Do you want to go with Jesus? Or, do you want Jesus to go? These are the most important questions you could ever answer.

20

Twelve Long Years of Weakness

When Jesus had again crossed over by boat to the other side of the lake, a large crowd gathered round him while he was by the lake. Then one of the synagogue rulers, named Jairus, came there. Seeing Jesus, he fell at his feet and pleaded earnestly with him, 'My little daughter is dying. Please come and put your hands on her so that she will be healed and live.' So Jesus went with him. A large crowd followed and pressed around him. And a woman was there who had been subject to bleeding for twelve years. She had suffered a great deal under the care of many doctors and had spent all she had, yet instead of getting better she grew worse. When she heard about Jesus, she came up behind him in the crowd and touched his cloak, because she thought, 'If I just touch his clothes, I will be healed.' Immediately her bleeding stopped and she felt in her body that she was freed from her suffering. At once Jesus realised that power had gone out from him. He turned around in the crowd and asked, 'Who touched my clothes?' 'You see the people crowding against you,' his disciples answered, 'and yet you can ask, "Who touched me?"' But Jesus kept looking around to see who had done it. Then the woman, knowing what had happened to her, came and fell at his feet and, trembling with fear, told him the whole truth. He said to her, 'Daughter, your faith has healed you. Go in peace and be freed from your suffering.' (Mark 5:21–34).

O nce before we noticed Mark using a 'split-screen' technique in telling the story of Jesus' ministry. He introduces one event, and then, to convey the sense of the passing of time, he describes a second incident. In this section we come to a moving and vivid illustration of this way of story-telling.

It begins with Jairus, the synagogue ruler, pleading with Jesus to heal his daughter. She is already at death's door (vv. 22–23). Jesus went with her father immediately. There was no time to lose, it seemed. But as the crowd surged forward with them *en route* to Jairus' house, Jesus suddenly stopped and asked, 'Who touched my clothes?' (v. 30).

EVERYONE TOUCHED HIM

No wonder the disciples were exasperated. This was ridiculous! Of course someone touched his clothes – he was in a crowd. Everyone was brushing against him. What else did he expect?

They should have known better. Jesus stood his ground and looked around the faces in the crowd. To everyone's amazement (and to the horror of Jairus, now panic-stricken that Jesus had stopped), a woman stepped forward, trembling with fear, and 'told him the whole truth' (v. 33).

'The whole truth' was that she had suffered from internal bleeding for twelve years, had spent all her savings on 'cures', and was actually getting worse. She was drained of financial resources; worse, she was now drained of all her physical energy. Jesus was her last hope. She had thought, 'If I just touch his clothes, I will be healed' (v. 28). So she had come up behind him, anonymously she had thought, and touched him. Immediately the bleeding ceased.

Why, then, did Jesus stop? Why did he raise Jairus' blood pressure and bring such obvious embarrassment to this woman? As we will see, he wanted to teach Jairus a lesson; but he also wanted to give instruction to the woman in the crowd. She needed to know exactly why she had been healed. Jesus was not content that her body should be made whole; he wanted to make her faith clear and strong too.

WEAK FAITH MADE STRONG

This woman had believed that Christ's garments could heal her. Jesus made clear that it was he himself, not his garments, that had power to heal. That was why he was conscious that something had happened. Such was his sensitivity that he could distinguish this woman's touch of faith from the pushing and shoving of the crowd. They put their weight into him; she had taken strength and power out of him (v. 30).

Our Lord does not explain how he knew this. But he does seem to suggest that he had voluntarily and immediately responded to this woman's grasping for healing. But unless she realised that it was his power, not his clothes, which had healed her, she would remain diseased spiritually, even although healed physically. She would forever see Jesus superstitiously as a healer, rather than intelligently and truly as a Saviour.

NOT TOUCH, BUT FAITH

The woman had also believed that she could be healed by touching Jesus – and, indeed, when she touched him, she was healed. But Jesus had drawn her out of the crowd lest she hopelessly confuse her physical touching and what lay behind it – her simple trusting. So Jesus explains, 'Your faith has healed you' (v. 34). It was not because she had come near enough to touch him, but because she had trusted in him that she had been cured.

The church has been very slow to learn the obvious lesson from this story. In the history of the Christian faith people have often substituted nearness to physical objects for saving faith. So-called relics of the saints, or even of Christ, have been paraded before people, or purchased by them, as though they could contribute to their salvation. But Jesus once and for all delivered us from such misunderstandings. It is not his garments which save us; not even touching them could save us (are there not people who might give their right hand for the sacredness of the privilege of touching the Turin Shroud, just in case it might still be the grave cloth of Jesus?). Only faith saves us, because only faith draws on the power of Jesus Christ as Saviour.

OPEN DISCIPLESHIP

This woman also seemed to believe that she could be healed by Jesus secretly. If only she could touch him in the crowd, no one would know. She is a delightful example of how naive we can be about discipleship. How on earth could she have kept her recovery secret? Jesus called her out of the crowd to encourage her to take her stand with him. She did not need to be ashamed to confess what had happened. The sooner she did so the greater would be her joy! If she had been ashamed to confess Christ now, she might never have known the full life which he had given to her.

Mark translates Jesus' farewell words as: 'Go *into* peace' (v. 34, emphasis added). That was exactly what she did. She had entered into a new life of wholeness, both physically and spiritually. Now she was to 'go into' it with joy, praising God for all he had done for her. She had 'tried the broken cisterns' and found that 'the water failed'. That day she had discovered that 'none but Christ can satisfy'. It was the greatest discovery of her life. She came for healing and found grace. Instead of slinking away, she was called to rejoice openly in God's grace.

Has Christ ever called you out of the crowd?

21

Twelve Brief Years of Life

While Jesus was still speaking, some men came from the house of Jairus, the synagogue ruler. 'Your daughter is dead,' they said. 'Why bother the teacher any more?' Ignoring what they said, Jesus told the synagogue ruler, 'Don't be afraid; just believe.' He did not let anyone follow him except Peter, James and John the brother of James. When they came to the home of the synagogue ruler, Jesus saw a commotion, with people crying and wailing loudly. He went in and said to them, 'Why all this commotion and wailing? The child is not dead but asleep.' But they laughed at him. After he put them all out, he took the child's father and mother and the disciples who were with him, and went in where the child was. He took her by the hand and said to her, 'Talitha koum!' (which means, 'Little girl, I say to you, get up!'). Immediately the girl stood up and walked around (she was twelve years old). At this they were completely astonished. He gave strict orders not to let anyone know about this, and told them to give her something to eat (Mark 5:35–43).

Jairus had come to Jesus in the greatest crisis of his life. His daughter was dying. She was only twelve years old, and her life was all that mattered to her father now. That was why he must have been overwhelmed with frustration when Jesus stopped to speak with – a woman! It emerged that she had been healed by Jesus. Why couldn't he just ignore her and get home with him? Furthermore, she had been suffering from haemorrhaging for twelve years – couldn't she have waited another half an hour and allowed his daughter to live? Even now servants were coming from his house to tell him that his daughter had died (v. 35).

The fact that Mark records the length of the woman's illness and the age of Jairus' daughter is probably significant (vv. 25, 42). In both cases it amounted to twelve years. Was Jesus trying to teach the synagogue ruler the meaning of compassion? For this poor woman had been drained of energy during the same years in which Jairus' daughter had grown and been healthy. Certainly Jesus was planning to strengthen the faith of Jairus by his teaching to the woman.

A FATHER'S FAITH

Jairus had some kind of faith. Presumably he had heard Jesus speak in the synagogue at Capernaum. We do not know whether he approved altogether of what Jesus had said. He had also heard of, and perhaps seen with his own eyes, some of the miracles. In his desperation, he now threw himself on Jesus' mercy. He appealed to his willingness to come to his aid. He knew that it was not a matter of 'can you?' but 'will you?' (v. 23).

TESTING

True faith grows by testing. The good workman tests his work to make sure that it will do all he intends it to do, and take whatever strains it may experience. For that reason, among others, Jesus stopped to speak to the woman he had healed – to test Jairus' faith, as well as hers.

While Jesus was speaking to the woman, messengers had come with the sad news that the little girl had died. Perhaps concerned to see Jairus in the company of Jesus, and anxious in case he should act like a drowning man grabbing at a straw, they encouraged him not to 'bother the teacher any more' (v. 35) and to 'come home with us'.

Here was a real test for weak faith. What did Jairus really think of Jesus? Was he, as his servants seemed to indicate, just another teacher? Would he be as helpless as the next man when face to face with life's ultimate reality? Was faith in Jesus good coinage for this life only?

Jesus overheard the servants' words, but ignored them and

encouraged Jairus to do the same. He gave two commands: Do not fear! Believe! The first was to reassure Jairus that the enemy of death was not stronger than Jesus. The second was to encourage him to hold on to Christ and trust him implicitly. Jairus realised he had no other option. He was 'driven' to trust Jesus in his utter helplessness. That is what true faith means.

STRENGTHENED FAITH

Jesus was urging Jairus to follow the example of Abraham. He too had been faced with an impossible situation: his wife was barren and beyond the age of child-bearing. Abraham himself was as good as dead. Yet God had promised them a son! Paul tells us that Abraham faced the facts of the situation, but he did not allow his actions or thoughts to be determined by his circumstances. Instead he kept his eye fixed on the promise God had given him (*Rom.* 4:18–21). He grew strong in faith as a result.

Jairus was being challenged to do the same. In order to encourage him, Jesus told those who were 'mourning' in the house that the little girl was not dead but merely sleeping. Her condition was only temporary.

That was perfectly true. But faith and unbelief understood it in different ways. The crowd ridiculed Jesus (v. 40) – surely one of the saddest statements in the whole Bible. They thought they knew better. Jesus had not even seen the body. But to Jairus it was a word of hope. Jesus believed his daughter would be restored.

In the face of derision, Jairus sided with Jesus. His faith triumphed because he trusted in a triumphant Saviour who showed himself to be Lord of life and death.

THE SECRET

Jesus raised the little girl back to life. He took her by the hand and said, 'Arise!' And she did! No wonder the witnesses were astonished. But why did Jesus act so secretly, taking only the child's parents and his three closest disciples with him (vv. 37, 40)? Surely if he had done this in full view of those who mocked him the effect would have been astonishing. He would not only have subdued their pride, he would have created a springboard for evangelism which would have swept thousands into the kingdom of God.

But, of course, that is not true. Those who will not trust Jesus' word will not trust his deeds. The Gospel assumes throughout that intimate knowledge of Jesus is not given to those who despise him. Here one of Jesus' earlier words was being fulfilled: those who do not have (faith) will find that even what they have (the opportunity to have faith, and to see Jesus work graciously in a time of need) will be taken from them (see *Mark* 4:25).

No doubt the talk in the local inn that evening was about how Jairus' daughter had been 'asleep'. 'Strange,' some of them would say, 'it was just what that Jesus said. Give him his due.' Unbelievers found another way of explaining what really happened that afternoon. That was why Jesus gave strict orders that her resurrection should be kept a secret among those who believed.

Notice what Jesus did in that little room. He took the little girl's hand (v. 41). By doing so – and touching a dead body – Jesus himself became ritually unclean (just as he had done when the woman with the haemorrhage had touched his garment [cf. *Lev.* 15]). He shared in her death in order to deliver her from it.

Later, on Calvary, Jesus would share again in death. This time it was our death. He would become 'unclean' for our sake, and bear God's judgment against our sin. In a sense what he was doing here was but a preview of what he would do then. It was also a preview of what he will do at the end of time, when he will take us by the hand and say, 'Arise!' That will not be in secret, but in public: 'Every eye will see him.' Even those who mocked him that day will see him – and will mourn, this time for themselves (cf. *Rev.* 1:7).

22

Rejection in Nazareth

Jesus left there and went to his home town, accompanied by his disciples. When the Sabbath came, he began to teach in the synagogue, and many who heard him were amazed. 'Where did this man get these things?' they asked. 'What's this wisdom that has been given him, that he even does miracles! Isn't this the carpenter? Isn't this Mary's son and the brother of James, Joseph, Judas and Simon? Aren't his sisters here with us?' And they took offence at him. Jesus said to them, 'Only in his home town, among his relatives and in his own house is a prophet without honour.' He could not do any miracles there except lay his hands on a few sick people and heal them. And he was amazed at their lack of faith (Mark 6:1–6a).

Jesus had been in his adopted town of Capernaum, where at least some of his followers had their homes (*Mark* 1:21–34). Now he paid a return visit to Nazareth, the scene of his childhood (*Luke* 2:51). He was 'accompanied by his disciples' (v. 1).

A visit home is always an occasion to look forward to. There is family to visit and there are old friends to see. But Jesus was not visiting for old times' sake. He had brought his disciples with him because he was engaged in kingdom work. That emerged very clearly when, on the Sabbath, he was invited to preach to the local synagogue congregation.

AMAZEMENT

Mark does not tell us what the Scripture reading was that day, nor does he mention the theme of Jesus' sermon. Some students of the

Gospels have argued that this incident is identical with the one recorded in Luke 4:14ff. In that case, the Scripture reading was taken from Isaiah 61:1ff. But it seems more likely that Luke records an earlier visit. Here Mark envisages a return visit during which Jesus found his townspeople no more responsive than they were at the beginning of his ministry.

The amazement of the people was obvious. Wherever Jesus preached people recognised the note of authority and authenticity in his message. He preached biblically, simply, graciously and powerfully. They must have felt what we too feel when we hear God's word properly expounded: 'So that's what this passage means. It's so clear. Why didn't I see it before?'

RESENTMENT

But amazement was only part of their response. Sadly, it was coupled with resentment: 'They took offence at him' (v. 3).

There were several elements in this. While Jesus had done miracles elsewhere (in Capernaum, for example, which was some twenty miles north), he did very few miracles in Nazareth. How could he, asks Mark, for people who simply would not trust him? (v. 5).

Were the people piqued that Jesus would not put on a demonstration of power for his own folk? They knew that he had worked remarkable miracles elsewhere, but they taunted him about it: 'He even does miracles, how come he's so wise?' (v. 2). One can sense the terrible small-town mentality gone badly wrong as they closed ranks in opposition to Jesus.

Much of what they said smacks of pride. Other people might be taken in by Jesus, but they knew better. The implication of their words (vv. 2–3) is plain: 'Who does he think he is, speaking with such assurance about God's word and about himself? We'll show him!' Then in the consciousness that even this would not hurt him as deeply as they wanted to, they twisted the knife in the wound: 'Isn't this *Mary's* son? (v. 3, emphasis added). The innuendo – to a Jew – was plain: even if a man's father were dead, he was still *his father's* son. To refer to Jesus as 'son of Mary' was to cast a stigma on his mother, and on himself. It was to raise doubts about his legitimacy.

Isaiah had prophesied accurately when he said that the Messiah would be 'despised and rejected by men' (*Isa.* 53:3). He was, indeed, 'without honour' (v. 4).

Jesus had suffered the subtle attacks of the Pharisees with their contorted theological arguments. Here, in Nazareth, the abuse had no subtle nuances. It was open, brazen rejection. They resented and despised him. They could not tolerate one who had come from among them and yet was so different from them. In that respect, Nazareth was a miniature of world history.

DETRIMENT

But their resentment proved to be to their detriment. Jesus had said that the measure we use would be the measure used for us (*Mark* 4:24). That was tragically true for the Nazarenes. For where people did not trust him, Jesus would not do any miracles. Mark says, 'He *could not* do any miracles there' (emphasis added) – not in the sense that it was physically impossible, for he did heal some sick folk (v. 5), but that it would have been morally and spiritually inconsistent. Where the kingdom of God is rejected it is inappropriate for the King to share its new life and joy.

Jesus was 'amazed at their lack of faith' (v. 6). This is the only occasion Mark records such a reaction to unbelief. The people of Nazareth enjoyed so many advantages. The Son of God had lived among them in childhood. He had preached to them with power. He had carried out some miracles. It seems likely that he had even returned to them after an earlier rejection (*Luke* 4:28). But they were blind to his identity, deaf to his message, and hardened their hearts against him. Mark does not record any further visits to Nazareth. Perhaps there were none. Even what they had was taken from them (*Mark* 4:25). Let us learn from their sad example.

23

Sent Out by Jesus

*Then Jesus went round teaching from village to village. Call-
ing the Twelve to him, he sent them out two by two and gave
them authority over evil spirits. These were his instructions:
'Take nothing for the journey except a staff – no bread, no
bag, no money in your belts. Wear sandals but not an extra
tunic. Whenever you enter a house, stay there until you leave
that town. And if any place will not welcome you or listen
to you, shake the dust off your feet when you leave, as a
testimony against them.' They went out and preached that
people should repent. They drove out many demons and
anointed many sick people with oil and healed them* (Mark
6:6b–13).

J esus had been rejected in his home town of Nazareth. But
rejection is never a reason for the servant of God to despair (see
2 Corinthians 4:1–6). Jesus' heart was set on obedience to his
Father, wherever that led him and whatever it might cost him. So
he did not lose heart. Instead he moved on and began to teach in
the various villages (v. 1). He saw rejection in Nazareth as the
indication of God's providence to spread the good news of
the kingdom of God elsewhere.

FEARLESS OR FOOLISH?

Later in the New Testament period, the early church learned
from Jesus' example. It kept a proper balance between a fearless
perseverance and a foolish persistence. So, here, Jesus tells his
disciples to leave the town which does not welcome them.

There is a lesson here for the work and witness of the contemporary church. By and large we have lost the sense of urgency
which these early disciples had. As a consequence we often
lose their sense of flexibility. We allow ourselves to be engaged in
ways and spheres of activity just because we have always done
things in this way and in that place. Striking the balance between
perseverance and mere tradition is not easy; but it is vital to the advance of the kingdom of God. We always need to be asking if we
are using the resources God has given us in the best possible ways.
If we retained a sense of the urgency of our task as Christ's
witnesses, we would be more likely to be flexible in order to serve
him fruitfully.

Clearly this section creates something of a 'pause' in Mark's
rapid account of Jesus' life. Its central theme, however, is Jesus'
preparation and commissioning of his disciples (*Mark* 3:14). Two
things predominate.

AUTHORITY

Jesus sent out his disciples with his own authority (v. 7). In
Jewish law the one who was sent by another carried the authority
of the one who sent him. It was just as if the sender himself had
come. Consequently, the treatment received by the 'sent one'
(which is what the word 'apostle' means) was understood as the
treatment accorded to the sender. These disciples would therefore
have been recognised as representatives of Jesus in the fullest
possible sense – and those who received or rejected them would
have realised they were receiving or rejecting Jesus himself.

This principle was true of the apostles in a special sense. That
was why they were able to give the New Testament writings to the
church as authoritative Scripture. But there is a secondary sense in
which this principle is true for all Christians. We represent Jesus.
The reaction of men and women to us as his brothers and servants
is their reaction to him (see *Matt.* 25:40, 45). That places on our
shoulders a tremendous responsibility to represent him properly. It
also gives us a sense of spiritual authority and dignity – it is King
Jesus we represent.

MANNER OF LIFE

This responsibility lies behind the further instructions which Jesus gave to the apostles. They were to undertake their mission with the minimum of personal supplies (vv. 8–9). They were men with one purpose, and nothing should be allowed to detract from it. Their message was an urgent one: the kingdom of God was near, in Jesus; men should therefore turn away from sin and live in obedience to God (v. 12). Everything about their bearing should indicate that their visit would be brief – the villagers must respond now!

For the same reason, when they were welcomed into a village they were to live in the same house until they left. Jesus was not merely concerned that his disciples would turn up their noses at the food or lack of home comforts they received. That certainly would have brought disgrace on their message. More likely, he was concerned that his disciples should not appear to be on a merely social visit – one night with one family, another with another family, and so on. They were there on the Lord's business, not on holiday. There were times for rest, but this was not one of them.

In a nutshell, the apostles, as Christ's representatives, were to do as Jesus himself would have done. The tone of their conversation, the style of their lives, everything about them was to reflect their Master; everything was to give expression to the seriousness and urgency of the message they brought from him.

Even the way they left the village was to express the significance of their visit. If they were rejected, they were to shake the dust of the village from their feet as a prophetic sign. Orthodox Jews visiting Gentile countries did exactly this when they left – shaking off any 'contamination' they might have contracted during their visit. In this action they indicated that the foreign country was outside the sphere of God's holy people and divorced from his grace. In the same way, Jesus was saying that a town which was geographically within the sphere of God's covenant might spiritually be a stranger to it.

What was true then of towns and villages can become true today of denominations, congregations and individuals. The test is: how do we respond to the message Christ has sent to us in his word? How do we react to his authority? How do we treat those he sends us as his servants? Are we willing to repent?

24

A King Enslaved

King Herod heard about this, for Jesus' name had become well known. Some were saying, 'John the Baptist has been raised from the dead, and that is why miraculous powers are at work in him.' Others said, 'He is Elijah.' And still others claimed, 'He is a prophet, like one of the prophets of long ago.' But when Herod heard this, he said, 'John, the man I beheaded, has been raised from the dead!' For Herod himself had given orders to have John arrested, and he had him bound and put in prison. He did this because of Herodias, his brother Philip's wife, whom he had married. For John had been saying to Herod, 'It is not lawful for you to have your brother's wife.' So Herodias nursed a grudge against John and wanted to kill him. But she was not able to, because Herod feared John and protected him, knowing him to be a righteous and holy man. When Herod heard John, he was greatly puzzled; yet he liked to listen to him. Finally the opportune time came. On his birthday Herod gave a banquet for his high officials and military commanders and the leading men of Galilee. When the daughter of Herodias came in and danced, she pleased Herod and his dinner guests. The king said to the girl, 'Ask me for anything you want, and I'll give it to you.' And he promised her with an oath, 'Whatever you ask I will give you, up to half my kingdom.' She went out and said to her mother, 'What shall I ask for?' 'The head of John the Baptist,' she answered. At once the girl hurried in to the king with the request: 'I want you to give me right now the head of John the Baptist on a platter.' The king was greatly distressed, but because of his oaths and his dinner guests, he did not want to refuse her. So he immediately sent an executioner with orders to bring John's head. The man went, beheaded John in the prison, and brought back his head on a platter. He presented it to the girl, and she gave it to her mother. On hearing of this, John's disciples came and took his body and laid it in a tomb (Mark 6:14–29).

We come now to a new section in Mark's Gospel. It extends from 6:14 to 8:30 and records a period of relative withdrawal on the part of Jesus. Mark introduces it with ominous words: Herod had heard of the activity of Jesus and his disciples. No one could predict how Herod would respond. Jesus wisely chose to find some place of relative obscurity beyond Galilee, at least for the time being.

The family name 'Herod' is synonymous in Scripture with opposition to the gospel. It was this Herod's father (Herod the Great) who had perpetrated the massacre of the innocents recorded in Matthew 2:16–18. In turn, Herod the Great's grandson, Herod Agrippa, died in the wake of his blasphemy (*Acts* 12:20ff). The Herod mentioned here bore many of the family traits.

JOHN RESURRECTED?

Why should the name of Jesus strike such fear into Herod's heart? Rumours were already spreading about his identity. The powers of the promised new age were already visible in his ministry. Some thought that he might be Elijah, whose return had been promised as the forerunner of the Day of the Lord (*Mal.* 4:5). Others thought he must be one of the prophets returned from the dead.

But there was another view: could he be John the Baptist, raised and returned (v. 14)? That was Herod's private conviction. But it was not a conclusion based on spiritual understanding. It was the conviction of a guilty conscience, for Herod was the one who had pronounced the death sentence on the Baptist's life: 'John, the man I beheaded, has been raised from the dead' (v. 16). In Jesus he saw the same God-ordained threat to his indulgence in his sin. Jesus would now become the object of his evil plans. Later in the Gospel, that opposition would come to its bitter fruition (see 12:13; *Luke*

23:8–12). Jesus knew that the time for his final passion had not yet come, and so he withdrew from Herod's territory.

But why had Herod put John to death? Here Mark explains for the sake of his readers who, presumably, had little knowledge of recent Palestinian history.

John the Baptist had consistently and fearlessly preached his message of repentance. He had applied it with equal consistency to the religious and the irreligious, the great and the lowly – including Herod. Nor had John spoken only in generalities or of trivialities. He had preached that Herod's present marriage to Herodias was contrary to God's law, and thus should be dissolved.

HEROD'S SIN

Herod had married Herodias, his brother's wife. That was clearly contrary to the law of Moses which prohibited marriage to a brother's wife (*Lev.* 18:16; 20:21).

Furthermore, Herodias, as her name suggests, belonged to the same family as Herod. She was, in fact, his niece. The law of Moses prohibited the marriage of an aunt and her nephew (*Lev.* 18:13). Certainly some in John's time believed that this was a principle which applied to parallel relationships (aunt and nephew being parallel to uncle and niece). So Herod's marriage could also be regarded as incestuous. There were probably many religious people who were shocked by this. No doubt some of the leaders spoke together privately about it. But John, perhaps alone, had brought the word of God to bear on the situation without compromise. Herod had sinned; he must repent. Repentance could mean only one thing: he must return to living according to God's law and repair all the damage he had done to others as far as that was possible. Notice exactly what John had been saying: 'It is not lawful for *you* to have your brother's wife' (v. 18, emphasis added). He had not spoken privately behind Herod's back. He had the courage to speak openly and plainly to him about his sin.

HEROD'S CONFLICT

John's preaching had affected Herod and Herodias in different ways. It enraged Herodias. She 'nursed a grudge against [him] and wanted to kill him' (v. 19). By contrast, Herod experienced a range of conflicting emotions. He feared John and actually protected him against his wife's plots. He was moved by John's preaching. Indeed he actually 'liked to listen to him' (v. 20). Perhaps Herod instinctively knew that John the Baptist was the one man who appeared in his court who told the unadorned truth. Clearly Herod admired John. And no wonder, for John was perhaps the first real man he had ever met. So he was torn between his admiration for John, who was all that Herod knew he himself ought to be – but was not, and his bondage to his desire for Herodias.

HEROD'S DOWNFALL

The manner in which the issue was finally settled is very revealing. Like John, Herodias knew Herod's weaknesses better than he did himself. She knew that sin never exists in isolation. Not only was Herod an adulterer; he was full of self-importance and pride. He threw a party which seems to have turned into a ghastly drunken orgy. The men present were prepared to turn the occasion into one of unbridled lust. Herodias was not above using such an occasion for her own ends. She sent in her daughter, Salome, to dance before them. In a moment of foolish public boasting, Herod was so carried away that he promised her anything in return for her performance.

Imagine, for a moment, the noise and revelry, the crude comments of these men, flaming with lust. You can almost hear the silence falling as Salome immediately responded to his foolish offer: 'Give me right now the head of John the Baptist on a platter' (v. 25).

Herod was trapped. His men knew it; Salome knew it; Herodias knew it; Herod knew it. There was only one way of escape. He must 'lose face' before all these men and break his drunken promise. But the cost was too high. He would rather lose John than his own pride and desire for influence.

Notice two important lessons this story is meant to teach us.

(i) *Herod had put off his decision to follow God's word.* He was 'not quite ready for it'. But in the event, the decision was forced on him at a time when he was least ready to make it. In dealing with our sins, there is never a time when we are 'more ready'. We must deal with them now, or we may not be able to deal with them later.

(ii) *Herod seemed to be the prisoner of one particular sin.* In his case it was sexual sin. But no sin exists in isolation. Like so many men, Herod discovered that failure to overcome one diagnosed sin is simply the symptom of failure to deal with sin in general. His spiritual life was eventually ruined by the sin of pride.

No wonder Herod's conscience was so tender when he heard about the ministry of Jesus. But this was more a sense of alarm than a spirit of repentance. The tenderness in his conscience did not last. When he reappears in the Gospels, it is as a hardened man. That was why, when Jesus was brought before him during his trial, he had nothing to say. For rather than seeking forgiveness, Herod wanted to be amused by Jesus: he 'hoped to see him perform some miracle' (*Luke* 23:8). So he 'plied Jesus with many questions, but Jesus gave him no answer' (*Luke* 23:9). The real Herod was then displayed: he 'ridiculed and mocked him' (*Luke* 23:11). Having rejected the preaching of John, he ended life ridiculing the One whom John had said was greater than himself. In the end, God had no more to say to Herod.

The lesson is crystal clear. Unless we silence sin, sin will silence conscience. Unless we heed God's word, the day may come when we despise God's Son – and then God will have nothing more to say to us.

25

The Faithful Shepherd

The apostles gathered round Jesus and reported to him all they had done and taught. Then, because so many people were coming and going that they did not even have a chance to eat, he said to them, 'Come with me by yourselves to a quiet place and get some rest.' So they went away by themselves in a boat to a solitary place. But many who saw them leaving recognised them and ran on foot from all the towns and got there ahead of them. When Jesus landed and saw a large crowd, he had compassion on them, because they were like sheep without a shepherd. So he began teaching them many things. By this time it was late in the day, so his disciples came to him. 'This is a remote place,' they said, 'and it's already very late. Send the people away so that they can go to the surrounding countryside and villages and buy themselves something to eat.' But he answered, 'You give them something to eat.' They said to him, 'That would take eight months of a man's wages! Are we to go and spend that much on bread and give it to them to eat?' 'How many loaves do you have?' he asked. 'Go and see.' When they found out, they said, 'Five – and two fish.' Then Jesus directed them to have all the people sit down in groups on the green grass. So they sat down in groups of hundreds and fifties. Taking the five loaves and the two fish and looking up to heaven, he gave thanks and broke the loaves. Then he gave them to his disciples to set before the people. He also divided the two fish among them all. They all ate and were satisfied, and the disciples picked up twelve basketfuls of broken pieces of bread and fish. The number of the men who had eaten was five thousand (Mark 6:30–44).

The disciples whom Jesus had sent out on mission for the kingdom of God (see 6:6–13) now returned and reported to him. In view of the possibility of opposition from Herod, and the sheer hustle and bustle of life (v. 31), Jesus invited them to spend some time quietly together, resting. He was concerned for their well-being as his servants, and in this respect he sets before the church an example to follow.

Thus, the disciple band set sail for a quiet spot. But it was not to be. Such was the impact made by their ministry that people would not let them out of their sight. By the time they had landed, a huge crowd had gathered (v. 34).

COMPASSION

Jesus' reaction to this scene gives us the clue to understanding the miracle which follows. He was filled with compassion for the people because they were like shepherdless sheep (v. 34). As the boat pulled into shore, that was probably what these thousands of people literally looked like, their white clothes set against the background of the green grass (v. 39). As they rushed towards the landing-place, they seemed for all the world to be like a huge flock of sheep who lacked order, discipline and leadership. They needed someone to guide them. They were hungry and thirsty for spiritual nourishment; they were straying and lost. How like poor, wandering sheep they were!

SHEPHERDLESS SHEEP

They were supposed to have 'shepherds'. There were priests and teachers of the law, but they had failed to nourish them. Then there was Herod, the king. He should have been the shepherd of the people. Perhaps the setting of this story following the description of Herod is quite deliberate on Mark's part. Herod had thrown a banquet for the rich and famous, and during it had slain John who had been a true shepherd of God's flock. Instead of denying himself for the sake of the people, as their true shepherd, Herod had indulged himself and ignored them.

Jesus stood in marked contrast. Whereas Herod had fed his own lusts, Jesus had compassion on the people and fed them, spiritually and physically. He proved himself to be the Good Shepherd. This is the message of the miracle of the feeding of the five thousand.

FEED THE SHEEP

First, Jesus teaches his disciples that their responsibility is to be shepherds of the people. They are to feed the five thousand (v. 37)! We can almost hear their protests echoing through two thousand years of history. Jesus must be joking! It would take the equivalent of many thousands of pounds to buy even the basics to give them a meal (think of the cost of a wedding reception!).

Of course the disciples could not feed them, at least, not in their own strength. But in the strength of Christ they did feed them. What they took out to the people, in a way they never understood, was able to satisfy their hunger. For the disciples, this was but a foretaste of what Jesus planned to do in them and through them in the years to come.

But, secondly, notice how Jesus is the Shepherd of the people. Quite deliberately he gives expression to the thought that had crossed his mind at the first sight of this huge crowd of people: they were uncared for sheep; he would shepherd them. He would reveal himself to them as the Shepherd of Israel (*Ezek.* 34:23).

He arranged the people in groups of hundreds and fifties (v. 40) – a reminder of the way in which the flock of God had been organised in the Exodus (*Exod.* 18:21). Then, just as the Lord had given them manna in the wilderness, so Jesus fed these, his sheep.

Perhaps this is why Mark included the incidental piece of information that the people sat on 'green grass' (v. 39). It is, of course, another little piece of evidence linking this Gospel to one of the disciples who had been an eyewitness of the event (Peter). But did Mark also see it as an extension of the picture of Jesus as the Good Shepherd of his people, making them 'lie down in green pastures' (*Psa.* 23:2)? It seems very likely. The Shepherd of the Galilean lakeside was the fulfilment of David's most intimate picture of his Lord.

There is another reason why Mark describes this miracle at this point in the Gospel. The previous section, on Herod, had raised the question: Who is Jesus? But it had then gone on to describe the murder of John the Baptist. Why did Mark not include the answer to that question then? Because he knew that the next section of his Gospel would answer it. Jesus is the One who has compassion; Jesus is the One who meets men's needs. He is the Good Shepherd who one day will lay down his life for his sheep. Perhaps some of those whom Jesus fed went home that day, singing with new meaning:

> *The Lord's my Shepherd, I'll not want.*
> *He makes me down to lie*
> *In pastures green: he leadeth me*
> *the quiet waters by.*

26

Jesus Meets All Needs

Immediately Jesus made his disciples get into the boat and go on ahead of him to Bethsaida, while he dismissed the crowd. After leaving them, he went up on a mountainside to pray. When evening came, the boat was in the middle of the lake, and he was alone on land. He saw the disciples straining at the oars, because the wind was against them. About the fourth watch of the night he went out to them, walking on the lake. He was about to pass by them, but when they saw him walking on the lake, they thought he was a ghost. They cried out, because they all saw him and were terrified. Immediately he spoke to them and said, 'Take courage! It is I. Don't be afraid.' Then he climbed into the boat with them, and the wind died down. They were completely amazed, for they had not understood about the loaves; their hearts were hardened. When they had crossed over, they landed at Gennesaret and anchored there. As soon as they got out of the boat, people recognised Jesus. They ran throughout that whole region and carried the sick on mats to wherever they heard he was. And wherever he went – into villages, towns or countryside – they begged him to let them touch even the edge of his cloak, and all who touched him were healed (Mark 6:45–56).

The story of the feeding of the five thousand ends with unexplained abruptness in Mark's Gospel: 'Immediately Jesus made his disciples get into the boat and go on ahead of him to Bethsaida' (v. 45). Why the immediacy? And why the separation?

Five thousand people represented the population of two of the largest towns in that region. Perhaps Jesus was concerned that if the real secret of the feeding of the multitude became commonly known it would just be a matter of moments before these people would proclaim him to be their long-hoped-for Messiah. He knew that his own disciples had hardly begun to grasp his real ministry as yet; how much less did the people in general understand? So, rather than be involved in a Galilean uprising, he sent his disciples away quickly, dispersed the crowd, and went alone into the hill country to pray (vv. 45–46).

COMMUNION

Mark represents Jesus as 'the Son of God' (1:1). Now he pictures him in fellowship in prayer with his Father. But he gives us no direct insight into the themes of Jesus' prayer-life. We are simply left to draw the conclusion that Jesus needed time alone with God.

How often we comment on this and hear sermons about it, yet how little we do – for ourselves or others – to put it into practice. Jesus was a man of constant prayer, and yet he also sought special times of fellowship with his Father, when the strategy of his life and ministry might be reviewed. We need to follow that pattern. We need to help others to do so as well. Not all mothers, for example, can send their little disciples away in order to have time alone with God! Not all husbands realise that their wives need such times, as they do themselves. At the very lowest level, our Lord's example is an encouragement to build seasons of special communion with God into our lives, and to do what we can to help others do so as well.

But the main point of this passage lies in the difficulties the disciples found themselves in (once again!). 'The wind was against them' (v. 48), and try as they might they could not reach the shore. Jesus had noticed this earlier in the evening, but it was not until three o'clock in the morning ('the fourth watch of the night') that he went to their help, walking miraculously over the water.

Mark tells us that Jesus 'was about to pass by them' (v. 48). That seems a strange comment until we remember that Mark is probably recording the very words he had heard Peter use in a sermon: 'We saw this strange figure coming to us across the water. We thought it was a ghost. It was about to pass us by, when we cried out.' Jesus reassured them by identifying himself: 'It is I. Don't be afraid' (v. 50). He climbed into the boat, the wind died down, and they reached the shore.

LESSONS

This incident was meant to teach the disciples two things.

(i) *Their own hardness of heart.* 'They had not understood about the loaves; their hearts were hardened' (v. 52). But what had they not understood about the loaves? They had not learned from the miracle who Jesus really was. Earlier in the day he had shown himself to be the Shepherd of his people. They should have known that he would not abandon them now in their troubles. They should have been trusting but instead they were terrified.

(ii) *The glory of their Master.* Jesus had identified himself with words which must have sounded like an echo in the ears of the disciples: 'It is I', or 'I am he', 'Do not fear'. Where had they heard those words before? Later they would remember that this was the way the Lord characteristically introduced himself to his needy people in the Old Testament. He was 'I Am', the Lord who banished his people's fears.

They should also have remembered what had just happened – when Jesus had organised the people in groups reminiscent of the days of the Exodus, in order to feed them. His actions were a hint to the disciples that just as God had led the people through the Red Sea so that they came to no harm, so Jesus would never let his people perish until their work was completed. Again, he had proved his utter trustworthiness to them. But, like us, they were all too slow to believe it.

ENDLESS NEEDS

The closing verses of this chapter underline one of the themes which Mark has been hinting at all through this section: the quantity and depth of the needs to which Jesus responded. Jesus' arrival in Gennesaret was the signal for an outpouring of need for him from the surrounding towns and villages. Graciously he healed them. Whether in the fourth watch of the night, or the blaze of the noonday sun, he cared for men and women.

Yet, it is apparently possible to see the power and grace of Jesus, and to have hearts which remain hardened. Nearness to him – like that of the disciples – is no guarantee of real trust in him. Even being the recipient of blessing from him is not always the same things as genuine faith in him. Like Herod with John the Baptist, it is possible for us to be hearers of God's word, yet to have hearts which are darkened and hardened towards it.

27

Men Without Grace

The Pharisees and some of the teachers of the law who had
come from Jerusalem gathered round Jesus and saw some of
his disciples eating food with hands that were 'unclean', that
is, unwashed. (The Pharisees and all the Jews do not eat
unless they give their hands a ceremonial washing, holding to
the tradition of the elders. When they come from the market-
place they do not eat unless they wash. And they observe
many other traditions, such as the washing of cups, pitchers
and kettles.) So the Pharisees and teachers of the law asked
Jesus, 'Why don't your disciples live according to the tradition
of the elders instead of eating their food with "unclean"
hands?' He replied, 'Isaiah was right when he prophesied
about you hypocrites; as it is written: "These people honour
me with their lips, but their hearts are far from me. They
worship me in vain; their teachings are but rules taught by
men." You have let go of the commands of God and are hold-
ing on to the traditions of men' (Mark 7:1–8).

The Gospel of Mark is punctuated by the appearances of the
Pharisees. We have already seen them in 2:16, 24 and 3:6 as
opponents of Jesus and his teaching. Now they have come down
from Jerusalem in order to spy on him. Mark indicates that they
came in sufficient numbers to gather round Jesus, perhaps to
isolate him from any popular support he might have had (v. 1).

No doubt they also wanted to scrutinise his every move, and
to do all in their powers to unnerve him. They were, after all,
accustomed to people being unnerved in their presence. How little
they really understood Jesus! He was free from the desire for praise

from men which plagued some of these Pharisees. Since he lived in the full light of his Father's holy presence, he would not be unnerved by their presence.

CAUGHT RED-HANDED!

Imagine the glee, then, in the Pharisees' hearts, when they caught some of the Lord's disciples beginning a meal without going through the ceremony of first washing their hands (v. 2). The fact that Mark says 'some' of the disciples were caught red-handed (or better, 'dirty-handed' in this instance!) suggests that these men were quite a mixed bunch.

Mark was writing for a largely Gentile audience, and so he takes time to explain the significance of this (vv. 3–4). We too wash our hands before meals, but for hygienic not religious reasons. These Pharisees were less concerned about hygiene and cleanliness than they were about the 'tradition of the elders'. As far as they were concerned, eating with unwashed hands was an indication of indifference to moral holiness. So the Pharisees washed everything – hands, cups and even the kettle!

How complicated the lives of the Pharisees must have been by comparison with the life of Jesus and his disciples. And how child-like the lives of the disciples must have seemed by comparison with the complexity of the Pharisees. That was not accidental. In fact, it takes us to the very heart of the difference between the Pharisees and Jesus. To them, God was a distant Law-maker who hemmed in the lives of the people. To Jesus, God was the Father of those who trusted in him. He wanted his children to live in open fellowship with him. God's laws express a Father's wisdom.

Read in one way, the Pharisees' words were simply expressions of concern that Jesus' disciples were not following the 'traditions'. But their question was a barbed one. Jesus himself was the object of their attack: 'Why don't *your* disciples live according to the traditions of the elders?' (v. 5, emphasis added). 'You are responsible for your disciples. They are flouting the traditions. That means *you* are flouting the traditions', was what these men were really saying.

Notice how Jesus replied: directly, penetratingly and biblically.

He quoted Isaiah 29:13 to expose three elements in the Pharisees' lives.

THE TRUTH ABOUT THESE PHARISEES

(i) *They were hypocrites.* 'You hypocrites', Jesus called them. The 'hypocrite' was an actor. In the ancient world, actors did not wear make-up to disguise themselves for their part. Instead, they wore masks representing the character. The real personality of the actor was hidden behind the mask he wore. That was the truth about these Pharisees. Their lips said one thing; their hearts spoke a different language altogether. They played a public role of being men devoted to God, when in fact their attitudes and actions demonstrated that they did not really know God at all. We do not need to belong to the sect of the Pharisees to share their sin.

(ii) *Their hearts were distanced from God.* They pretended to be near to God. Their whole lives were regulated by religious duties and activities. But the truth was that they had really set their hearts on someone else: themselves. Their hearts did not beat in time with the love and compassion of God for the needy. That, to Jesus, was the sure sign that they did not really know him.

(iii) *They placed tradition above Scripture.* Isaiah had accused the people in his day of so clinging to man-made traditions that, for all practical purposes, God's word was made subservient to man's word. Jesus saw the fulfilment of that in the Pharisees. To them the observation of man-made external rules had taken the place of inward spiritual graces. Holiness was being judged by what could be seen. But God measures holiness by what is in the heart.

It was not that they had replaced God's love by God's law. How could they, when love is the fulfilment of the law? No, they had replaced God's love with self-love, and God's law with man's tradition. Having made themselves their own gods, they were insisting that others follow them or perish. How thankful Christ's disciples must have been that he had the moral integrity to say as much.

Sadly, the Pharisees had begun as a group of people deeply

concerned for personal purity. Their theology was orthodox. But when a desire for holiness, coupled with an orthodox theology is linked to a heart that is closed to God's grace (however much they profess a theology of grace), tragedy results. That is as true today as it was then. Be warned.

28

Hypocrites Exposed

And he said to them: 'You have a fine way of setting aside the commands of God in order to observe your own traditions! For Moses said, "Honour your father and your mother" and, "Anyone who curses his father or mother must be put to death." But you say that if a man says to his father or mother: "Whatever help you might otherwise have received from me is Corban" (that is, a gift devoted to God), then you no longer let him do anything for his father or mother. Thus you nullify the word of God by your tradition that you have handed down. And you do many things like that.' Again Jesus called the crowd to him and said, 'Listen to me, everyone, and understand this. Nothing outside a man can make him "unclean" by going into him. Rather, it is what comes out of a man that makes him "unclean".' (Mark 7:9–16).

The Pharisees had renewed their efforts to trap Jesus. Ostensibly they were criticising his disciples; actually they were determined to undermine Jesus' influence on the people. Behind that lay an even more sinister motive. They recognised that Jesus' teaching would destroy their influence and especially their reputation. Jesus was calling into question everything on which they were resting their hopes for acceptance with God, namely the assumption that – in contrast with 'sinners' – they were acceptable to him because of who they were and what they had done. It was Jesus' teaching on grace that so enraged them! Jesus taught that God saves sinners. The Pharisees taught, by contrast, that by definition sinners would not be saved.

GRACE OR MERIT?

What was at stake, then, in this central conflict in Jesus' ministry was nothing less than the way of salvation. Behind that, of course, lies the very nature of God himself. The Pharisees saw him as one who would be pleased with their keeping of the traditions. Only *that* would sustain them in covenant relationship with God, they believed. Jesus, by contrast, taught that he was a gracious Father, willing to forgive sinners. The Pharisees stumbled at this because it called into question everything they stood for. To follow Jesus, for a Pharisee, would have meant a completely new view of God *and* a completely new attitude to themselves.

There was another reason the Pharisees were so critical of Jesus' teaching. He taught that God graciously saves sinners. But, they argued, if that is so, men will live as they please; they will flout the law of God and yet still be able to enjoy the salvation of God. If only they had been able to see their own hearts clearly they might have seen that the reverse is always the case: it is the man who has been accepted by God's grace who devotes the rest of his life to pleasing him. The man who has no assurance that he is accepted by God will always live a lie, pretending to be better than he is – either before God or men.

At this stage, Jesus did something which few of his contemporaries would have dared to do: he exposed those who opposed him for the hypocrites that they really were. He showed how, for all their proud boasting in their traditions, they were living in disobedience to God's word.

CORBAN

Sometimes men would take a sacred vow to devote something (money, possessions) to the Lord. The devoted thing then became 'Corban' (v. 11), or set apart for God. That was a perfectly good and indeed godly practice.

But these Pharisees trusted the principle of Corban and gave it precedence over God's law. God had commanded his people to love and honour their parents (*Exod.* 20:12). While in normal circumstances a parent will do what he or she can to help children as they grow up, there are also times when sons or daughters should help their parents. Think, for example, of relatively poor parents whose children 'do well'. As the parents grow old and are perhaps in some need, how fitting it is that children should offer whatever help they can to the father and mother who have poured out their lives' energy for their children. It is a beautiful thing to see such care, and a joy to children when they are able to repay in a different coinage the love of their parents.

Jesus envisages a situation like that arising. Here is a young man. He does not anticipate that his parents will ever need his help. So, in his desire to be wholeheartedly devoted to God, he pronounces his possessions 'Corban'. His parents can no longer benefit from them.

But what if some unexpected tragedy strikes, and the parents stand in need? Surely in these circumstances a way must be found to honour father and mother? The ruling of the Pharisees was that nothing could be done, even to alleviate sickness. The tragedy was that the Pharisees actually led those they advised to breach one of the great commandments. Under the guise of religious faithfulness they encouraged disobedience to the law! On the surface they seemed highly spiritual; but Jesus said: 'You have set aside the commands of God in order to observe your own traditions' (v. 9).

Should we not, then, be prepared to put the Lord and his work before father and mother? Indeed we should – and must. Jesus himself taught that (see Luke 14:26). But that never involves indifference to, or rejection of, the command of God to honour them.

This was just one illustration of the way in which Jesus believed the Pharisees were actually driving people away from God and his word. That was why Jesus spoke with such unusual emphasis. He 'called the crowd to him', he summoned them to listen to him and understand what he was saying (v. 14). Holiness is not a matter of externals, but of the heart. It is what comes out of our hearts that makes us unclean, not what goes in.

How very slow the Christian church has been to take Jesus' teaching to heart. But it is too easy for us to point the finger at 'the church'. What about ourselves? Have we substituted the traditions of men for the word of God, and insisted that others do the same?

29

Outside In, or Inside Out?

Again Jesus called the crowd to him and said, 'Listen to me, everyone, and understand this. Nothing outside a man can make him "unclean" by going into him. Rather, it is what comes out of a man that makes him "unclean".' After he had left the crowd and entered the house, his disciples asked him about this parable. 'Are you so dull?' he asked. 'Don't you see that nothing that enters a man from the outside can make him "unclean"? For it doesn't go into his heart but into his stomach, and then out of his body.' (In saying this, Jesus declared all foods 'clean'.) He went on, 'What comes out of a man is what makes him "unclean". For from within, out of men's hearts, come evil thoughts, sexual immorality, theft, murder, adultery, greed, malice, deceit, lewdness, envy, slander, arrogance and folly. All these evils come from inside and make a man "unclean".' (Mark 7:14–23).

The controversy between the Pharisees and Jesus had erupted once again. Jesus had begun to expose their hypocrisy. In ostensibly 'protecting' God's law with their traditions, they had effectively weakened its radical demands. The effect of their teaching was to give their own regulations priority over the sacred law of God – as Jesus had demonstrated in his discussion of 'Corban'.

Our Lord was concerned about the way in which the people were being led astray by these false shepherds. So he turned from the Pharisees and summoned the crowd to come nearer to listen to what he had to say. He emphasised the importance of his teaching for each of them ('Listen to me, *everyone*', emphasis added), and urged them to think through its implications ('understand this', v. 14). Sin is not the result of our environment, but of the evil in our own hearts. 'Nothing outside a man can make him "unclean" by going into him. Rather, it is what comes out of a man that makes him "unclean" ' (v. 16).

SUPERFICIALITY

A major error of the Pharisees was their superficial view of sin. They had almost regulated sin out of existence in their lives – or so they thought! But their regulations were simply shutters which blinded them to the heart-searching nature of the law of God (see Matthew 5:21–48). How foolish they were to think that real holiness and godliness were matters of outward performance! How short-sighted to think that mechanical obedience was what pleased the living God! Yet how common their idea of sin was, and is.

The most alarming thing to Jesus was how widespread this view of sin had become. The respect, even fear, in which the Pharisees were held was indication enough of that. Even more alarming was the surprise of his disciples at the 'proverb' or 'parable' he spoke. It seemed almost revolutionary to them, never mind to the common people (vv. 17–18). They, too, had been overly impressed by skin-deep religion.

INSIDE, NOT OUTSIDE

Jesus patiently explained himself. 'If you will only stop to think about it,' he said, 'you will see that food cannot make you a sinner, nor can abstaining from certain foods make you holy, for it all goes "in one end and out the other" ' (v. 19)! Food never enters a man's heart.

CLEAN FOOD

In case his earliest readers failed to grasp the implications, Mark spelled them out. Jesus was declaring all foods 'clean' when he said this. As Christians we are at liberty to eat any food. There may be times when we will abstain from all food, when we fast in order to devote ourselves in a concentrated way to God. There may be foods we will refrain from eating because of their effects on us (the fact that we may eat any food does not mean we are obliged to eat all varieties). We may refrain from eating certain foods on certain occasions because we are conscious of the effect our eating may have on others (see *Acts* 15:20; *Rom.* 14:14–23; *1 Cor.* 8:1–13). But we remain free to eat all foods as Christians.

The important thing for Mark was the freedom of conscience implied in these words. That freedom is a joy to possess, whether or not we exercise it in any given situation (we do not always need to use our liberty in order to possess it). But that was precisely the kind of freedom which disturbed the Pharisees. Like all legalists who mix 'merit' with 'mercy' in salvation, they would rather carry the burden of these regulations (*Luke* 11:46) than the light and easy yoke of Jesus' freedom (*Matt.* 11:28–30).

UNCLEAN HEARTS

But if Jesus declared all foods 'clean', he also revealed that all hearts are 'unclean'. It is the heart of man (the centre of his being, not the central organ of his anatomy) which is corrupted and pumps sin through every area of his life. It is a factory of evil, including both outward acts and inward thoughts: 'The heart is deceitful above all things and beyond cure. Who can understand it?' (*Jer.* 17:9).

The tragedy of the Pharisees was that they did not know themselves. They had never really asked God to search their hearts to see if there was any offensive way in them (*Psa.* 139:23–24). They did not realise that, at worst, their environment simply 'triggered off' their sinful hearts. It was never the root cause of sin. No amount of insulation from 'the world' could ever protect them from the power of sin in their hearts.

Jesus did not mean that outward actions are of no importance – that only the thought counts. For him evil actions are rooted in evil hearts. If we are to deal with the actions we must also deal with the root cause.

GUARD THE HEART

Here Jesus is teaching something many Christians forget. Mere abstinence from certain activities can never make us holy. The battle against sin must be fought within. Since sin finds different outlets in each of us, one individual may need to guard himself in circumstances which do not threaten another individual in quite the same way. But in every heart lie the seeds of every possible sin. Therefore we must root out sin. We must guard our hearts, because out of them come the great issues of life (*Prov.* 4:23).

30

For All Peoples

Jesus left that place and went to the vicinity of Tyre. He entered a house and did not want anyone to know it; yet he could not keep his presence secret. In fact, as soon as she heard about him, a woman whose little daughter was possessed by an evil spirit came and fell at his feet. The woman was a Greek, born in Syrian Phoenicia. She begged Jesus to drive the demon out of her daughter. 'First let the children eat all they want,' he told her, 'for it is not right to take the children's bread and toss it to their dogs.' 'Yes, Lord,' she replied, 'but even the dogs under the table eat the children's crumbs.' Then he told her, 'For such a reply, you may go; the demon has left your daughter.' She went home and found her child lying on the bed, and the demon gone (Mark 7:24–30).

In this section of the Gospel of Mark we have already seen that Jesus was under pressure from two different sources: Herod, who feared that he was John the Baptist risen from the dead and returned to haunt him; and the Pharisees, who relentlessly pursued Jesus in their efforts to destroy the influence of his teaching. Eventually these two groups would come together in fulfilment of the words of Psalm 2 (see *Acts* 4:25–30). In the meantime, Jesus continued to keep on the move in order that his Father's plan for his life should not be thwarted by men

There is a lesson for us in this. Our Lord knew that his life had been mapped out for him by the Father. It had been foreordained or predestined that he should be crucified. Jesus knew that God's purposes would be fulfilled. Yet, at the same time, he knew he had to live consistently within those purposes. God's sovereign plan did not absolve him of the responsibility to live faithfully and carefully. That is no less true for us too.

Jesus therefore travelled beyond his own country, to the region of Tyre (v. 24). Notice that Mark tells us he wanted his presence there to be kept secret. But it was only a matter of time before the 'secret' was out and someone else in need had been drawn to Jesus.

A GENTILE WOMAN

Central to the miracle story which follows is that the person who came to Jesus in such need was first, a woman and, secondly, a Gentile. Furthermore, it was not her son who was in need, but her daughter, who was under the influence of an evil spirit. In the ancient Jewish world this was a combination of need beneath the dignity of any true rabbi. In that context we see Jesus restoring this woman and her daughter to the dignity for which God made woman at the beginning – to live as the image of God (*Gen.* 1:26–27).

How much the woman from Syrian Phoenicia understood about Jesus is not at first made clear. She certainly believed he could help her daughter, for she begged him to cast the demon out of her life.

STRANGE RESPONSE

Jesus' response has often been a puzzle to students of Scripture. The woman fell at Jesus' feet in her desperation (v. 25). Yet Jesus' reply sounds cold and almost harsh: 'Let the children eat all they want . . . for it is not right to take the children's bread and toss it to the dogs [that is, the household pets]' (v. 27).

Two explanations are possible. It may be that Jesus was saying: 'The message I bring is first of all to be given to the Jews, not to you Gentiles.' In which case, the woman's reply suggests that she instinctively saw that Jesus had come to be the Saviour of the world and not just the Saviour of his own people, the Jews.

The other possible interpretation is this: Jesus had come to this region with his disciples to find rest and haven from the danger of being seen as merely a miracle-worker. The disciple band had gathered to enjoy the fellowship of a family. Should he, the head of the family, interrupt the 'meal' in order to feed the 'household pets'?

If this second interpretation is the right one, Jesus' words are more of a parable than a 'put down'. In speaking this way he was testing out the nature of the woman's trust in him. Did she see him merely as a medicine-man or a magician like so many others? She gave him the answer he was looking for. It revealed a mixture of deep personal respect for Jesus himself, and the firm determination of faith to enter into its privileges: 'Even the dogs under the table are allowed to eat the children's crumbs' (v. 28).

What had this woman seen in Jesus' reply which encouraged her to persist in her prayer? Was it his use of the word 'first' (v. 27)? He had not closed the door to faith on her part; rather he was gently putting his shoulder to the door to test how firm her faith was. Was it strong enough and real enough to open the door? In fact it was, and Jesus granted her request. She went home to discover her daughter delivered, just as Jesus had said.

THE SAVIOUR OF THE WORLD

Like so many other stories in Mark's Gospel, this one should not be read in isolation. It gives us preliminary hints that Jesus has come for the world, not only for the Jews. But it also occurs in the context of the stubborn resistance of the Pharisees to Jesus. All their education and rigorous efforts to keep the 'traditions of the elders' had blinded them to what this simple foreigner saw in Jesus: she needed him, and she knew he was able to bring salvation to her and her family. The Pharisees would have thought of her not as a household pet, but as a 'Gentile dog', and despised her. The hardness of their attitude to others was really a symptom of the hardness of their hearts to Jesus. They had never been brought to see their need of him. Therein lay the greatest tragedy of their lives. Hardening of the spiritual arteries is a fatal disease.

31

The Deaf Hear, the Dumb Speak

Then Jesus left the vicinity of Tyre and went through Sidon, down to the Sea of Galilee and into the region of the Decapolis. There some people brought to him a man who was deaf and could hardly talk, and they begged him to place his hand on the man. After he took him aside, away from the crowd, Jesus put his fingers into the man's ears. Then he spat and touched the man's tongue. He looked up to heaven and with a deep sigh said to him, 'Ephphatha!' (which means, 'Be opened!'). At this, the man's ears were opened, his tongue was loosened and he began to speak plainly. Jesus commanded them not to tell anyone. But the more he did so, the more they kept talking about it. People were overwhelmed with amazement. 'He has done everything well,' they said. 'He even makes the deaf hear and the mute speak.' (Mark 7:31–37).

O n more than one occasion already we have noticed that the structure of Mark's Gospel has its own significance. In general terms it is reminiscent of the structure of Peter's preaching of the good news about Jesus. But we have also seen that some incidents are recorded side by side because they present us with the challenge of two different ways of responding to Christ: in faith or in hardness of heart.

This section of the Gospel, 6:1 to 7:37, seems to follow a pattern which is repeated in 8:1–30. Both these sections begin with a feeding miracle, and end with a miracle of eyes being opened. In this section, it is physical ears and lips which are opened; in the later section it is Peter's spiritual ears and lips that are opened by God to confess Jesus as the Messiah. It is almost as though Mark is preparing us for the great central point in his Gospel when the question 'Who is Jesus?' receives its definitive answer. From that point onwards, the rest of the Gospel will explain the work which Jesus has come to do in his capacity as Messiah.

Jesus and the disciples now made their way back through Sidon to the Sea of Galilee and into the region of the Decapolis (where Legion had so faithfully borne his witness to the Saviour). One incident which took place at that time remained firmly embedded in Peter's memory. It appears in no other Gospel. Perhaps it had special significance only for Peter, because he saw in it a parallel to his own spiritual experience.

WITHOUT SPEECH OR HEARING

Whatever the reason for its inclusion in Mark's Gospel, this is one of the most beautiful, as well as being perhaps the most unusual of all the miracles. Picture the scene: a man who is deaf and almost completely dumb is being hurried along by his friends to meet Jesus. Perhaps they are all in such a state of excitement that they have not even explained to their friend what they hope Jesus will do. Excitedly they beg Jesus to heal him.

What does Jesus do? The first thing he does is to take this man away from the crowd. What he was about to do needed to be done privately lest it be misunderstood as some kind of ritualistic mumbo-jumbo. He put his fingers into the man's ears, spat, and touched the man's tongue, looked up to heaven, sighed, and said (in Aramaic, his everyday language), 'Be opened' (v. 34).

SIGN LANGUAGE

The man could not hear Jesus and he was also incapable of verbal communication. So Jesus 'spoke' to him in the language he could understand – sign-language. The fingers placed in his ears and then removed meant, 'I am going to remove the blockage in your hearing.' The spitting and the touching of the man's tongue meant, 'I am going to remove the blockage in your mouth.' The glance up to heaven meant, 'It is God alone who is able to do this for you.' Jesus wanted the man to understand that it was not magic but God's grace that healed him.

The deaf and dumb man was immediately able to speak and hear (v. 35). Why, then, did Jesus urge him and his friends not to speak about what had happened? After all, how could they avoid speaking about it? Clearly the Lord was deeply concerned that his real identity should not be confused. Again he was to be disappointed by the response of those whose lives he had so signally blessed.

ALL THINGS DONE WELL

Yet, hidden in the friends' disobedience is an important lesson for us to learn. For the response of the people to what had happened was to say that Jesus 'has done everything well' (v. 37). There is something quite eloquent in such testimony to him. Perhaps it serves to remind us that even when our witness is not all that it should be, God is able to bring praise to his Son through it.

What, then, did the people find so amazing? The most obvious thing was that Jesus had healed the man. But the manner in which he had done it was also extraordinary. He had done it quietly, modestly and, most of all, graciously. His sign-language was, in a sense, an acted parable of his incarnation – he had entered into this man's world of silence and spoken the only language he could understand.

DEEP EMOTION

But Mark's account includes one element on which we have passed no comment. He tells us that as Jesus looked up to heaven, it was 'with a deep sigh' (v. 34). This Gospel is very sparing in its description of Jesus' expressions of emotion. What, then, did this sigh mean? Is it an indication of the energy which Jesus expended in setting the man free? Yet Jesus healed people on other occasions without such sighs. It is more likely that this is an expression of the deep sorrow and anger our Lord felt at the ravages of the Fall in the lives of men. The sigh was the sigh of the heart of God for his needy creation.

Many years before, Isaiah had prophesied that one of the blessings of the messianic age would be that 'the ears of the deaf [would be] unstopped . . . and the tongue of the dumb [would] shout for joy' (*Isa.* 35:5–6). That day those Scriptures had been fulfilled in the Decapolis. This man, made to hear the music of God's creation and to speak the praises of the Creator, had been unable to do either. All that was left for him was a stammering attempt to express the deep inadequacies of his humanity for the service of God or man. He shared in the pains of the fallen creation. But now Jesus Christ had made him whole. He was restored, in some measure, to what he was created to be. No wonder the people proclaimed that Jesus 'has done everything well' (v. 37).

PROPHETIC ACTION

Like many other miracles, this one is also a prophecy. It is a glimpse into what Jesus Christ intends to do when he comes again to exercise his reign over all the powers of darkness. By comparison with that day we are all spiritually deaf and only barely stammer the praises of our Creator. It will not always be so. The day is coming when the stammerer will be the eloquent proclaimer of his Father's praise, and the deaf will hear the voice of Christ with crystal clarity.

But that day did not lie only in the future for this man. The joy and power of it came upon him the day he met the Lord Jesus. He began then to hear the voice of God and to speak his praises. So it is for all those who enter with him into the kingdom which Jesus Christ brought so near.

If he had known them, there is no doubt the deaf and dumb man would have sung Charles Wesley's words:

> O for a thousand tongues to sing
>   My great Redeemer's praise,
> The glories of my God and King,
>   The triumphs of His grace!
>
> Hear Him, ye deaf; His praise, ye dumb,
>   Your loosened tongues employ,
> Ye blind, behold your Saviour come;
>   And leap, ye lame, for joy!
>
> My gracious Master and my God,
>   Assist me to proclaim,
> To spread through all the earth abroad
>   The honours of Thy Name.

32

The Messiah's Kingdom

During those days another large crowd gathered. Since they had nothing to eat, Jesus called his disciples to him and said, 'I have compassion for these people; they have already been with me three days and have nothing to eat. If I send them home hungry, they will collapse on the way, because some of them have come a long distance.' His disciples answered, 'But where in this remote place can anyone get enough bread to feed them?' 'How many loaves do you have?' Jesus asked. 'Seven,' they replied. He told the crowd to sit down on the ground. When he had taken the seven loaves and given thanks, he broke them and gave them to his disciples to set before the people, and they did so. They had a few small fish as well; he gave thanks for them also and told the disciples to distribute them. The people ate and were satisfied. Afterwards the disciples picked up seven basketfuls of broken pieces that were left over. About four thousand men were present. And having sent them away, he got into the boat with his disciples and went to the region of Dalmanutha. The Pharisees came and began to question Jesus. To test him, they asked him for a sign from heaven. He sighed deeply and said, 'Why does this generation ask for a miraculous sign? I tell you the truth, no sign will be given to it.' Then he left them, got back into the boat and crossed to the other side (Mark 8:1–13).

We have already noticed that there is a kind of parallel running through the structure of this section of Mark's Gospel. The feeding of a multitude is followed by a sea voyage, conflict with the Pharisees, a discussion which has bread as its theme, leading to a remarkable healing and climaxing in a confession of faith. We will see later that this repeated pattern is of considerable significance for Mark. Through it he is indicating how slow of heart the disciples were to recognise and trust in Christ.

Here in this section, Jesus feeds 'another large crowd' (v. 1). There are obvious similarities between 8:1–13 and 6:30–43. In both cases the pattern of the miracle is similar; in both cases the motivation of Jesus is the same – compassion; in both cases there is a plentiful supply of food, miraculously created from a meagre supply of bread and fish.

TWO FEEDINGS

It is often said today that somehow the narrative of Jesus' ministry became confused at this point, and this passage betrays a confusion in the memory of the disciples, or perhaps simply a repetition by the author because of a special point he wants to make.

A little thought underlines how impossible that is. For one thing, miracles in which thousands of people are fed from a handful of loaves are too memorable for anyone to think it happened twice if it happened only once. The idea that a confusion in memory took place is ludicrous. But further, the discussion which follows in 8:14–21 assumes there were two feedings. If there was only one, not only is the second story confused, the passage which follows it is a complete fabrication.

MESSIANIC BLESSINGS

What is the message of this miracle? It demonstrates the compassion of Jesus, as we have seen. But it is interesting to see this miracle in the context of the ancient promises God had given to his people about the blessings the Messiah would bring when he inaugurated his kingdom. He would supply bread for the hungry. Here is how Isaiah put it: 'You who have no money, come, buy and eat! . . . Why spend money on what is not bread, and your labour on what does not satisfy? Listen, listen to me, and eat what is good, and your soul will delight in the richest of fare' (*Isa.* 55:1–2). When Jesus' coming had been promised, Mary had praised God as one who had 'filled the hungry with good things' (*Luke* 1:53). Like all the miracles, this miracle points us to the identity of our Lord.

NO OTHER RESOURCES

There is another emphasis here. In the earlier feeding miracle it seems that the disciples' 'bank balance' was in very good order. 'Are we to go and spend that much [that is, eight months of a man's wages] on food?' they asked.

Among twelve of them that sum amounted to two or three weeks' wages. It is not impossible that they had such a sum. It is also possible that this was at a time before Judas Iscariot began to siphon off the funds for himself (*John* 12:6). At the time of the second feeding, however, the disciples had insufficient resources. There was nowhere to buy food in this remote area, even if they had the money. Christ himself was their only resource. For the disciples this lesson was one they needed to learn over and over again.

SIGNS OF THE KINGDOM

This second feeding miracle also seems to have been set in the region of the Decapolis, on the far side of the Sea of Galilee. That distinguishes it from the first miracle not only geographically but also ethnically and religiously. This crowd was probably a mixed group of Jews and Gentiles, perhaps none of them deeply committed, but awakened by the presence and teaching of Jesus, and hungry to listen to him. In this case, the feeding of the multitude foreshadows the gathering together of those from every nation under heaven to the heavenly feeding of God's people. But it also points to the 'feeding' of the people of God in the church today. Already Jesus was hinting (as perhaps the woman from Syrian Phoenicia had begun to see) that he would break down barriers which separated men and women from fellowship with one another.

No sooner had Jesus left than the Pharisees reappeared, this time questioning him, testing him and seeking to trap him. In particular, they wanted some 'sign from heaven' to authenticate his ministry (v. 11). For the second time in two chapters, Mark records the deep sighs of Jesus. This time they were of profound anguish at the bitter opposition of these men to himself and his message. Did they want a sign? His whole life and ministry signified his identity. No sign would ever convince such hard-hearted men, therefore none would be given. They demanded signs; Jesus showed compassion. If they did not recognise that this was the way God was revealing himself in Jesus, then they must remain in their blindness.

It seems altogether possible that those who were present at the miracle of the feeding did not come to know of its miraculous nature until long after, if ever. But the disciples knew, for Jesus used them as his instruments in it. As for the unbelieving Pharisees, they never came to see the power of God in Jesus.

Our own times are no different. But, wonderfully, Jesus is no different either. He is still able to take the inadequate resources we bring to him, bless them, and use us as the instruments of taking his blessings to a needy world. Although our resources be small, and we be few in number, the Lord Jesus is not limited in power. Indeed, he chooses to take the weak things of the world to confound the things that are mighty (*1 Cor.* 1:26–31).

33

No Bread!

The disciples had forgotten to bring bread, except for one loaf they had with them in the boat. 'Be careful,' Jesus warned them. 'Watch out for the yeast of the Pharisees and that of Herod.' They discussed this with one another and said, 'It is because we have no bread.' Aware of their discussion, Jesus asked them, 'Why are you talking about having no bread? Do you still not see or understand? Are your hearts hardened? Do you have eyes but fail to see, and ears but fail to hear? And don't you remember? When I broke the five loaves for the five thousand, how many basketfuls of pieces did you pick up?' 'Twelve,' they replied. 'And when I broke the seven loaves for the four thousand, how many basketfuls of pieces did you pick up?' They answered, 'Seven.' He said to them, 'Do you still not understand?' (Mark 8:14–21).

Jesus and his disciples were, once again, on their way back to the other side of the Sea of Galilee, following the feeding of the four thousand. It is not difficult to imagine the scene that follows. Jesus' mind was still full of the experiences of the past hours; perhaps as he enjoyed the natural restfulness of this crossing he allowed his thoughts to roam. Did he think about the feeding, and the picture this had presented of what would one day take place in his Father's kingdom? This was 'the joy that was set before him' for which he would 'endure the cross' before being set down at his Father's right hand (*Heb.* 12:2).

ONE LOAF

As the boat made its way slowly across the Sea, Jesus sensed frustration among the disciples. Perhaps they were blaming each other for something they had just discovered: they had brought only one loaf of bread with them! At the very least they should have been able to see the humour in the situation. They had just been part of a miracle in which four thousand people had been given enough bread to satisfy their hunger – and they had forgotten to bring bread (of all things!). But, apparently, some of them were really quite irritated. How fickle we are.

YEAST

Jesus quietly intervened: 'Be careful. Watch out for the yeast of the Pharisees and that of Herod' (v. 15). What did he mean? Clearly his mind was still full of the events of his encounter with the Pharisees. Since his disciples' conversation was about bread, Jesus used the 'language' of their discussion to make his point more memorable for them. A tiny amount of yeast affects the whole lump of dough into which it is mixed. The evil and hypocritical hearts of the Pharisees and Herod influenced their whole lives. 'Beware of the yeast of unbelief!' Jesus was saying.

His warning was as necessary as it was timely. The disciples' reaction indicates that their minds were already full of anxiety about themselves and frustration with the providences of their own lives. Just when their hearts should have been lifted up in the joy of being with Christ, they were discontented. How like the Pharisees! They thought that Jesus was blaming them for having so little bread! They, like the Pharisees, were dragging Jesus down in their own minds to their own level!

PATIENT CARE

With perfect patience, Jesus began to pastor his disciples by asking them a series of questions designed to bring them to understand what he was saying. He led them from the content of their conversation ('Why are you talking about having no bread?' v. 17), to their spiritual condition – their spiritual blindness and their continued hardness of heart (v. 18). Slowly he brought to the front of their minds what he had done in the feeding miracles (vv. 19–20). How could they be anxious about having only one loaf, when with them was the One who had now fed a total of nine thousand people with twelve loaves, leaving nineteen baskets still full! They had seen his compassion for those who were in need; could they not trust him to care for them too?

Perhaps into the minds of the disciples came another occasion when they had crossed the Sea with Jesus, and had given violent expression to the distrust and fear in their hearts by asking him: 'Teacher, don't you care if we drown?' (*Mark* 4:38). In essence that question revealed the same kind of unbelief which characterised the Pharisees and Herod: the refusal to yield to the tender mercy of God in Jesus; the desire to hold on to one's own life and rule it, rather than abandon oneself to the rule and provision of the Lord.

Sometimes we think that only tragedy of major proportions could create hardness of heart and spiritual blindness in our lives. Jesus teaches his disciples otherwise. Here *too little bread* was a sufficient cause to show just how hard their hearts and how blind their spiritual understanding could be. Unbelief is like leaven: small, but influential; apparently insignificant, but all-pervasive in its influence.

CONTENTMENT

One of the great marks of true spiritual growth is this: if we know that Christ is with us, we will not wriggle under frustrating providences. Having only one loaf was hardly a matter of life or death. Yet its significance grew out of all proportion until it filled the minds of the disciples with frustration, and blinded them to Jesus' presence and teaching. If their hearts and eyes had been fixed on him, they might have been able to smile at their foolishness instead of blame one another for it. The lesson the author of Ecclesiastes taught is one which the disciples needed to learn: 'Better one handful with tranquillity than two handfuls with toil and chasing after the wind' (*Eccl.* 4:6). Knowing and trusting Jesus Christ enables us to live like that, and to say with Paul: 'I know what it is to be in need, and I know what it is to have plenty. I have learned the secret of being content in any and every situation, whether well fed or hungry, whether living in plenty or in want. I can do everything through him who gives me strength' (*Phil.* 4:12–13).

34

The Second Touch

They came to Bethsaida, and some people brought a blind man and begged Jesus to touch him. He took the blind man by the hand and led him outside the village. When he had spat on the man's eyes and put his hands on him, Jesus asked, 'Do you see anything?' He looked up and said, 'I see people; they look like trees walking around.' Once more Jesus put his hands on the man's eyes. Then his eyes were opened, his sight was restored, and he saw everything clearly. Jesus sent him home, saying, 'Don't go into the village.'

Jesus and his disciples went on to the villages around Caesarea Philippi. On the way he asked them, 'Who do people say I am?' They replied, 'Some say John the Baptist; others say Elijah; and still others, one of the prophets.' 'But what about you?' he asked. 'Who do you say I am?' Peter answered, 'You are the Christ.' Jesus warned them not to tell anyone about him (Mark 8:22–30).

'Do you have eyes but fail to see?' Jesus had recently asked his disciples (8:18). The stories which follow immediately in Mark's account of the ministry of Jesus describe eyes being opened. There is little doubt that the disciples were meant to learn something about their relationship with Jesus from this miracle story.

A blind man was brought to Jesus in Bethsaida. As on other occasions, people begged Jesus to heal (v. 22). His response again reveals his extraordinary care for and sensitivity to individuals in their need. Later in the Gospel, Mark tells us how Jesus healed a blind man in full public gaze (10:46–52). But here he 'took the blind man by the hand and led him outside the village' (v. 23).

There was a personal and a symbolic reason for this. The Lord's action was a perfect illustration to the disciples of what he wanted to do with them in their spiritual blindness: take them gently by the hand, and lead them on. But there was presumably another reason. Perhaps it was that Jesus understood the personality of this man. Instinctively he knew that to heal him in public would be as painful to him as his present blindness. So he took him outside the village, to a place where they could be quiet together. We would dearly love to know what passed between them during that walk! If you have ever met someone with whom you could share anything, perhaps you have had a taste of the privilege that was given to this unsighted man. Did he pour out the story of his life to Jesus, in answer to his gently probing questions? Did he find himself able to express to Jesus thoughts and fears which he had kept hidden beneath the surface of his mind, even from himself? That seems very likely.

MEN LIKE TREES WALKING

The unique element in this miracle now took place. Jesus spat on the man's eyes, put his hands on him, and then asked: 'Do you see anything?' (v. 23). The question itself is unique. Jesus does not seem to have anticipated complete restoration of the man's sight. When he replied, 'I do see people, but hazily – like trees walking', Jesus placed his hands on the man a second time. Then 'he saw everything clearly' (v. 25).

What is the significance of this? Was it that this man was a particularly 'difficult case' for Jesus? Hardly!

Was this miracle then – like others – a sign? Yes! But to whom? To the man? No! – to the disciples. And this is confirmed by the fact that Jesus had already asked them about their vision of him (v. 18). He was now leading them by the hand to the point at which their sight would become much clearer, and Peter would confess 'You are the Christ' (v. 29). Their spiritual understanding did not come instantaneously, but gradually. They, too, needed the second touch from the hands of their Master.

It would be a great mistake for us to make this miracle, and its message to the disciples, the basis for any doctrine of spiritual experience; for example, the necessity of some kind of 'second touch' in order to enjoy normal Christian experience. Later in the Gospel, Mark records how Bar-Timaeus was given his sight immediately; we do not make his experience the basis for any doctrine of 'one touch experience'. We should avoid the temptation to do the same here. It may be that Jesus' command to this man, 'Don't go into the village' (that is, don't go there immediately) was intended to give him time to cope with his experience of healing. We need to do the same, lest we turn our individual experience into a norm for all Christians.

CLEARER SIGHT

Nevertheless, the lesson for the disciples was this: only as Jesus keeps on opening your eyes to him will you see him clearly. They did have some spiritual vision; but it needed to be healed and sharpened. That would be an ongoing process in their lives as Jesus continued to perfect what he had begun. Indeed, if the 'second touch' symbolised a definite experience for the believer, it would be that of glorification, when we will no longer see only fragments of Christ, but his full glory revealed before us. In the meantime, our spiritual vision needs to be sharpened. That is why Paul prayed for the Ephesian Christians (who had already received spiritual sight):

> I keep asking that the God of our Lord Jesus Christ, the glorious Father, may give you the Spirit of wisdom and revelation, so that you may know him better. I pray also that the eyes of your heart may be enlightened in order that you may know the hope to which he has called you, the riches of his glorious inheritance in the saints . . . (*Eph.* 1:17–18).

He recognised that coming to Christ is just the beginning of clear seeing. That is why the prayer so many Christians use before reading a passage of Scripture is not just for beginning believers, but for us all: 'Open my eyes, that I may see wonderful things in your law' (*Psa.* 119:18).

35

Who is Jesus?

Jesus and his disciples went on to the villages around Caesarea Philippi. On the way he asked them, 'Who do people say I am?' They replied, 'Some say John the Baptist; others say Elijah; and still others, one of the prophets.' 'But what about you?' he asked. 'Who do you say I am?' Peter answered, 'You are the Christ.' Jesus warned them not to tell anyone about him (Mark 8:27–30).

Mark has now brought us to the turning point in his Gospel. His purpose in writing it has been to enable us to identify Jesus for ourselves.

In the first words of the Gospel Mark had indicated who Jesus was: the Son of God (*Mark* 1:1). But in the Roman world for which he wrote, being the 'son of God' might mean a variety of things – after all, Caesar himself was regarded as divine! It was essential to explain precisely what he meant. That is why throughout the opening chapters of the Gospel, he has posed the question of Jesus' identity in a variety of ways. When Jesus forgave the sins of the paralytic man who was lowered through the roof, it seemed as if he were claiming a divine identity. Yet the same Jesus who forgave sins ate and drank with tax collectors and 'sinners'! 'How could any true servant of God do that?', the Pharisees asked.

Soon the disciples found themselves enquiring about Jesus' true identity, when he stilled the storm on the Sea of Galilee: 'Who is this? Even the wind and the waves obey him' (*Mark* 4:41). Later in the Gospel, we find that King Herod and many of the people were asking the same question too (*Mark* 6:14–16).

But here we come face to face with the issue of Jesus' identity – on which the entire Gospel depends. For now it is Jesus who asks his disciples questions about his identity.

Notice that there are two stages in the way in which Jesus interrogates them.

WHO DO MEN SAY JESUS IS?

First of all, Jesus asked his disciples what others were saying about him (v. 27). The answer they gave is illuminating. Some people were saying he was John the Baptist or Elijah, and others apparently listed a variety of Old Testament prophets, including Jeremiah (*Matt.* 16:14).

What was the significance of this? Clearly the people recognised several things about Jesus. He was a prophet. No one could possibly speak as he did unless God had sent him. Like the Old Testament prophets, Jesus spoke with the direct authority of God – people could sense that as they sat and listened to his teaching.

God had promised that one day he would give the people a prophet like Moses (*Deut.* 18:17). Perhaps Jesus was the one? Then, again, God had promised 'I will send you the prophet Elijah before that great and dreadful day of the Lord comes' (*Mal.* 4:5). Could it be that Jesus was the long-promised returning Elijah? Or was he, as King Herod had thought, John the Baptist returned from the dead (*Mark* 6:16)?

It is interesting to notice with which of the prophets the people tended to associate Jesus. Elijah and John the Baptist were men with the mark of the desert on their lives. We tend to contrast them with the grace of Jesus' ministry. But here we are given a hint that even the people who did not really understand who Jesus was, understood this: Jesus belonged to the same on-going purpose of God as these men. There was the note of eternal reality in his every word and action.

Was it simple ignorance on the part of the people – or was it perhaps wishful thinking – that they identified Jesus as a preparatory figure? After all, if he were only the forerunner of the messianic day of judgment which Malachi had foretold, then 'the end' had not yet come. There was still time. Things were not quite that serious, yet. If this were the attitude of the people, they were in grave peril.

WHO DO YOU SAY I AM?

It was one thing for the disciples to record the opinions of others. But what about their own convictions? Jesus now faced them with that issue. Who did they think Jesus was? Speaking apparently for the whole disciple band, Peter responded that Jesus was not merely another prophet; he was the *final* prophet, the promised Christ! He was the Son of the living God!

We must not dilute the full force of these words. They come from the lips of an orthodox Jew. Peter and the others had been taught the Old Testament from their childhood. They knew the significance of reciting the great creed of Israel 'The Lord our God, the Lord is one' (*Deut.* 6:4). So his confession of Jesus as the Son of God was a breakthrough of monumental proportions. He was saying something revolutionary, not only about Jesus, but about the nature of God! Far from being an 'easy' confession, the kind of thing we might expect from an uneducated first-century Palestinian fisherman, it was the complete opposite. It was the last thing in the world Peter would have been 'programmed' to say by birth or environment.

What had driven Peter and his companions to this conclusion? We can hazard a guess (although Mark does not tell us in so many words). It must have been the same evidence of Jesus' life and ministry which Mark has placed before us already in the Gospel. That point is worth emphasising. You do not need more information than Mark has already given to you by this point in his narrative to begin to confess Jesus as Christ and as the Lord of your life. He is the one in whom the promises of the Old Testament have reached their fulfilment. His words and works express the authority of God himself. He is the Son of God!

WARNING

Jesus closes this section with a warning. His disciples are to tell no one what they have heard and seen (v. 30). Why? Should Peter's confession not have been the launching pad for a new evangelistic initiative? Should they not now go throughout the land and eventually to Jerusalem proclaiming openly that the Son of God had come?

Jesus knew that the people would not understand that message. More, he knew that his disciples did not really understand the significance of that message – yet. Certainly, Peter had seen that Jesus was the Christ, the Son of God. He had, at last, seen the answer to the question of Jesus' identity. What he did not yet understand was the nature of Jesus' ministry. In the coming days, Jesus would patiently unfold that to him. But as yet, Peter's poor spiritual vision was only partly healed. Like the blind man of Bethsaida, he needed a second touch from Jesus, in order to see properly. The first touch had enabled him to see Jesus' identity. The second would help Peter to see 'everything clearly' (*Mark* 8:25). This 'second touch' is described in the rest of Mark's Gospel.

36

Cross-bearers

*He then began to teach them that the Son of Man must suffer
many things and be rejected by the elders, chief priests and
teachers of the law, and that he must be killed and after three
days rise again. He spoke plainly about this, and Peter took
him aside and began to rebuke him. But when Jesus turned
and looked at his disciples, he rebuked Peter. 'Get behind me,
Satan!' he said. 'You do not have in mind the things of God,
but the things of men.' Then he called the crowd to him along
with his disciples and said: 'If anyone would come after me,
he must deny himself and take up his cross and follow me. For
whoever wants to save his life will lose it, but whoever loses
his life for me and for the gospel will save it. What good is it
for a man to gain the whole world, yet forfeit his soul? Or
what can a man give in exchange for his soul? If anyone is
ashamed of me and my words in this adulterous and sinful
generation, the Son of Man will be ashamed of him when
he comes in his Father's glory with the holy angels.'*
(Mark 8:31–38).

We have reached the turning point in the Gospel of Mark.
Jesus has given his disciples fresh revelation. Their eyes
have been opened. They now know that Jesus is the Christ. That
also marked a turning point for Jesus in his sharing of his mission
with them. Now that they knew who he was, they must also learn
what kind of Messiah he had come to be. The words with which
this section begin are, therefore, highly significant: 'He then began
to teach them that the Son of Man must suffer. . .' (v. 31). Only
when they recognised his identity could they begin to struggle

with the way in which their Lord intended to fulfil that identity. He was going to be a suffering Messiah. Mark adds that Jesus 'spoke plainly about this'. It is clear from the response of Peter that the disciples were left in no doubt about the implications of the statement, even if they were slow to believe that things would really happen that way.

SUFFERING SERVANT

How had Jesus come to this conclusion? Mark does not explain. But we know from the Gospel narrative that Jesus identified not only with the promised Messiah; he was also the Suffering Servant, of whom Isaiah had spoken in various parts of his prophecy – the One who would come and be rejected by his own people and die with sinners, but then triumph and be honoured by God (*Isa.* 52:13–53:12).

Immediately Simon Peter took hold of Jesus and began to rebuke him for speaking like that! For a moment he had forgotten himself and had begun to speak with the accents of Satan. Jesus rightly rebuked him. His mind was set in a worldly pattern, not in a godly pattern (v. 33).

Yet, in another sense, Peter had not 'forgotten himself'. The sad truth was that he was quick-witted enough to see what the implications of Jesus' suffering would be – and he was actually concerned about himself! For Jesus then went on to explain the implications of his identity for those who would follow him. It would mean taking up the cross, losing one's life for the sake of the gospel! No wonder Peter had been so defensive! Jesus seemed to be saying that unless his disciples were willing to commit themselves to this principle of his own life, he would be ashamed of them (v. 38).

What was it that Peter had failed to see before which now, for the first time, dawned on him?

THE MESSIAH'S MINISTRY

(i) *Sacrifice.* He did not appreciate that Jesus' Messiahship and salvation had sacrifice at its heart. He had never brought together the Old Testament teaching on the Messiah who would bring in the new day of the kingdom of God, and the Suffering Servant who would give justification and forgiveness to God's people. He had thought (in his spiritual blindness) that God's kingdom would come in power, majesty and glory. But Jesus was saying that it would come through rejection, humiliation and shame. What stunned Peter's mind was this thought: God's only Messiah is a Suffering Servant.

(ii) *Submission.* Peter also failed to see that at the heart of Jesus' ministry lay his complete submission to God's word. Like Satan in the wilderness temptations, Peter was saying to Jesus: 'Yes, you are the Messiah; but choose the way of power to inaugurate your king-dom' (*Matt.* 4:1–11). He did not appreciate that the plan of God is never 'up for negotiation'; it has to be submitted to with a whole heart. Yes, Peter admired Jesus. What he did not yet seem to understand was that Jesus was determined that every moment of his life would be lived in obedience to the Father's plan. Such radical commitment was simply beyond Peter's present experience.

(iii) *Conformity.* Peter had not yet fully understood that follow-ing the Messiah meant conformity to the Messiah. Now it dawned on him: a life of discipleship with Jesus would necessarily involve radical self-denial. The Gospels suggest that this was something Peter found difficult to accept. It seemed just too grim to be true. In fact, so painful was this message to him that on one occasion he responded: 'Look, we have left everything to follow you' (*Matt.* 19:27). Was there not another side to discipleship?

DISCIPLESHIP IS TWO-SIDED

In fact, Jesus already indicates here that there are two sides to discipleship. Yes, there is the cross-bearing, the self-denial, the sharing in his sufferings. But Jesus is no man's debtor. Those who lose their lives for his sake will gain them; those who are not ashamed of him or his words will look forward to meeting him again in the assurance that he will not be ashamed of them. Follow-ing the crucified Christ means following the conquering Christ who will share with all his people the blessings of his conquest.

Later in his life, Simon Peter seems to have meditated a great deal on Jesus as the 'stone'. To those who believed, this stone was precious. But to others it became a stumbling stone (*1 Pet.* 2:4–10). He knew himself how near he had come to falling on it and being destroyed by it. He learned – the hard way – that there is no other Christ to follow than the Crucified One.

That is just as true for us as it was for him.

37

Transfigured

And he said to them, 'I tell you the truth, some who are standing here will not taste death before they see the kingdom of God come with power.' After six days Jesus took Peter, James and John with him and led them up a high mountain, where they were all alone. There he was transfigured before them. His clothes became dazzling white, whiter then anyone in the world could bleach them. And there appeared before them Elijah and Moses, who were talking with Jesus. Peter said to Jesus, 'Rabbi, it is good for us to be here, Let us put up three shelters – one for you, one for Moses and one for Elijah.' (He did not know what to say, they were so frightened.) Then a cloud appeared and enveloped them, and a voice came from the cloud: 'This is my Son, whom I love. Listen to him!' Suddenly, when they looked round, they no longer saw anyone with them except Jesus. As they were coming down the mountain, Jesus gave them orders not to tell anyone what they had seen until the Son of Man had risen from the dead. They kept the matter to themselves, discussing what 'rising from the dead' meant (Mark 9:1–10).

Jesus' summons to wholehearted discipleship had emphasised the cost of following him. Cross-bearing, self-denying loyalty would be the principle of the Christian life. Yet he had already hinted that there was another side to discipleship. Those who lost their lives for his sake would actually gain them. Now, however, Jesus indicates – with tantalising brevity – that the life of discipleship looks forward to sharing in the glory of the Messiah. He said,

'Some who are standing here will not taste death before they see the kingdom of God come with power' (v. 1).

All kinds of explanations have been offered for these highly enigmatic words. To what did Jesus refer?

INTERPRETING SCRIPTURE

It is worth pausing to ask a general question at this stage: How should we go about answering a question like that in the course of our study of the Bible? We should first of all look for 'clues' within the passage and its context which will help us to understand the author's words through his mind, not our own twentieth-century minds. Are there any such clues in this passage? The most obvious one lies in the words of verse 2. Six days after Jesus had spoken, he took Peter, James and John to witness his transfiguration.

Here Mark clearly draws a connection between what Jesus said and what Jesus experienced on the Mount of Transfiguration. He seems to be suggesting that the explanation of this cryptic saying lies in what took place at the end of that week. There three of the disciples ('some who are standing here', v. 1) saw the power of God's kingdom, indeed its glory in an altogether new way. It was as though they caught a glimpse of all that Jesus would be when his kingdom finally came. He was transfigured. His glory was seen. His power and kingly majesty were momentarily visible. It was a foretaste of that day when his kingdom would come with power in his resurrection (when he was 'declared with power to be the Son of God', *Rom.* 1:4). It was a foretaste, too, of the day of his final glory.

ON THE MOUNTAIN

What, then, did these three disciples witness? As Jesus appeared in the radiance of glory, Elijah and Moses came to speak with him. These two great figures of the Old Covenant spoke with Jesus about his forging of the New Covenant in his blood. Luke tells us that they spoke about Jesus' 'exodus', or departure in Jerusalem (*Luke* 9:31). His death would be the new Passover; the salvation of his people would be the new Exodus. What a fascinating conversation this must have been – paralleled only by Jesus' exposition of the Scriptures on the Emmaus Road on the day of his resurrection! (See Luke 24:13–35.)

PETER'S EXCITEMENT

Clearly Peter became so excited he simply had to say something. But how inappropriate his words turned out to be (v. 33). He planned to build three shelters. Did this mean that he wanted to erect three 'tents of meeting' here on the mountain on the assumption that the final age had now dawned? Whatever his motive, he had forgotten the words which Jesus had so recently spoken about the cross. Or, had he? Was he perhaps saying in his heart of hearts: 'This is it. The kingdom has come. There is no need for the pathway of suffering and shame. We can stay here with Moses, Elijah and Jesus'?

No wonder God spoke so powerfully, and mercifully in deed and in word. The cloud of the glory-presence of God descended and covered them. The voice from heaven spoke, pointing to Jesus. Did Peter not yet understand who Jesus was, or the significance of Moses and Elijah appearing with him? This glorious moment was not an escape from the cross, but the preparation for it. These two figures should not be thought of as in any sense on a level with Jesus – they were simply witnesses to him. Oh, Peter, focus your attention on Jesus, the Son!

As though to underline this, Moses and Elijah disappeared from view. Only Jesus remained. Peter, James and John had been present at one of the most sacred moments in the whole history of salvation. They had seen 'the kingdom of God come with power' (v. 1).

Jesus told them to keep this to themselves until after his resurrection, and they did. But from time to time these three disciples quietly discussed with one another what they had seen and what their Master had said. They still did not fully understand the presence of God's kingdom in Jesus. Only after the resurrection would their eyes be fully opened. Then they would understand that the power of God would be made known through the weakness of the cross, and the glory of Christ made known only through his shame.

THE VOICE STILL SPEAKS

Would you not give your right arm for the privilege of hearing that voice from heaven bear testimony to Jesus? That is a natural feeling for any Christian. Yet it was not the view Simon Peter eventually took. Later he was to write that the testimony of Scripture to the Lord Jesus is as clear and powerful as any word we might hear from the heavens (2 Pet. 1:17–19). By this he meant that, if we would see the glory of Jesus Christ now, we must read Scripture just as eagerly as Peter would have lingered on the mountain top. The same voice speaks in both places! The same testimony is given: Jesus is God's Son; listen to him!

38

What About Elijah?

As they were coming down the mountain, Jesus gave them orders not to tell anyone what they had seen until the Son of Man had risen from the dead. They kept the matter to themselves, discussing what 'rising from the dead' meant. And they asked him, 'Why do the teachers of the law say that Elijah must come first?' Jesus replied, 'To be sure, Elijah does come first, and restores all things. Why then is it written that the Son of Man must suffer much and be rejected? But I tell you, Elijah has come, and they have done to him everything they wished, just as it is written about him' (Mark 9:9–13).

As the three disciples, Peter, James and John, made their way down from the mountain where Jesus had been momentarily transformed and they had seen his power and glory, one thing puzzled them. He had told them not to mention what they had seen until after his resurrection. Why was this such an enigma? It is natural to assume that it was because they still did not fully understand his mission. Doubtless that is true; but there is more to their puzzlement than this. Like the Pharisees, the disciples believed in a future resurrection (see, for example, John 11:23–24). But for the disciples the resurrection was a sign of the end of the world. It was the forerunner of the final judgment and the new age. If the resurrection was so near, they asked, 'Why do the teachers of the law say that Elijah must come first?' (v. 11).

In their minds was the prophecy which had been given through Malachi:

See, I will send you the prophet Elijah before that great and dreadful day of the Lord comes. He will turn the hearts of the fathers to their children, and the hearts of the children to their fathers; or else I will come and strike the land with a curse (*Mal.* 4:5–6).

As a result, the reappearance of Elijah was expected by many people before the coming of the Messiah and the end of the ages. Interestingly, some of Jesus' contemporaries thought he must be Elijah, because his presence and power did seem to be a sign that God was bringing in his kingdom (see 8:28).

The disciples therefore were puzzled: if the resurrection was to take place soon, what about the promised coming of Elijah? Were the teachers wrong?

WHO IS ELIJAH?

'No', answered Jesus. They were not wrong in their expectation; but they were short-sighted in their interpretation of the prophecy. Elijah does come first and his work is restoration (v. 12). But, says Jesus (notice how gently he leads them to a true understanding of the Scriptures!), that Old Testament passage cannot be isolated from other passages about God's kingdom. Scripture also says that the 'Son of Man must suffer much and be rejected' (v. 12). How can these things be harmonised?

John the Baptist was Elijah. The restoration in which he engaged was not a physical restoration, because the kingdom he served was not a political one. He preached a restoration of repentance, of changed hearts, not of worldly power and might. The response to him was but a foreshadowing of the response there would be to the Messiah – rejection.

To the 'inner circle' of the disciples who heard this, Jesus' words must have been breathtaking in their significance. Now all the Scriptures made sense. The political and worldly interpretations which had been placed on the hope of the Messiah's kingdom were overturned. Elijah had already come! But the people had been blind to him, just as they would be also to the One whose kingdom the new Elijah had proclaimed.

The resurrection of which Jesus had spoken was not that of the end of the world, but rather that of the beginning of the new world, and of the new race of men and women who would be followers of

Jesus. Then, but not before then, would it be fitting to share with others what had been revealed on the mountain top. The resurrection of which he spoke was his own victory over the powers of darkness and death.

SLOW TO UNDERSTAND

This section underlines a theme we have already noticed running through Mark's Gospel. Jesus' disciples trusted and loved him. They really did believe that he was the Christ. But how little they understood what that really meant. They had been guilty of interpreting the Scriptures in terms of the traditions they had heard and their own ideas. Now, almost daily, it seemed as though Jesus was showing them things in the Scriptures they had been blinded to before. That was a ministry he would continue even after his resurrection (*Luke* 24:25–27, 34).

There is a lesson for us here. We are also prone to interpret God's word badly. Our great need is for Jesus himself to explain to us what it means. He is the One who can touch our eyes again and again, to help us to see (cf. *Mark* 8:22–26). He uses all kinds of instruments to do so: sermons, books, study groups, private reading, friends and so on. But in the last analysis it is only Jesus himself who can open our eyes to see what the Lord is saying to us in his word. That is why the promise he has given to the church of the presence of the Holy Spirit – Jesus' own Spirit – as our teacher, is so priceless. It is his presence that makes our hearts burn within us as the Scriptures are expounded (*Luke* 24:34)!

39

Man's Failure, Christ's Faith

When they came to the other disciples, they saw a large crowd around them and the teachers of the law arguing with them. As soon as all the people saw Jesus, they were overwhelmed with wonder and ran to greet him. 'What are you arguing with them about?' he asked. A man in the crowd answered, 'Teacher, I brought you my son, who is possessed by a spirit that has robbed him of speech. Whenever it seizes him, it throws him to the ground. He foams at the mouth, gnashes his teeth and becomes rigid. I asked your disciples to drive out the spirit, but they could not.' 'O unbelieving generation,' Jesus replied, 'how long shall I stay with you? How long shall I put up with you? Bring the boy to me.' So they brought him. When the spirit saw Jesus, it immediately threw the boy into a convulsion. He fell to the ground and rolled around, foaming at the mouth. Jesus asked the boy's father, 'How long has he been like this?' 'From childhood,' he answered. 'It has often thrown him into fire or water to kill him. But if you can do anything, take pity on us and help us.' '"If you can"?' said Jesus. 'Everything is possible for him who believes.' Immediately the boy's father exclaimed, 'I do believe; help me overcome my unbelief!' When Jesus saw that a crowd was running to the scene, he rebuked the evil spirit. 'You deaf and mute spirit,' he said, 'I command you, come out of him and never enter him again.' The spirit shrieked, convulsed him violently and came out. The boy looked so much like a corpse that many said, 'He's dead.' But Jesus took him by the hand and lifted him to his feet, and he stood up. After Jesus had gone indoors, his disciples asked him privately, 'Why couldn't we drive it out?' He replied, 'This kind can come out only by prayer' (Mark 9:14–29).

The artist Raphael's unfinished last work was a painting of the dual scene of the Mount of Transfiguration and the valley below it. On the mountain top, the light of glory shines as Christ appears in his majesty; in the valley there is only gloom and darkness because the disciples have no power to help a dire case of human need (v. 18).

DISCIPLES' FAILURE

An argument had broken out between the disciples and the teachers of the law. The focus of the argument involved helping this young boy who was deaf and dumb, and also suffered from seizures of a severe and destructive nature. His father had come to Jesus' disciples asking them to drive out the evil spirit in his son, and to set him free for life. But they could not do it. Perhaps it was their failure which had led to their argument with the teachers of the law. But just then, Jesus arrived.

Mark vividly captures the pressures and frustrations of Christ's life in these verses. On the mountain top he had been faced with the spiritual short-sightedness of his disciples. Here in the valley he was confronted by unbelief, and asked, 'O unbelieving generation, how long shall I stay with you? How long shall I put up with you?' (v. 19). That cry from the heart is very significant. It underlines for us the very real disappointment which Jesus felt with his disciples. He did not 'soft-pedal' his reactions. Nor did he allow them to think of their failure as a justifiable inadequacy ('We're only human, after all'). No; it was *unbelief*.

THE BOY'S CONDITION

Clearly Jesus did not regard this boy's condition as 'ordinary' epilepsy (not that any epilepsy can be 'ordinary' for those who suffer from it). He shared with the father the conviction that the cause of these seizures, and of the boy's hearing and speech defects, was demonic. This was confirmed when the lad was brought to Jesus and was immediately convulsed by the evil spirit.

The Lord asked how long he had been in this condition. The

answer, 'from childhood', and the description of how the spirit often seemed to throw him into the fire or into water must have moved Jesus deeply. He was an only son (*Luke* 9:38); he had been afflicted in this way since his childhood; the seizures came 'often' (v. 21). As a deaf mute, he could not hear the words of comfort his father must often have mouthed to him and could not speak to share the inner despair he must so frequently have felt.

JESUS IS LORD

Notice that Jesus did two important things: first he rebuked the evil spirit (v. 25). As King and Judge of all things, Jesus issued his judgment of guilt and condemnation on this spirit; then he commanded the spirit to leave and never to return. He declared the boy to be permanently free from such demonic influence for the rest of his life. In doing so he not only dealt with the root of his need but also brought him into a fearless enjoyment of freedom!

So violent was the departure of the spirit that the crowd thought for a moment that the boy was dead (v. 26). But when Jesus took him by the hand, 'he stood up'. The word here is the word for 'resurrection'. The boy had truly been given life. But, as we shall see, the use of 'resurrection language' is a signpost from Mark about the ultimate significance of this miracle.

CONVERSATIONS

Running alongside the action in this story are two important conversations: one between Jesus and the boy's father, the other between Jesus and the disciples.

(i)   *The need for faith.* Disappointed by the disciples' failures, the father had asked Jesus to help, 'if you can'. Jesus challenges the weakness of his faith: 'Everything is possible for him who believes' (v. 23). But what does he mean? Does he mean that the boy will be delivered if the father has faith? Or, does he mean that the boy can be delivered because Jesus has faith and is therefore able to set him free? Either interpretation is possible. In any event, the father's weak faith was strengthened. 'I too believe' he said, 'because you have such perfect trust in the power of God, help me to cast out my unbelief and trust fully in him' (v. 24).

But why did Jesus place such emphasis on faith? Because he wanted the blessing this family was about to receive to be experienced in the context of personal trust in him and love for him. That is always his way, whether he brings physical deliverance to us or not.

(ii) *The nature of faith.* Why had the disciples been unable to drive out the demon (vv. 18, 28)? Only prayer could do this, replied Jesus (v. 29). The disciples had relied on their own strength, or perhaps on their past achievements (for example, Mark 6:13) instead of calling on the power of God. But that is what faith in action is. Faith is man in his weakness trusting God's promise in his word. Only through such weakness is the strength of God seen.

Jesus delivered this boy by 'weakness', that is by relying in prayer on the power of God. The result was that the boy experienced a resurrection. Jesus' actions pointed forward to the time when he would conquer all the powers of darkness – in the weakness of the cross and the triumph of his own resurrection. At the same time he was laying down the principle of all spiritual service in God's kingdom: God uses the weak things of this world to destroy the influence of the things which are mighty. In this way the glory is always his.

40

Understanding Jesus

They left that place and passed through Galilee. Jesus did not want anyone to know where they were, because he was teaching his disciples. He said to them, 'The Son of Man is going to be betrayed into the hands of men. They will kill him, and after three days he will rise.' But they did not understand what he meant and were afraid to ask him about it. They came to Capernaum. When he was in the house, he asked them, 'What were you arguing about on the road?' But they kept quiet because on the way they had argued about who was the greatest. Sitting down, Jesus called the Twelve and said, 'If anyone wants to be first, he must be the very last, and the servant of all.' He took a little child and had him stand among them. Taking him in his arms, he said to them, 'Whoever welcomes one of these little children in my name welcomes me; and whoever welcomes me does not welcome me but the one who sent me' (Mark 9:30–37).

This section in Mark's Gospel, beginning with the confession of Simon Peter at Caesarea Philippi (8:27–30) presents the turning point of Jesus' ministry. From this point onwards, Jesus is on the Via Dolorosa to Jerusalem. Now, in Mark's account, the miraculous becomes rare. The focus of attention is on the cross, and the implications it carries for Jesus' disciples. This explains why Jesus valued privacy so highly (v. 30): 'because he was teaching his disciples' that he would soon be crucified in Jerusalem.

THE DISCIPLES' DIFFICULTIES

In the course of the narrative, three significant things are said about the disciples.

(i)   *They could not understand Jesus.* To us, what he taught them
seems plain enough. How could they fail to grasp the fact that
he was going to die? But we know now what they did not know.
Nothing could have been more repugnant to their minds than to
believe what he was telling them. He was saying, quite literally,
that he already was betrayed. Although the event had not been
accomplished, it was certain. But, since Jesus was still with them,
how could they take in that he was already handed over to be
crucified?

What was particularly difficult for them to grasp was that Jesus
was interpreting the Old Testament Scriptures in a quite different
way from the way they had been taught them. He spoke of himself
as the 'Son of Man' (v. 31). That enigmatic title could simply mean
that he was the faithful servant of God (like Ezekiel). But it is also
a reference to the figure described in Daniel 7, who receives
honour and glory from 'The Ancient of Days' (see *Dan.* 7:9–14).
Yet, Jesus seemed to identify the destiny of this Son of Man with
that of another Old Testament figure – the Suffering Servant of
Isaiah 52:13–53:12.

How could the figure of glory (the Son of Man) also be the
figure of shame (the Suffering Servant)? They simply could not
understand. Only later would they see that it was through his
death as Suffering Servant that he entered into his glory as Son of
Man.

We have not rightly understood the identity of Jesus until we
have seen that he is both.

(ii)   *They were afraid to ask Jesus.* The disciples did not really
understand Jesus. They were afraid to ask him what he meant.
Why should that be – since Jesus was surely the most approachable
of men? The answer lies in the fact that their Master's repeated
stress on his passion underlined just how central it was in his own
thinking. Yet they were his disciples; they should have known what
his mission was. But the implications were just too enormous for
them to accept. It is not really surprising that they hesitated to
raise the subject with him.

But there was probably another element which induced fear
in their hearts: the seriousness with which Jesus spoke, and the

strength of his commitment to his task. Their own spirits were not really in tune with Jesus' spirit. It frightened them to hear him speak like this, because his commitment was a silent summons to them to share it. But now, as later, they found the message of the cross was a stumbling block. They were not the last disciples to react like that.

(iii) *They argued about position.* As though to drive home the spiritual weakness of the disciples, Mark records the sad story of their argument.

Mark gives the impression that Jesus had almost been isolated from the disciples after his announcement. No doubt his commitment to the cross showed on his face. It was a time when none of the disciples felt able to walk alongside him.

But Jesus was far more conscious of what the disciples were doing than they had imagined (how foolish they and we can be!). When they were settled in Capernaum he asked a question to which their answer was an embarrassed silence (v. 34). They had been arguing about which one of them would be the greatest in the kingdom. Jesus had just spoken about his own forthcoming shameful rejection, but meanwhile the disciples, supposedly his followers, had been arguing about their status.

If we did not know our own hearts we would find it difficult to believe that this really happened. But any disciple who knows himself hears the echoes in his own life of such unfaithfulness.

Jesus once again took time to teach them the principles of the kingdom of God. It is one in which service, not personal kudos, is the central theme. The disciple is recognised not by the honour he gives to those who are important in the world's eyes, but by how he responds to those who possess neither position nor importance – like children. You can almost picture Jesus, just at this point. He called the youngest boy in the home they were in, and bringing him into the middle of the discussion, turned to the disciples and said: 'It is only when you learn to welcome little ones like this that you have really learned to welcome me. And only when you have learned to welcome me, have you welcomed the Father who sent me.'

Jesus spoke in Aramaic. In that language the word for 'child' also serves as the word for 'servant' (rather like the French *garçon*). Was he saying: 'It is only when you learn to receive me as the Servant of the Lord in my acts of humility, that you will really be submitted to God'?

If it is still true today that your attitude to those who have no 'standing' in society, reflects your attitude to the Lord Jesus, what kind of disciple are you?

41

Sons of Thunder

'Teacher,' said John, 'we saw a man driving out demons in your name and we told him to stop, because he was not one of us.' 'Do not stop him,' Jesus said. 'No-one who does a miracle in my name can in the next moment say anything bad about me, for whoever is not against us is for us. I tell you the truth, anyone who gives you a cup of water in my name because you belong to Christ will certainly not lose his reward. And if anyone causes one of these little ones who believe in me to sin, it would be better for him to be thrown into the sea with a large millstone tied around his neck' (Mark 9:38–42).

In three successive chapters of his Gospel, Mark records Jesus' teaching on the reason for his coming. He is going to Jerusalem to die, in order to fulfil the prophecies of Scripture. He is the Suffering Servant of whom Isaiah had spoken. He is the One who will be wounded and bruised for the sins of men.

Shortly after each of these statements, Mark also records some response on the part of the disciples. Each response shows how poorly they grasped what their Lord was teaching them. In Mark 8:32, Peter responded in words which reminded Jesus of the temptations he faced in the wilderness at the beginning of his ministry. Later, in Mark 10:35, it was James and John who showed their true colours by seeking advancement in the kingdom of God, instead of exercising commitment to the cross of Christ. Here, it is John on his own.

We know John, affectionately and rightly, as 'the apostle of love'. It is instinctive to think of him in terms of the graciousness of his life. Yet that seems to be far from the whole truth about him. For

Jesus gave John (and his brother James) the nickname 'Boanerges' (*Mark* 3:17). Notice that it was Jesus who gave them this name! It means 'sons of thunder'. It hardly indicates that by nature John was meek and gentle. On the contrary, he was a firebrand! In this story we have an illustration of how his fiery zeal was misplaced.

MISPLACED ZEAL

John, and perhaps the other disciples too, had seen someone driving out demons by using the name of Jesus. John's words betray the attitude of his heart towards this man: 'he was not one of us' (v. 38). So he had rebuked him and told him to stop. On his return, he reported his diligence to the Master. He had made sure there would be no 'unauthorised use' of Jesus' name!

We can understand John's feelings. We may well have shared them ourselves in other connections. Here he was an 'official' representative of Jesus, discovering that someone else was able to do all he could (and more) but lacked the 'title' he possessed. Perhaps the sting in the tail for John was that just a few days before the other disciples had been powerless to help a man's demon-possessed son. Now, as though to rub salt into the wounds, someone else was casting out demons!

Jesus showed extraordinary restraint and patience with John. He reminded him that ministry in Jesus' name was not the prerogative of the few, but the privilege of all those who belonged to the kingdom. Anyone who shared in the work of that kingdom (as this man was obviously doing) would not 'in the next moment say anything bad about me' (v. 39).

NOT AGAINST JESUS

From this strange incident, Jesus drew an important lesson for his followers: 'Whoever is not against us is for us' (v. 40). But what does this mean? Was Jesus taking a *laissez-faire* attitude to discipleship? Do we not meet people who tell us that they have 'nothing against Christ, personally', yet seem far removed from being his disciples? Is Jesus saying that these too are really on his side?

What had concerned Jesus was that John's response to this man had been totally negative because John's chief interest had been his own exclusive relationship to Christ and his commission from him. He had manifested a deep-seated 'them-and-us' mentality because he was anxious to safeguard his own role. His real concern had not been for Christ's honour and kingdom. So Jesus had explained: 'The real issue is not whether this man is one of your group, John, but whether he is for me or against me.' Later, the apostle Paul would try to introduce a similar principle into the church at Rome: 'Accept one another, then, just as Christ accepted you, in order to bring praise to God' (*Rom.* 15:7).

Perhaps the reason Jesus was so gentle with John was that John's words were as much a confession as a statement. Did he realise in the light of what Jesus had just said (vv. 33–37) that he had done a shameful thing? Was that why Jesus had gently pressed home his point: 'John, even the person who only gives someone a cup of cold water in my name – never mind casts out demons – will not lose his reward.' In the last analysis, it is more important that the servants of God are devoted to Christ than that they are 'one of us'. Indeed, our Lord adds, if we cause one of those who belong to him to sin, we will receive the most terrible of judgments. Better to be thrown into the sea with a stone round your neck than to bring such offence.

Do we really take that seriously? Or do we, however secretly, despise what Jesus says here? Would Jesus give you the same nickname he had given to John – son of thunder? Is that how you are known by other Christians? It is not a compliment!

42

Christianity is Serious

'If your hand causes you to sin, cut it off. It is better for you to enter life maimed than with two hands to go into hell, where the fire never goes out. And if your foot causes you to sin, cut it off. It is better for you to enter life crippled than to have two feet and be thrown into hell. And if your eye causes you to sin, pluck it out. It is better for you to enter the kingdom of God with one eye than to have two eyes and be thrown into hell, where "their worm does not die, and the fire is not quenched." Everyone will be salted with fire. Salt is good, but if it loses its saltiness, how can you make it salty again? Have salt in yourselves, and be at peace with each other' (Mark 9:43–50).

In the previous section of this chapter we noticed Jesus warning his disciples not to cause any of his 'little ones' to stumble. It is clear from the context that Jesus did not have children exclusively in mind. All those who serve Christ are in view. If we cause them to sin, we deserve the most severe of judgments. For indifference to those for whom Christ has died is indifference to Christ himself. If he gave his life for them, we belittle him if we belittle them.

The theme of stumbling is continued in the passage which follows; but this time Jesus is warning his disciples against the danger of stumbling themselves by their failure to deal with sin.

FIRE OF CONDEMNATION

Jesus spoke with great seriousness and concreteness about sin. He does not treat it lightly, nor does he offer cheap and easy remedies.

On the contrary, only when we aim at the complete eradication of sin are we likely to have any success against its influence. We are faced with two alternatives: kill sin, or sin will eventually kill us.

There can be no reconciliation between the Christian and sin, and no platform for negotiation. If we do not engage in the effort to conquer it, we may be sure that it will conquer us. We must put out the fires of sin in our hearts, or we will find ourselves exposed to the flames of hell and separation from God, permanently (vv. 44, 48).

It is not an accident that Jesus speaks about sin in relation to the hand, the eye and the foot (vv. 43–47). He is not really suggesting that we engage in acts of self-mutilation in order to be free from sin. Rather, he is underlining the fact that sin is not a 'spiritual' reality which has no relation to daily life. On the contrary, we express our sinfulness through what we do with our hands, what we gaze at with our eyes, where we go to on our feet. The Christian gospel, therefore, summons us to present our bodies to the Lord, as offerings of holiness (see *Rom.* 6:13, 19; 12:1–2). The battle for purity is serious, and it is life-long. According to Jesus, the alternative to winning that battle is the loss of our whole life, in the flames of condemnation.

FIRE OF PURIFICATION

But there is another 'fire' of which Jesus speaks: the fire of purification; 'everyone will be salted with fire' (v. 49).

In the Old Testament, the sacrifices made in the temple were seasoned with salt (*Lev.* 2:13). Jesus seems to be saying here that as we offer our lives to Christ, we too will become like those sacrifices. But we will be seasoned with fire, not salt – the trials which will purge away all the dross of our Christian lives so that only those who have taken Christ's summons seriously will remain standing. Perhaps this is the background to what Peter was later to write about the importance of not being surprised by the fiery trial (*1 Pet.* 1:6–7; 4:12). Through it our faith will emerge, tested and purified for Christ's glory.

SALT OF CONSECRATION

A further word association occurs in verse 50. The mention of being 'salted' (v. 49) leads to the 'saltiness' of Christians. We are to have 'salt' in ourselves.

In Jesus' world, of course, salt was a basic commodity essential to life itself. It was said that 'the world cannot survive without salt' because of its value as a food preservative. What a tragedy, then, if salt were to lose its saltiness.

Our Lord's point is that unless we maintain the purity of our own lives (plucking out the eye, etc.) and are purified by the flames of testing, and remain faithful to Christ, our lives will have no preserving influence on this corrupt world. If we begin to fall into the same patterns of life as those which are characteristic of the world, we will never be able to point men and women to another world.

In view of this, Jesus adds, by way of application: 'be at peace with each other' (v. 50). Does that seem an anticlimax after his great summons to moral purity? Not at all. It is precisely in the ability of Christians to love one another truly and humbly from the heart that the community of believers is distinguished from the back-biting or back-scratching communities of the world. Being at peace with one another is a reflection of the God-given peace we have first received from Jesus Christ. Jesus never down-played the powerful witness of true Christian fellowship. Neither should we.

Jesus leaves us here with some heart-searching questions: Am I treating sin casually? Am I willing to be cleansed through fiery trials? Am I living the kind of life which will make a real impact on society? Am I really preserving loving relationships with my fellow-Christians?

43

Divorce

Jesus then left that place and went into the region of Judea and across the Jordan. Again crowds of people came to him, and as was his custom, he taught them. Some Pharisees came and tested him by asking, 'Is it lawful for a man to divorce his wife?' 'What did Moses command you?' he replied. They said, 'Moses permitted a man to write a certificate of divorce and send her away.' 'It was because your hearts were hard that Moses wrote you this law,' Jesus replied. 'But at the beginning of creation God "made them male and female". "For this reason a man will leave his father and mother and be united to his wife, and the two will become one flesh." So they are no longer two, but one. Therefore what God has joined together, let man not separate.' When they were in the house again, the disciples asked Jesus about this. He answered, 'Anyone who divorces his wife and marries another woman commits adultery against her. And if she divorces her husband and marries another man, she commits adultery' (Mark 10:1–12).

The ministry of Jesus in Galilee had come to an end. He now continued his work in Judea as he prepared for the final journey to Jerusalem and for the suffering he had already predicted he would experience (*Mark* 9:31). Crowds followed him and listened to his teaching. But with them came the little deputation we have now become accustomed to meeting – 'some Pharisees' (v. 2).

These men came to 'test' Jesus. Mark uses this verb on four occasions. Three times it refers to the Pharisees (*Mark* 8:11; 10:2; 12:15). But its first use in the Gospel describes the activity of Satan (*Mark* 1:13). That is highly significant. Mark means us to ask, 'Where did I see this kind of testing before? Why, it was when Satan tested Jesus in the wilderness!'

The parallel stretches beyond the use of the same verb. The Pharisees' activity involved the same mishandling of Scripture which had characterised Satan's approach to Jesus (see *Matt.* 4:1–10).

SCRIPTURE TWISTING

The Pharisees questioned Jesus about the legitimacy of divorce. It was one of the major debating points among them, and divided them into two schools of thought. One took a relatively easy-going attitude, allowing divorce for almost any reason; the other took a much stricter line. It is interesting to notice what 'sins' really concerned these men.

But Jesus was wise to them. He knew that they would try to gain some 'leverage' out of his reply. He pointed them back to Scripture. Now he would put *them* to the test! 'What did Moses command you?' he asked (v. 3). Immediately they replied that 'Moses permitted divorce' (v. 4). Little did they realise that they had already revealed the inner workings of their hearts, and indicated they were out of tune with the Author of Scripture.

The Pharisees referred to what Moses had said in Deuteronomy 24:1–4, which should be read in this connection. They argued that there Moses gave permission for divorce to take place if a man found something 'indecent' in his wife. The point of debate among the Pharisees was merely over what constituted something 'indecent'.

But this reply neglected the context in which these verses of Scripture were written, and indeed their wider context in the whole word of God. Moses' words were intended to create a legal barrier to men sinning as they pleased. They were meant in part to protect the rights of women. Rather than giving permission for divorce, they were intended to restrict the ease with which divorce would take place. Moses' words reminded men of the solemn vows of commitment taken in marriage. But the Pharisees had twisted this. What was intended to be a barrier against licence, some of the Pharisees had turned into a bridge to easy divorce.

JESUS' INTERPRETATION

Jesus recognised that divine laws on divorce had been issued in the Old Testament. But those laws were intended to restrict man's rebellion against God's fundamental law of marriage, given in Genesis 2:24. There marriage was viewed as a life-long and exclusive relationship between one man and one woman. God had not changed his mind about that. The purpose was still the same: a man is united permanently to his wife in marriage (v. 8); no man should ever separate them (v. 9).

TALK FIRST ABOUT MARRIAGE

Jesus raised the discussion on to a different plane altogether. The Pharisees wanted to talk about divorce; he insisted on talking about marriage. Their primary interest lay in seeing how far they could go and still remain within the letter of the law. Jesus' primary interest was in restoring men to the lifestyle for which they had been made. In that context one man, one woman marriage was not a restriction of liberty, but the sphere of its enjoyment and development. It was a gift from the Father. The reason the Pharisees found this so unpalatable was because their hearts were so hardened against the Father.

The Pharisees may have been stunned by what Jesus said. The disciples certainly were. When they were alone with him they questioned him about his teaching. Asking Jesus questions was admirable. But their questions revealed the extent to which their thinking too had been influenced by their environment. Matthew's account suggests they regarded Jesus' standards as impossible. It would be better not to marry if this were the expectation (*Matt.* 19:10)!

Jesus did not change his stance in order to please his disciples. Indeed, he emphasised that someone who divorces his partner and remarries is committing adultery.

Mark assumes here the teaching found elsewhere in the New Testament that marital unfaithfulness or blatant desertion may end a marriage in any case (*Matt.* 19:9 and *1 Cor.* 7:15ff). In such circumstances a Christian may act as though his or her spouse were dead (the Old Testament punishment for such marital sin was death, leaving the individual free to remarry). But such exceptions simply recognise the reality of sin, they do not excuse it. Indeed, they underline the deep solemnity of marital sin.

We can almost hear the protests of the disciples echoing across the centuries (they were no different from twentieth-century people, in this respect). Jesus, however, did not waver. He knew that the stability of family and society life depended on the marriage institution being honoured. If this basic creation design were overthrown, moral, spiritual, psychological and social chaos would result.

How devastatingly relevant to the present day these words of Jesus are! How like the disciples some modern Christians have become. But Jesus did not change the Maker's instructions then – nor has he done so since. We should be grateful that he pointed men back to the original design for life in God's kingdom. Only when we follow that design does marriage 'work' as it should. And when a marriage begins to fail, only re-treading, and re-following the Maker's instructions can repair and save it.

44

Children and the Kingdom of God

People were bringing little children to Jesus to have him touch them, but the disciples rebuked them. When Jesus saw this, he was indignant. He said to them, 'Let the little children come to me, and do not hinder them, for the kingdom of God belongs to such as these. I tell you the truth, anyone who will not receive the kingdom of God like a little child will never enter it.' And he took the children in his arms, put his hands on them and blessed them. (Mark 10:13–16).

M ark has just recorded an incident which revealed the unbiblical thinking of the Pharisees. Now he shares with us another story of spiritually narrowed heart arteries. But this time the culprits are the disciples! Jesus had earlier warned them to watch out for 'the yeast of the Pharisees' (*Mark* 8:15). Here we see one of the reasons why.

Some parents were bringing their children to Jesus for his blessing. Normally they would have brought them to one of the recognised rabbis for that purpose. Jesus seems to have been moved by the fact that these parents wanted *him* to receive and pray for their children. It was an expression of their recognition of his grace and their trust in him.

DISCIPLES OUT OF LINE

The disciples, however, were less than impressed and rebuked them (Mark interestingly uses the masculine pronoun, indicating that it was not just mothers who brought their children to Christ!).

Young children had no standing in society. Who did these parents think they were, adding to the Master's burdens?

The truth of the matter was that this reflected the prejudices of the disciples, not the attitude of Jesus. He was 'indignant' when he saw what was happening (v. 14). That is strong language indeed. Jesus, angry with his disciples? Surely that was something to be reserved for the Pharisees? That is exactly why Jesus was so indignant: his disciples were doing the very thing for which he so consistently opposed the Pharisees! They misrepresented the character of God. They distorted his grace and they diluted his holiness. The disciples were now doing the same thing in connection with Jesus. By their actions they were saying 'This is what Jesus is like. He has no time for you or your children!' No wonder their Master was so deeply moved. What to the disciples was an exercise of their authority was to Jesus a complete distortion of the kingdom of God!

NOT A REWARD BUT A GIFT

In this context, Jesus said two things.

(i) *The kingdom belongs to such.* He urged the children to come, or be brought to him, because 'the kingdom of God belongs to such as these' (v. 14).

Sometimes this statement has been read as though Jesus had said, 'The characteristics of these children have a spiritual parallel. If that spiritual parallel is present in your life, then the kingdom of God belongs to you.' But that is not what Jesus says in verse 14. It is what he says in the next verse (v. 15). In verse 14, Jesus is saying: 'I am the King in the kingdom of God. I belong to these children and all those who are like them.' These children should not be held back from him precisely because Jesus and his kingdom belong to them!

Does this mean that all children belong naturally to the kingdom of God? That can hardly be the case, for Scripture teaches us that naturally we are the children of wrath, not the children of the kingdom (*Eph.* 2:3). What, then, did Jesus mean?

Part of the answer lies in identifying those about whom he is

speaking. They belonged to parents who were sufficiently committed to Jesus to take their little ones to him in public for his blessing.
That blessing was the blessing of the king. As he prayed for them,
Jesus asked that they would receive the blessings of the new
covenant in his blood (v. 16).

Did this mean that irrespective of their response to Jesus these
children were automatically guaranteed salvation? Christians have
often misinterpreted Jesus' words here because they are afraid that
is the implication of taking them at their face value. But if we
remember the context in which Jesus speaks we will not make that
mistake. He is speaking about children whose parents are already
disciples (and will in turn 'disciple' them). Such parents know they
need to teach their children the responsibilities of kingdom life, as
well as the privileges of kingdom possession. If the blessings of
God are rejected in disobedience, they are forfeited. Nothing that
is said here implies any other position on the part of Jesus.

(ii) *Receiving the kingdom.* This becomes all the clearer when we
notice the wider application Jesus draws from this incident:
'anyone who will not receive the kingdom of God like a little child
will never enter it' (v. 15).

Sometimes these words are also misunderstood, as though Jesus
meant we must be willing, submissive and generally angelic if
we are to enter the kingdom! But quite apart from being a naive
reflection on the ways of children, that would be to teach that
certain qualities qualify us for salvation in God's kingdom! That
would be a denial of the gospel.

Children had no standing in Jesus' society. If they were to
receive anything it could not be on the basis of their present rights,
but only as a gift. Similarly, if any of us is to receive the kingdom of
God it must be as a completely unmerited gift from God. If we do
not receive the kingdom that way, 'like a little child' (v. 15), it will
never belong to us.

The thrust of Jesus' words about the kingdom belonging to
children is this: the kingdom of God is a gift, not a right; it is given
by grace, not earned by qualifications. Christ gives it as he chooses.
He had chosen to give it to these children, who were brought in
faith by their parents.

No wonder he was indignant with the disciples. They were in danger of turning the gospel of the gift of the kingdom into a Pharisaic message about earning the kingdom.

In our concern to emphasise our responsibility to repent and believe, we must never make the mistake of the Pharisees – or the disciples. We do not need to 'guard' the grace of God (as the Pharisees and the disciples here tried to do). It will guard itself by the new life it produces in us.

45

Rich, but Sad

As Jesus started on his way, a man ran up to him and fell on his knees before him. 'Good teacher,' he asked, 'What must I do to inherit eternal life?' 'Why do you call me good?' Jesus answered. 'No-one is good – except God alone. You know the commandments: "Do not murder, do not commit adultery, do not steal, do not give false testimony, do not defraud, honour your father and mother."' 'Teacher,' he declared, 'all these I have kept since I was a boy.' Jesus looked at him and loved him. 'One thing you lack,' he said. 'Go, sell everything you have and give to the poor, and you will have treasure in heaven. Then come, follow me.' At this the man's face fell. He went away sad, because he had great wealth (Mark 10:17–22).*

Jesus had been speaking about receiving the kingdom of God as a little child. While his words were still clearly embedded in his disciples' memories an incident occurred which vividly illustrated what he had taught them. A young man ran up to him and asked him on bended knee what he needed to do in order to have eternal life. Luke's Gospel underlines just how remarkable this was by telling us the man was a 'ruler' (that is, in the local synagogue, *Luke* 18:18). Here, surely, was a wonderful opportunity for Jesus to establish a bridgehead into a whole community by making this respected young man one of his disciples!

But Jesus never pursued slick and easy methods of evangelism. In fact, the disciples must have thought his initial response to this man was frankly disappointing! He began to discuss theology with him! With apparent respect, this young enquirer had addressed Jesus as 'Good teacher' (v. 18). Jesus' curious reply was to ask him why he had called him 'good' since no one was good except God.

Only as we follow through the conversation between them does Jesus' response to the rich young man begin to make sense. He had asked Jesus about eternal life in God's kingdom. Painstakingly, Jesus led him, and later his own disciples, through a series of lessons which were (and are) vital for all who would enter into eternal life.

ETERNAL LIFE!

(i) *Knowledge of God.* Later, in his great prayer in John 17, Jesus distilled the essence of eternal life. It is to 'know you, the only true God, and Jesus Christ, whom you have sent' (*John* 17:3). Eternal life means knowing the Father and the Son. It means knowing the Father through the Son, because the Son is equal with the Father and is the One who makes him known (*John* 1:1–2, 18).

When Jesus said, 'Why do you call me good, when we both know that God alone is good?' (v. 18), he was pressing home the question: 'Do you really know God? Your words suggest that you see an intimate relationship between God and myself. Do you really see that?'

(ii) *Knowledge of ourselves.* This is the point of Jesus' apparently casual reference to the law of Moses (v. 19). Already he had taken the measure of the man. That is probably why the commandments he refers to would test whether his understanding of the law was outward and merely formal, or inward and spiritual. Would the young man see that these commandments revealed sinful motives as well as sinful actions (see *Matt.* 5:21–48)? Would he see that Jesus had said nothing about his relationship to the living God – that this question was only 'for openers'?

The young man revealed the sad superficiality of his self-understanding. He volunteered the information that he had kept these commandments from boyhood. He was like Paul before the full force of the law showed him the real nature of his heart. He thought he was alive, when in fact he was spiritually dead (*Rom.* 7:9). 'As for legalistic righteousness' he too was 'faultless' (*Phil.* 3:6). But he was blind to what he was really like inside.

JESUS LOVED HIM, *BUT* . . .

Do not think for a moment that this young man was a rogue. The reverse was the case. He was an earnest, sincere, religious, devoted young man. As far as he understood his own heart he had kept the commandments. In every human respect he was the kind of man most of us secretly admire, but fail to imitate. That was why Jesus 'looked at him and loved him' (v. 21). But something was missing – one thing which amounted to everything. His life was still centred on himself rather than on the kingdom of God.

With a surgeon-like cut, Jesus expertly, and unexpectedly, exposed the man's need: 'Go, sell your possessions, give everything to the poor, and then come and follow me. You will then have treasure in heaven' (v. 21).

One sentence was enough to teach this young man the truth about himself that had been hidden all these years. He had out-wardly kept the commandments; but there was a god in his life which he prized more than the knowledge of the true God: 'he had great wealth' (v. 22). Sadly, with his heart deception now unveiled, he turned round and went back to the idol worship from which he had almost escaped. Only, now he knew the truth about himself.

Here was a man who had great wealth, and was not willing to take the 'risk' of faith by leaving it for the sake of greater wealth. What was his mistake? He made his greatest ever decision on the basis of this life rather than on the basis of eternal life. If only he had remembered the story of Moses which must have been read to him so often 'from boyhood'! He counted 'disgrace for the sake of Christ as of greater value than the treasures of Egypt, because he was looking ahead to his reward' (*Heb.* 11:26). Moses calculated on the basis of eternal arithmetic. This young man relied on the inaccurate calculator he had always used: wealth. He stands as a perpetual monument to the fact that if we have everything, but have not Christ, we ultimately have nothing. The special tragedy of his life – as he made his way home sadly – was that now he knew it.

46

All for Jesus

Jesus looked around and said to his disciples, 'How hard it is for the rich to enter the kingdom of God!' The disciples were amazed at his words. But Jesus said again, 'Children, how hard it is to enter the kingdom of God! It is easier for a camel to go through the eye of a needle than for a rich man to enter the kingdom of God.' The disciples were even more amazed, and said to each other, 'Who then can be saved?' Jesus looked at them and said, 'With man this is impossible, but not with God; all things are possible with God.' Peter said to him, 'We have left everything to follow you!' 'I tell you the truth,' Jesus replied, 'no-one who has left home or brothers or sisters or mother or father or children or fields for me and the gospel will fail to receive a hundred times as much in this present age (homes, brothers, sisters, mothers, children and fields – and with them persecutions) and in the age to come, eternal life. But many who are first will be last, and the last first' (Mark 10:23–31).

The whole of Jesus' attention had been given to the rich ruler who had come to him seeking eternal life. Now, as the young man turned away sadly, clinging to his possessions rather than responding to Christ's invitation, Jesus turned to his disciples. There must have been sadness in his eyes and on his face. There was certainly deep sadness in his words, as he commented on what they had all witnessed: 'How hard it is for the rich to enter the kingdom of God!' (v. 23).

NEEDLES AND CAMELS

His words astonished the disciples – despite all they had just seen. After all, the rich had many advantages. From a human point of view it seemed to be so much easier for them to live lives which pleased God. They did not have the fears and anxieties which the poor knew; they had time on their hands to spend in religious learning and actions ('idle rich' doubtless some of the disciples would say).

The disciples had still not learned the real meaning of the conversation between Jesus and the young man. So their Lord underlined it for them with one of his most memorable sayings: It is as difficult for the rich to enter God's kingdom as it is for a camel to go through the eye of a needle!

Various efforts have been made to find the source of this statement – was there a city gate somewhere in Jesus' time known as 'The Needle's Eye' through which camels came and were unloaded in order to enter? Is this some kind of well-known proverbial saying? But the source of the illustration makes no difference to its message. Jesus is saying, in the most vivid fashion possible, that in terms of natural ability it is utterly impossible for a rich man to enter the kingdom of God!

CAN ANYONE BE SAVED?

The response of the twelve was open-mouthed incredulity. If this were so, surely nobody could be saved! That was probably the response Jesus expected. Having already taught the disciples (in his conversation with the ruler) the significance of the true knowledge of God and the knowledge of themselves, he now wanted to show them the knowledge of God's grace. What man could never do, God alone can do (v. 27).

What did Jesus mean? He meant that eternal life not only has God as its goal, it has God as its source and beginning. Only he can give it! Only when he gives us new hearts, to abandon everything for Christ, will we be free from our personal forms of idolatry and yield to the principles of the divine kingdom (*Ezek.* 36:25–27). The message of the encounter with the rich young ruler in Mark's

Gospel teaches the same lessons as Jesus' encounter with Nicodemus in John's Gospel (3:1–21). Eternal life, the kingdom of God, salvation – these can be ours only when we are cast on the mercy and grace of God to give them to us.

LEFT EVERYTHING?

Significantly, it is Simon Peter who blurts out what was on the minds of most of the disciples: 'We have left everything to follow you!' (v. 28).

Did Peter never get his sentence finished? Was he going to ask a question about where they stood? He did not need to. Jesus understood his consternation. He knew that even for his own disciples the radical challenge he had just issued must have brought deep self-questioning about their own level of commit-ment to him. We can almost hear Peter saying, 'Lord, we're not rich men; we have not left such treasures; but, Lord, we have left everything we had!'

Our Lord's response contains some of the greatest words of encouragement to be found anywhere in Scripture. Yes, he recog-nises that to follow him will involve many in suffering persecution (v. 30). But will that 'sacrifice' involve 'loss'? By no means. Jesus promises that whatever his disciples sacrifice for his sake and for the spread of the gospel will be given back to them 'a hundred times as much in this present age . . . and in the age to come, eternal life' (v. 30).

MULTIPLICATION NOT SUBTRACTION!

It is a staggering promise, and, to a casual reader of the Gospels, an impossible one. We can understand 'pie in the sky when you die' ('in the age to come, eternal life!'), but 'pie now'? That is what Jesus seems to be promising.

From outside the kingdom, where the reality of its power is an unknown quantity, the promise appears ludicrous. Yet thousands, millions of Christians throughout the ages could testify how this promise has come true in their lives. Christ has never been their debtor. He has supplied all their needs. Even when becoming a

Christian has meant leaving family, or being rejected by them, Christ has given back a hundred families to his servants. It is one of the most stubborn facts of history that this promise has been fulfilled. Christ, as the great explorer David Livingstone once said, was a gentleman, and has kept his word.

This was something the rich young ruler never discovered, as far as we know. It is one of the 'secrets of the kingdom of God'. Is it one on which you have ventured everything?

47

Towards Jerusalem

They were on their way up to Jerusalem, with Jesus leading the way, and the disciples were astonished, while those who followed were afraid. Again he took the Twelve aside and told them what was going to happen to him. 'We are going up to Jerusalem,' he said, 'and the Son of Man will be betrayed to the chief priests and teachers of the law. They will condemn him to death and will hand him over to the Gentiles, who will mock him and spit on him, flog him and kill him. Three days later he will rise.'

Then James and John, the sons of Zebedee, came to him. 'Teacher,' they said, 'we want you to do for us whatever we ask.' 'What do you want me to do for you?' he asked. They replied, 'Let one of us sit at your right and the other at your left in your glory.' 'You don't know what you are asking,' Jesus said. 'Can you drink the cup I drink or be baptised with the baptism I am baptised with?' 'We can,' they answered. Jesus said to them, 'You will drink the cup I drink and be baptised with the baptism I am baptised with, but to sit at my right or left is not for me to grant. These places belong to those for whom they have been prepared.' When the ten heard about this, they became indignant with James and John. Jesus called them together and said, 'You know that those who are regarded as rulers of the Gentiles lord it over them, and their high officials exercise authority over them. Not so with you, Instead, whoever wants to become great among you must be your servant, and whoever wants to be first must be slave of all. For even the Son of Man did not come to be served, but to serve, and to give his life as a ransom for many' (Mark 10:32–45).

Chapters 8, 9 and 10 of Mark's Gospel are punctuated by Jesus' three-fold announcement of his impending suffering and death (8:31–32; 9:31; 10:33). There is a growing sense in the narrative that Jesus is steadily making his way to fulfil his destiny. Mark pictures Jesus striding out in front of his disciples and those who accompanied them. There was 'something about him' now that had a profound effect on them all. It was not that he had resolved something which had been troubling him. It was more a sense of almost frightening determination in his whole bearing. The disciples (who must have assumed by this time that they knew Jesus 'inside out') were 'astonished'; the others who were with them were 'afraid' (v. 32). The degree of commitment which Jesus manifested was something they had never encountered before. They could not fully understand it; but it unnerved them just because it drew them into its own orbit. They sensed that his commitment required their commitment!

DETAILED PROPHECY

Taking the disciples aside, Jesus explained his mission in greater detail than before. They were going to Jerusalem – and Jerusalem was where he would die! He, the Messiah, would be treated with contempt by his own people. They would hand their own promised Messiah over to the Gentiles to be mocked and spat upon, flogged and eventually executed (vv. 33–34).

Now his followers were in possession of almost all of the details which would be fulfilled so soon. How did they react?

On similar occasions they had reacted very badly. As Mark records their 'spiritual pulse rate' in response to these revelations of Jesus, it had been very poor. On the first occasion Peter had tried to divert Jesus; on the second, the disciples had begun to argue about which one of them was the greatest. By now, however, they would surely have learned their lesson.

SELFISH REQUESTS

Sadly, they had not. As the journey continued, James and John realised the significance of what they had just heard. Their

Messiah was going to suffer in Jerusalem, and then he was going to rise again! This could mean only one thing: the messianic age, promised in the Old Testament Scriptures, was almost here. The messianic banquet would soon be served. Now was the time to stake their claim for a place of honour in the coming world, beside Jesus himself! It may well be that these brothers had usually found themselves in the places of honour when the disciples ate together – some people seem to have a knack of always sitting next to the central character!

Jesus immediately took them to task. They did not really understand what they were asking. Nor did they understand how insensitive their selfishness was in the light of what Jesus was about to do. Like Peter before them, they were looking for a crown without a cross, glory without suffering, honour without humility.

THE WINE AND THE WATER

This is the point of the question Jesus asked them: 'You cannot drink of my cup and be baptised with my baptism, can you?' (v. 38, where the question is phrased in such a way as to expect 'no' as the answer). On the cross, Jesus would drink the cup of God's wrath against sin, he would be baptised (or overwhelmed) with the waters of God's judgment! But the brothers were undeterred – what did Jesus know about what they could and could not do? Yes, they could share both his cup and his baptism. They did not pause to reflect on the meaning of either.

With a hint of sadness, Jesus assured the disciples that they would indeed drink a cup and receive a baptism of suffering. But it was the prerogative of his Father, not his own, to bestow the places of honour at the messianic banquet. Did they not yet understand? Had they not learned yet to imitate him, and seek honour for the Father rather than for themselves?

CHAIN REACTION

When the others heard what had happened – perhaps from the two sheepish brothers reporting their conversation with Jesus – they proved themselves to be no better. They were furious. Their own pride was hurt. It was time for Jesus to step in once more to underline the principle they had so badly failed to keep.

What was that principle? It was very simple. The way of the disciple is different from the way of the world. In the kingdom of God, true greatness is measured by our service, not by the number of our servants. It is seen, not in how high up the ladder we have climbed, but how far down the ladder we are prepared to climb for the sake of others. True discipleship has at its heart letting go of our desire for honour in this world, in order to bestow honour on others.

But discipleship is also a 'modelling' process. It means being like Jesus! He came to serve others, not to be served by them. He came to give his life for others. If James and John and all the others really were going to be his disciples, then it was time they began to live like their Master.

The 'simple' words of Jesus are always the most difficult, aren't they?

48

A Blind Beggar

Then they came to Jericho. As Jesus and his disciples, together with a large crowd, were leaving the city, a blind man, Bartimaeus (that is, the Son of Timaeus), was sitting by the roadside begging. When he heard that it was Jesus of Nazareth, he began to shout, 'Jesus, Son of David, have mercy on me!' Many rebuked him and told him to be quiet, but he shouted all the more, 'Son of David, have mercy on me!' Jesus stopped and said, 'Call him.' So they called to the blind man, 'Cheer up! On your feet! He's calling you.' Throwing his cloak aside, he jumped to his feet and came to Jesus. 'What do you want me to do for you?' Jesus asked him. The blind man said, 'Rabbi, I want to see.' 'Go,' said Jesus, 'your faith has healed you.' Immediately he received his sight and followed Jesus along the road (Mark 10:46–52).

Passover was approaching. It was time for pilgrimages to Jerusalem for the annual feast. What this meant to the Old Testament believer is recorded in the fifteen 'Songs of Ascents' (*Psa.* 120–134). They perfectly express the wide variety of spiritual experience involved in travelling there. No doubt some of those psalms were sung on the way, as pilgrims lifted up their eyes to the hills, contemplated the danger of their journey (especially on the road between Jericho and Jerusalem – see Luke 11:30!) and as they arrived in the city (see *Psa.* 121, 122).

Jesus was in the middle of such a crowd of pilgrims. They were now in Jericho (v. 46). It was here, just outside the city gate, that Jesus met Bartimaeus, the man whose blindness condemned him to a world of darkness and poverty, and reduced him to beggarhood.

BARTIMAEUS

We do not know how Bartimaeus had heard about Jesus. It seems likely that Jesus' name was on the lips of many of the pilgrims as they talked together. The stories of his teaching and healing must have figured prominently. Had Bartimaeus put two and two together, in order to conclude that this Man was no ordinary teacher or healer? Had he heard how Jesus claimed to be the One on whom the Spirit of the Lord had been promised to rest, who would give sight to the blind (*Luke* 4:18)?

As he heard the crowds passing by, Bartimaeus learned that Jesus was with them. This might well be the only opportunity he would ever have. At the top of his voice he shouted out, 'Son of David, have mercy on me!' (v. 48).

Naturally the crowd told him to hold his tongue (wouldn't you have done the same?). They were there for the spectacle of seeing Jesus on his way to Jerusalem. Many of them must have realised that a confrontation of monumental proportions might result. Bartimaeus had only nuisance value under such circumstances.

The blind beggar cried out all the more. Nothing would stop him. Jesus heard him. He stopped, and called him.

Was it the same people who had sought to silence him who now told him to 'cheer up'? Did their words indicate a sadness in Bartimaeus' cry which now touched their hearts? Or were they interested only in the 'sport' of the occasion? Mark gives us no answer. His attention is now completely focused on the encounter between Jesus and Bartimaeus.

WHY CALL ON JESUS?

Jesus' question perhaps appears naive: 'What do you want me to do?' (v. 51). But its simplicity is deceptive. It went straight to the heart of the matter. Why had Bartimaeus called on Jesus? Did he need financial assistance? How much – or how little – did he believe Jesus could do for him? He answered immediately. There was only one thing he wanted from Jesus: his sight. His request for it was the evidence that he believed Jesus could provide it. And he did. Bartimaeus could see immediately. And, says Mark, 'he

A Blind Beggar

followed Jesus along the road' (v. 52). What a scene that must have been!

THE GOSPEL IN ACTION

This is the penultimate miracle in Mark's Gospel, a further visual presentation of the presence of the kingdom of God. It gathers together several important lessons.

No miracle in this Gospel more vividly illustrates the promise God had given through the prophet Joel. When God establishes his kingdom 'everyone who calls on the name of the Lord will be saved' (*Joel* 2:32). Bartimaeus encountered Jesus' power, not on the basis of his strength, but in the context of his weakness. The crowd around him believed (rightly) that he had nothing he could contribute to what Jesus was doing. They did not understand that this was not a disqualification from calling on the Lord's name (in effect, it was they, and not Bartimaeus, who were blind). Bartimaeus brought nothing but his need. But in doing so he fulfilled a fundamental law in God's kingdom: there is no other way to come to Jesus but on the basis of our need and his adequacy to meet it fully.

JESUS HAD TIME

A further element emerges in this story. Jesus had time for Bartimaeus. When we recall the context – the sense of fear in the disciples' hearts as they watched Jesus go to Jerusalem with such awe-inspiring determination – our Lord's tender care for one blind beggar is profoundly moving. His willingness to stop, when his own heart must have been heavy with sorrow; his concern that Bartimaeus should share his need, when not even his own disciples seemed capable of sharing his own need – all this emphasises the gracious character of the Saviour. It stands also in marked contrast to the events of the previous section, when the disciples had fought among themselves for the places of honour and Jesus reminded them that true greatness lies in humble service. If that is so, then Jesus' greatness never stood out more clearly than when he called this helpless man out of his darkness and into the light of a new and more glorious day.

Throughout Mark's Gospel there is an underlying message for the church in Rome, and for the church in all ages. Jesus has not changed, he is still the same. He still stops for those who call on his name, and he listens to our prayers for help.

49

Ride on in Majesty

As they approached Jerusalem and came to Bethphage and Bethany at the Mount of Olives, Jesus sent two of his disciples, saying to them, 'Go to the village ahead of you, and just as you enter it, you will find a colt tied there, which no-one has ever ridden. Untie it and bring it here. If anyone asks you, "Why are you doing this?" tell him, "The Lord needs it and will send it back here shortly."' They went and found a colt outside in the street, tied at a doorway. As they untied it, some people standing there asked, 'What are you doing, untying that colt?' They answered as Jesus had told them to, and the people let them go. When they brought the colt to Jesus and threw their cloaks over it, he sat on it. Many people spread their cloaks on the road, while others spread branches they had cut in the fields. Those who went ahead and those who followed shouted, 'Hosanna! Blessed is he who comes in the name of the Lord! Blessed is the coming kingdom of our father David! Hosanna in the highest!' Jesus entered Jerusalem and went to the temple. He looked around at everything, but since it was already late, he went out to Bethany with the Twelve (Mark 11:1–11).

E very schoolboy is supposed to know Julius Caesar's famous words before he crossed the River Rubicon, 'The die is cast'. It means that a point of no return has been reached. That was true now for Jesus. He had committed himself to going to Jerusalem. There was no turning back. Now his last days had arrived; the climactic activity of his life was about to begin.

Jesus knew that in the purposes of God he had already been handed over to be shamefully treated and crucified. He must have been conscious that the plotting of his death had been going on now for months (*Mark* 3:6). But he did not go to the cross as a helpless victim. All the Gospel writers emphasise that Jesus was the Lord and Master both of his disciples and of his own situation. It would be no accident that he would be arrested and crucified. In fact, those events were but further steps in fulfilling his own saving purposes. His majesty and authority begin to shine through from the moment of his entry into Jerusalem.

It seems likely that Jesus' commandeering of the colt was a prearranged action. Perhaps its owner was now with Jesus, so that his servants and neighbours would not think it strange for the animal to be taken to him for Jesus.

KINGLY ARRIVAL

But why did Jesus *ride* into Jerusalem? It was a more unusual act than we might at first think, because pilgrims usually made the last part of their journey to the city on foot. Nor is the explanation simply that he was tired from his journey (although he may well have been). No, his action was one of prophetic symbolism. It was the fulfilment of an ancient prophecy from Zechariah 9:9: 'Rejoice greatly, O Daughter of Zion . . . See, your king comes to you, righteous and having salvation, gentle and riding on a donkey, on a colt, the foal of a donkey.' This was no spur-of-the-moment idea on Jesus' part. For those who had eyes to see, it was a deliberate claim to be the One of whom the prophets had so clearly written.

The crowds of pilgrims who were also making their way to Jerusalem were caught up in what was happening, and began to sing and shout the words of some of the great pilgrim hymns of the psalter. They greeted him as one who had come in the name of the Lord. Cloaks and branches were thrown on the road as the joy of the crowd began to overflow into activity. Doubtless none of them knew that the animal on which Jesus sat had never been ridden before (v. 2). But some of the disciples knew – and knew also that the animals used in the Old Testament system of worship were invariably those which had not been employed in secular business. Hidden in the very heart of this symbolism was the message that Jesus had come to give his life as a ransom sacrifice for men's sins!

HUMBLE BEARING

Yet, for all Jesus' kingly bearing in his entry into Jerusalem, there is something else we should notice. He does not enter Jerusalem in pomp and circumstance. It is with meekness and lowliness that he enters the city which is to reject him.

These are virtually the only qualities in his own character to which Jesus ever drew attention. In the famous 'comfortable words' he invites us to come to him precisely because he is meek and lowly in heart (*Matt.* 11:28–30). The same qualities had become visible in Jesus' life when, catching sight of the city of Jerusalem, his heart had burst with sorrow and his eyes had filled with tears. He wept over its sin and unbelief (*Luke* 19:41–44). What a strange way for the Son of David to return to the seat of David's kingdom! Yet there never was a more regal entry into Jerusalem than on that day.

THE TRUE VICTOR'S TRIUMPH

Think, for a moment, what Mark's record would convey to those who read it first – the Christians in Rome. No doubt many of them had seen generals enter Rome in triumph to receive the accolades of victory. How stark the contrast between Roman glory and Jesus' humility must have seemed. How mighty and powerful the sword and political power by contrast with King Jesus! Yet we know that his kingdom was established, while the glory that was Rome disappeared into oblivion. We know that what Jesus did in Jerusalem established a kingdom which would outlast all the kingdoms of this world and break in pieces every man-centred kingdom which sets itself against it. Jesus had come to take his throne – but had committed himself to begin his reign from a cross.

What were Jesus' thoughts as he made his way to the temple that evening, and 'looked around at everything' (v. 11)? Did he remember the first time he had seen it, as a twelve-year-old boy (*Luke* 2:41–52)? Did he think back through the history of his people, and ponder some of the statements of the Psalms, about this place where God had made himself known? The temple had been destroyed before. In a day or two he would tell his disciples that it would soon be destroyed again. There was only one kingdom which would stand – the kingdom which would come soon, through his death and resurrection. With those thoughts, or similar ones in his mind, he realised it was late, and returned to Bethany. Now it was just a matter of time!

50

Prophet, Priest and King

*The next day as they were leaving Bethany, Jesus was hungry.
Seeing in the distance a fig-tree in leaf, he went to find out if it
had any fruit. When he reached it, he found nothing but leaves,
because it was not the season for figs. Then he said to the tree,
'May no-one ever eat fruit from you again.' And his disciples
heard him say it. On reaching Jerusalem, Jesus entered the
temple area and began driving out those who were buying and
selling there. He overturned the tables of the money-changers
and the benches of those selling doves, and would not allow anyone to carry merchandise through the temple courts. And as he
taught them, he said, 'Is it not written: "My house will be called
a house of prayer for all nations"? But you have made it "a den
of robbers".' The chief priests and the teachers of the law heard
this and began looking for a way to kill him, for they feared him,
because the whole crowd was amazed at his teaching. When
evening came, they went out of the city.*

*In the morning, as they went along, they saw the fig-tree
withered from the roots. Peter remembered and said to Jesus,
'Rabbi, look! The fig-tree you cursed has withered!' 'Have faith
in God,' Jesus answered. 'I tell you the truth, if anyone says to
this mountain, "Go, throw yourself into the sea," and does not
doubt in his heart but believes that what he says will happen, it
will be done for him. Therefore I tell you, whatever you ask for
in prayer, believe that you have received it, and it will be yours.
And when you stand praying, if you hold anything against
anyone, forgive him, so that your Father in heaven may forgive
you your sins.'*

*They arrived again in Jerusalem, and while Jesus was walk-
ing in the temple courts, the chief priests, the teachers of the law*

and the elders came to him. 'By what authority are you doing these things?' they asked. 'And who gave you authority to do this?' Jesus replied, 'I will ask you one question. Answer me, and I will tell you by what authority I am doing these things. John's baptism – was it from heaven, or from men? Tell me!' They discussed it among themselves and said, 'If we say, "From heaven", he will ask, "Then why didn't you believe him?" But if we say, "From men" . . .' (They feared the people, for everyone held that John really was a prophet.) So they answered Jesus, 'We don't know.' Jesus said, 'Neither will I tell you by what authority I am doing these things' (Mark 11:12–33).

Throughout Mark's Gospel, Jesus is always in complete control of every situation. Everything he does is stamped with the imprint of his gracious authority. In the previous section we noted how Jesus rode into Jerusalem as the prophesied king. Yet he came in meekness and lowliness, not in pomp and ostentation. But that meekness should not be misunderstood as weakness. Jesus entered Jerusalem as the promised Messiah. It is not surprising then that his actions revealed his authority as the prophet, priest and king whom God had sent.

PROPHET

He shows his authority as the prophet whom God has sent by the power of his word. When he spoke to the fig tree (v. 14), his word came true (vv. 20–21). He was hungry. The tree showed signs of bearing fruit – even though it was out of season. But when Jesus went to take the figs promised by the leaves, there were none. He spoke a word of judgment on the tree: no one would ever eat its fruit again. The next morning, as the disciples returned to Jerusalem, they saw the tree withered from its roots!

Was this an act of callous and spiteful malice on Jesus' part? In view of Mark's concern to show Jesus' regal grace, that is unthinkable. Rather, Mark saw in Jesus' action an acted prophecy. Israel, like the fig tree, showed the outward signs of bearing fruit, but those who approached it spiritually hungry found none. Although planted by God, and nurtured by his servants, the people of God were spiritually barren. Like vine branches which bore no fruit, they would be cast aside (*John* 15:6).

Many readers have been alarmed by this action of Jesus. It seems so severe. But it drives us to one of two conclusions: either Jesus was callous and cynical in his use of power, or the question of our spiritual fruitfulness is one of immense seriousness which we ignore at our peril. The Jewish people did ignore it, and within years were exposed to the withering judgment of God. How much we need to learn that, without exception, Jesus means what he says!

PRIEST

When Jesus arrived at the temple, he demonstrated his authority there as God's priest. The temple had apparently been turned into a market-place, where dishonest commercial exploitation was taking place. Had the priests any sense of dignity or authority they would have cleansed God's sanctuary long before. But it took the God-appointed priest to drive out those who were desecrating the house of God. It was meant to be 'a house of prayer for all nations' (v. 17, cf. *Isa.* 56:7); it had become a commercial market-place instead. Where God's name was to be praised it had been dishonoured and besmirched. That was something Jesus would not tolerate, even if, humanly speaking, it would cost him his life – as indeed it did (v. 18).

There are few more awe-inspiring passages in Scripture than this one. Here Jesus' holy wrath burned with frightening purity. Single-handed, he restored the place to its original purpose. As the true priest in the temple of God, he cleansed it for prayer.

Jesus is still the one priest in the church of God. His actions then must make us ask whether the church has learned its lesson yet. What blasphemy when the impression left by the church is that buying and selling in this world and its goods is its chief interest! We should not think that his careful scrutiny of the church is a thing of the past. Think of his words to the seven churches in Asia, appended to John's letter in Revelation 1. There Jesus is pictured again robed in his priestly garments (*Rev.* 1:12–16), scrutinising his temple, urging repentance before it is too late. He comes seeking spiritual fruit and true worship. Is that what is most noticeable about your life and that of your Christian fellowship?

KING

The final segment in the chapter records an incident in which Jesus' bearing as king is underlined. He was asked a 'trick question', in the hope that he would condemn himself out of his own mouth (v. 28): On whose authority did he act?

Jesus answered with a question of his own (we would do well to learn from him how to respond to cynical opponents of the gospel!). If the priests, lawyers and elders would answer his question, he would in turn answer their question. In fact, as they all knew, the right answer to his question provided the right answer to their question! 'Was John's baptism from heaven, or merely from men?' (v. 30).

If they replied 'from men', the religious leaders knew they would face an uprising against them, for John was regarded as a true prophet and martyr – with good reason. But, if they replied 'from God [heaven]' their failure to respond to his ministry would be inexcusable. Not only so, but Jesus himself had been recognised and baptised by John as the Messiah! To acknowledge that John's baptism was God-ordained would be to confess that Jesus was the Christ!

How pathetic these great theologians and leaders must have looked, as they said to Jesus: 'We don't know'! 'Then, you are incapable of recognising the source of my authority', said Jesus (v. 33).

What is the lesson? You will not truly confess Jesus as the Christ until you are willing to bow to his authority as your Saviour, Lord and Teacher.

51

The Owner's Son

He then began to speak to them in parables: 'A man planted a vineyard. He put a wall around it, dug a pit for the winepress and built a watchtower. Then he rented the vineyard to some farmers and went away on a journey. At harvest time he sent a servant to the tenants to collect from them some of the fruit of the vineyard. But they seized him, beat him and sent him away empty-handed. Then he sent another servant to them; they struck this man on the head and treated him shamefully. He sent still another, and that one they killed. He sent many others; some of them they beat, others they killed. He had one left to send, a son, whom he loved. He sent him last of all, saying, "They will respect my son." But the tenants said one to another, "This is the heir. Come, let's kill him, and the inheritance will be ours." So they took him and killed him, and threw him out of the vineyard. What then will the owner of the vineyard do? He will come and kill those tenants and give the vineyard to others. Haven't you read this scripture: "The stone the builders rejected has become the capstone; the Lord has done this, and it is marvellous in our eyes"?' Then they looked for a way to arrest him because they knew he had spoken the parable against them. But they were afraid of the crowd; so they left him and went away (Mark 12:1–12).

Jesus' authority had been demonstrated by his kingly entrance into Jerusalem, and challenged by the religious leaders as they had continued to question him. They had tried to assert their authority over him, but they could not compare with him morally, nor could they hold a candle to him theologically! In argument he was their Master! All their attempts to 'corner' him so far had fallen to the ground. But now Jesus brings the issue to a head himself, by telling a parable which so touched the consciences of the religious leaders that they felt 'he had spoken the parable against them' (v. 12). Despite all their deep-seated opposition against him, they were constrained by Jesus' authority to recognise that he was their Master and Judge.

REBELLIOUS TENANTS

Not all of Jesus' parables were so readily understood by his hearers. But they immediately recognised in this one an allusion to the picture of Israel which Isaiah had drawn – as the vineyard of the Lord (*Isa.* 5:1–7). Jesus married that to the daily experience of tenant farmers who laboured on the land of absent landlords. In the parable, the tenants were the religious leaders from whom spiritual fruit was expected (v. 2). The parable of the vineyard was, in fact, the spoken form of the parable of the fig-tree which Jesus had 'told' in the previous chapter.

The story which Jesus told moved beyond daily experience. Revolts by tenant farmers were not unusual. What would have been unusual was the fact that the owner in Jesus' parable sent servant after servant (vv. 2–5). Doubtless the religious leaders realised that the servants in the parable represented the prophets of the Old Testament. The final messenger was the owner's son. There was no doubting his identity. It was Jesus. He was now confronting them, in this semi-veiled manner, with the fact that he knew what their plan was: they intended to destroy him (v. 7)! Only their fear of men held them back (v. 12).

Notice again how Jesus controls the situation, and is master of every moment of his own life. Until this time he had carefully avoided unnecessary confrontation with the leaders. But now his time had almost come. He knew that he could issue these warnings and expose these wicked men, and yet still keep to God's timetable. He knew that this would not lead to his immediate or premature death, for one reason: these men lacked the courage of their convictions. Unlike Jesus, they were not prepared to die for their cause, and therefore out of fear of the crowd, they refrained from any action. They lacked 'moral courage'. But, then, how could such men have any?

REACTIONS

When God's word searches out men's motives and exposes their hearts, two reactions are always possible. Men may see themselves as they really are, repent from their sin, and turn to the Lord. We might think that would be the inevitable response to Jesus' own preaching.

But another kind of response is possible: we can harden our hearts against the one who exposes our need, and resolve with unmitigated bitterness to be rid of his influence. This was the pathway these Jews chose (see verses 7–9). Foolishly they thought they could emerge unscathed. But time proved Jesus right: the vineyard of God was given to others.

DISCARDED STONE FITS!

Jesus drew on Psalm 118:22–23 to paint the same picture in different colours. The psalm tells of one of the stones which had been brought to the building site for Solomon's temple. The stone was discarded as unfit for the sanctuary. Yet, those who rejected it did not realise that it was perfectly shaped and hued to be the capstone of the porch! The stone which the expert builders had rejected was the one which would hold everything together! Jesus, who would be despised and rejected by these leaders was actually essential for access into God's presence! This is God's way. Through what man counts as foolish, God shows that his folly is wiser than the wisdom of men, and his weakness stronger than the strength of men (*1 Cor.* 1:25).

APPLICATION

But the lesson of this parable cannot be confined to the religious leaders of Jesus' time. Paul explains that it applies to the church today (which is largely Gentile): branches were broken off so that we could be grafted into God's vine, the church. But while that is true, we must remember God's righteous judgment! Do not be proud and self-sufficient. Rather bow in reverent fear, for if God did not spare the natural branches, will he spare the grafted branches if they eventually show the same hardness of heart (see *Rom.* 11:19–21)? By no means!

God continues to send servants to us, to remind us of our debt to him. In a multitude of ways he reminds us that he looks for the fruit of grace in our lives. His servants may be preachers and teachers of his word; they may be those who remind us personally that we are to live for Christ; they may be the joys and sorrows of life, which encourage us to seek our only ultimate joy and strength in God and his grace. The question is: How do you respond to the messengers God sends? Do you welcome them, or do you seek to silence the voice of God in them?

52

The Opposition United

Later they sent some of the Pharisees and Herodians to Jesus to catch him in his words. They came to him and said, 'Teacher, we know you are a man of integrity. You aren't swayed by men, because you pay no attention to who they are; but you teach the way of God in accordance with the truth. Is it right to pay taxes to Caesar or not? Should we pay or shouldn't we?' But Jesus knew their hypocrisy. 'Why are you trying to trap me?' he asked. 'Bring me a denarius and let me look at it.' They brought the coin, and he asked them, 'Whose portrait is this? And whose inscription?' 'Caesar's' they replied. Then Jesus said to them, 'Give to Caesar what is Caesar's and to God what is God's' And they were amazed at him (Mark 12:13–17).

Jesus unites people. He took the already malformed clay of young men's lives and shaped them into a band of apostles who were eventually willing to live and die for him. But men are not always united by Jesus in that way. They can also be united in hostility towards him, even if otherwise they have little in common. This was the case with the Pharisees and the Herodians. Mark records that they were in league against him throughout almost the entire period of Jesus' public ministry (*Mark* 3:6). Together they plotted and schemed his destruction.

ENEMIES UNITED

Nowhere is this more evident than in the series of 'trick questions' with which Jesus was now faced. Here, the Pharisees, who stood for the old ways, and many of whom were 'hard-liners'; and the Herodians, whose life style was one of constant compromise rather than principle, forced themselves on Jesus once more. There was one person significant enough to bring them together – Jesus – but it was in sworn opposition to all that he taught and did. Sinking their differences, they were united in opposition to him, just as Herod and Pontius Pilate would be at the end of this week (see *Luke* 23:1–12).

That was not a phenomenon limited to the first century. In every age, indeed in the experience of every Christian, the time comes when opposites will be united against the gospel. The struggle for the survival of self-centred living will see to that!

FORKED TONGUES

The delegation came with a carefully thought out and pointed trick question. They reminded Jesus of his integrity (speaking, as the 'Red Indians' in the old western movies used to say 'with forked tongue'). In the light of his known impartiality, faithfulness and teaching ability, they had a question for him. But no sooner were these flattering words out of their mouths than they began to spew out the poisonous venom in their hearts: 'Is it right to pay taxes to Caesar or not?'.

There are several important features in this question. First of all it made room for only two answers: yes or no. Any other answer would seem to avoid the real issue. But, secondly, it was politically loaded. If Jesus answered 'yes', he would take the side of the Pharisees and Herodians, but they knew he would be setting himself against the profound popular hatred of the Roman taxation system. Taxes served as a constant reminder to the Jews that they were a broken and subjugated people. That was why the Zealots' refusal to pay them was regarded as an essential element in nationalistic loyalty. But, then, if Jesus answered 'no, it is wrong to pay taxes to Caesar', he would immediately be accused of treason. He was in a 'no-win' situation – at least the Pharisees and Herodians thought so.

SATANIC COLLUSION

Jesus' initial response is significant: 'Why are you trying to trap me?' he asked (v. 15). The verb Mark uses to translate Jesus' original statement (which would have been made in his native tongue of Aramaic) is used in the Gospel several times of the Pharisees. But the first time it occurs, it is used of Satan testing Jesus in the wilderness (*Mark* 1:13). It seems likely that the connection in vocabulary is deliberate on Mark's part: Jesus associated these testings with the efforts of Satan to stand in his way. But, as the rest of the passage shows, our Lord mastered his opponents as successfully as he had earlier overcome Satan in the desert.

MASTERLY REPLY

Jesus asked for a coin. The drama in his action is obvious. One can almost hear the crowd around him holding their breath, and a look of puzzlement beginning to come over the faces of his opponents as he asked his question: 'Whose image appears on the Roman coinage?' The answer, of course, was 'Caesar's'.

So what? Jesus responded with devastating simplicity: 'If this coin has Caesar's image on it, then it belongs to him – give him his due.'

Was he giving in to the Pharisees and Herodians so easily? On the contrary. Doubtless the hearts of his enemies began to dance with glee that they had at last cornered him, and forced him to 'save his skin' by compromising with the occupying forces. 'But' Jesus added, 'I see another "coin", bearing a different image – I see you men, the image of God stamped on your lives. So, I conclude, you must give to God what belongs to him – the whole of your lives.'

With one sentence Jesus exposed the truth about his enemies and demolished their efforts to trick him. He put the question of living under Caesar in its proper place: a distant second behind the more important question of living in the kingdom of God. The man who is devoted to God does not make the issue of his political freedom the number one priority in his life. He knows that he can serve God, freely in his heart, under the most oppressive of regimes. The fact that these men were hounding Jesus to death demonstrated how far they were from doing that. Exposed, defeated and humiliated, they could only crawl away to regroup on another occasion.

It makes you wonder if an enormous cheer went up from the crowd for Jesus, doesn't it? Certainly this is a passage which makes every disciple thrill with admiration for his Saviour.

53

Question and Answer

*Then the Sadducees, who say there is no resurrection, came to
him with a question. 'Teacher,' they said, 'Moses wrote for us
that if a man's brother dies and leaves a wife but no children, the
man must marry the widow and have children for his brother.
Now there were seven brothers. The first one married and died
without leaving any children. The second one married the
widow, but he also died, leaving no child. It was the same with
the third. In fact, none of the seven left any children. Last of all,
the woman died too. At the resurrection whose wife will she be,
since the seven were married to her?' Jesus replied, 'Are you not
in error because you do not know the Scriptures or the power of
God? When the dead rise, they will neither marry nor be given in
marriage; they will be like the angels in heaven. Now about the
dead rising – have you not read in the book of Moses, in the
account of the bush, how God said to him, "I am the God of
Abraham, the God of Isaac, and the God of Jacob"? He is not
the God of the dead, but of the living. You are badly mistaken!'*
(Mark 12:18–27).

In human warfare through the centuries a major tactic has been
to attack the enemy in waves, striking at him before he has the
opportunity to recover his defences. The same kind of assault is
characteristic of spiritual warfare. In this part of his Gospel, Mark
vividly describes how Jesus himself was the object of such attacks,
as wave upon wave of 'delegations' came to question him. In Mark
11:27 it had been the chief priests, the teachers of the law and the
elders; in Mark 12:13 it had been the Pharisees and the Herodians.
Now it was the Sadducees.

THE SADDUCEES

Many of Mark's readers probably knew very little about the internal struggles of the Jewish faith. To them a Jew was a Jew. Distinguishing the various nuances of Jewish religion was irrelevant to most people, as it still is today. It is necessary to know at least one thing about the difference between the Pharisees and the Sadducees, however, to understand this incident: Sadducees based their theology on the first five books of the Old Testament, and, in particular, they denied the doctrine of the resurrection. The question they asked Jesus has this background.

Another element in Old Testament teaching forms the background to their question. In Deuteronomy 25:5–10 (a section of the Old Testament which the Sadducees did accept as divinely inspired), God had made provision for a family to be raised up for a husband who had died childless. A near relative would marry his widow, and the first child would be counted as the dead man's. In this way the man's name and honour would not be lost. An example of this (called the Levirate law from the Latin word *levir*, brother-in-law) can be found in the story of Ruth.

TRICK QUESTION

The Sadducees' trick question was this: Suppose a situation arose where a married man died before his wife had a child, and his brother married her, but he also died childless . . . and so on, until six of his brothers had married the woman, and had all died childless . . . whose wife would she be in the resurrection?

This kind of argument is known technically by the Latin phrase *reductio ad absurdum* (reduction to the absurd). It tries to show that some basic belief cannot be true because its implications seem absurd or ridiculous. No doubt there was a good measure of chortling and winking as Jesus was asked the question. For this hypothetical (but, of course, possible!) story seemed to indicate that if God had given the Levirate law (which all agreed he had), it would be ridiculous to believe in the resurrection – just look at what might happen. So, the Sadducees were arguing, the doctrine of the resurrection is impossible.

Doubtless their question was an 'old chestnut' – the kind of question every Sadducee's son asked every Pharisee's son in primary school! No one had ever found an answer to it, and the Sadducees expected no one would.

That is, until they encountered Jesus and foolishly tried to trick him.

DIRECT SPEECH

What did Jesus say? Notice his reply, step by step:

(i) *The Sadducees were wrong.* Jesus speaks with prophetic brevity. Men who deny the resurrection are simply in error. As far as he was concerned certain things are non-negotiable. This is one of them. We conclude from this that all modern-day Sadducees who profess the Christian faith but deny the resurrection are opposed to the teaching of Jesus.

(ii) *Behind this error lies ignorance.* The Sadducees did not know the word of God or the power of God (v. 24). They did not understand the many testimonies in the Old Testament to the resurrection. They had so small a view of God that they seemed to think the world to come would be simply a continuation of the world as it is. If they had known the power of God to transform human life, they would have already known what Jesus was about to tell them.

(iii) *Jesus expounded Scripture to prove his point.* Pointedly, he refers to 'the account of the bush' (v. 26). The Jews did not possess personal copies of the Old Testament and therefore commonly referred to biblical passages in this general way. Why was this passage so significant? Because it was a part of Scripture which the Sadducees themselves held to be divinely inspired. If it taught the resurrection, the point was proved!

Jesus draws attention to the way in which God speaks of himself as the God of Abraham, Isaac and Jacob. But how does this prove he is the God of the living, not of the dead? Simply because God's covenant promise to save his people would not be of any significance if it were overcome and shattered by death. It would be a tawdry salvation which lasted only for this life. The commitment of God to his servants, Abraham, Isaac, and Jacob, Jesus argued, is itself adequate proof of the resurrection. If the Sadducees had known the power of God as those patriarchs had done, they would realise that hope in God is not for this life only. In a word, Jesus was saying, to deny the resurrection is simply to deny God and his true character. Deny the resurrection and you become a practical atheist.

KNOW YOUR BIBLE!

This passage teaches many important lessons. Perhaps the most practical is this: the man who knows the Scriptures and the power of God (as Jesus himself did) will always be able to give an answer for the hope he has in the gospel (*1 Pet.* 3:15). That is why a mind well-furnished with Scripture, which has spent time in meditation on its teaching, and is convinced of the power of its author, will see through all hypocritical objections to Christian faith, and be able to contend for the faith which has been given to the church (*Jude* 3).

54

The Greatest Commandment

*One of the teachers of the law came and heard them debating.
Noticing that Jesus had given them a good answer, he asked him,
'Of all the commandments, which is the most important?' 'The
most important one,' answered Jesus, 'is this: "Hear, O Israel,
the Lord our God, the Lord is one. Love the Lord your God with
all your heart and with all your soul and with all your mind and
with all your strength." The second is this: "Love your neighbour as yourself." There is no commandment greater than these.'
'Well said, teacher,' the man replied. 'You are right in saying
that God is one and there is no other but him. To love him with
all your heart, with all your understanding and with all your
strength, and to love your neighbour as yourself is more important than all burnt offerings and sacrifices.' When Jesus saw that
he had answered wisely, he said to him, 'You are not far from the
kingdom of God.' And from then on no-one dared ask him any
more questions* (Mark 12:28–34).

At one point in the Jewish Passover liturgy it seems that a series
of questions was asked in preparation for sharing in the
ceremony itself. Some careful students of Mark's Gospel have
noticed that it too records a series of questions just before the
Passover. There is a striking parallel between the Passover liturgy
and Mark 12:13–37: the questions involved points of law ('Is it
right to pay taxes to Caesar?', *Mark* 12:14); issues in which the
truth was ridiculed (the Sadducees' question about the woman
married seven times and the resurrection); questions of conduct
(which is the most important commandment?); and finally, a
question which the head of the house would put often seeking the
meaning of two passages which seemed contradictory (cf. 12:35–37).

[199]

If Mark is deliberately following this pattern, then the very way in which he composed the Gospel is meant to say to us: 'Here are the questions which lead up to the true Passover; and here is Jesus, the One who can answer all the questions which the Passover celebrations leave unanswered.' It is a very skilful way of showing the final adequacy of Jesus by contrast with the preliminary nature of all of God's deeds in the Old Testament.

LAWYERS AND LAWS

Here, in these verses, a teacher of the law appears who has obviously been listening to the previous debates. He was impressed by what Jesus had to say, and so he too asked a question: 'Which is the most important commandment?'

Questions about which laws are more important than others are of perennial interest of lawyers! This man's question was certainly not original, even though it may have been completely sincere – certainly Jesus treated it as a sincere question, and gave it a straightforward answer.

But, even if the question was sincere, Jesus also seems to indicate that his question was muddle-headed. Quite naturally the lawyer wanted to be able to list the laws of God in a clear order of priority, so that he would know exactly where he stood as he measured his life against them.

Jesus' answer underlined the fact that any man's attempt to measure himself against the law for his own reassurance is bound to lead to disaster, because the very first law requires comprehensive, universal, undiluted love for God with every ounce of one's being. And, it carries with it a clear implication – we are to love our neighbours as ourselves! In other words, Jesus' answer emphasised the fact that God is never satisfied with anything less than the devotion of our whole life for the whole duration of our lives.

WHOLEHEARTED DEVOTION

It is important for us to spell out the implications of what Jesus says in his quotation from Deuteronomy 6:4–5 (in vv. 29–30). God is to be the object of the devotion of my heart. The centre of my whole being must be directed towards him and his glory. He must come first in my ambitions and motives. I am to love him too with my soul – so that all my affections and emotions will be in tune with his will and set aflame with a desire to serve him. Then, I must give my thought life to him, seeking to keep my mind pure, and to have all my thinking disciplined and controlled by what he has revealed in Scripture. And all my strength and energy must be his.

MY NEIGHBOUR AND MYSELF

But, what does it mean to love our neighbours as ourselves? How can the same Jesus teach us to love self and to deny self (*Mark* 8:34)?

The answer lies in recognising that God made man as his image. To love God himself implies that we will also love everything which reflects him in any way. It would be inconsistent to love him but not those who bear his image (see *James* 3:9–10). In this sense, each man should have a proper love and respect for all that God has made him. Notice that loving ourselves is, in the last analysis, the expression of our love for God. That love should be reflected similarly in our attitude to others. We have a special motive for caring for others, as members of the kingdom of God. We know something about people they may not even know about themselves: they were made to reflect God's image and glory. Even when that image has been distorted in their lives, we love them, because we see what they were meant to be, and are moved with compassion.

Here was a law which lifted all law-keeping out of the 'legalism' into which it had sunk in Jesus' day. It was a law which called for total devotion, not merely punctilious observation of a few external rules.

NEAR, BUT NOT IN

The lawyer was clearly impressed by what Jesus said. He recognised that such heartfelt obedience to the Lord was far more important than any ritual in which he could engage without being obedient. Jesus commended him for his understanding, and added a comment designed to send the lawyer home deep in thought: 'You are not far from the kingdom of God' (v. 34).

What could that mean? Was this man not actually in the kingdom of God, lawyer though he was? Was there a step he still had to take? Indeed there was. He recognised Jesus as a great teacher (v. 32). But he was more. He was also the Saviour of those who realised they could not keep the law, and needed not a teacher but a Saviour. This man really was near the kingdom. He recognised great qualities in Jesus. We do not know whether he ever came near enough to Jesus to enter it. What a story he would have to tell if he did!

We are now nearing the end of Mark's record of the coming of the kingdom of God. It is surely time to stop and ask yourself: 'Am I near the kingdom now, or am I actually in it?'

55

Using God's Word

While Jesus was teaching in the temple courts, he asked,
'How is it that the teachers of the law say that the Christ is
the son of David? David himself, speaking by the Holy
Spirit, declared: "The Lord said to my Lord: Sit at my right
hand until I put your enemies under your feet." David him-
self calls him "Lord". How then can he be his son?' The large
crowd listened to him with delight. As he taught, Jesus said,
'Watch out for the teachers of the law. They like to walk
around in flowing robes and be greeted in the market-places,
and have the most important seats in the synagogues and the
places of honour at banquets. They devour widows' houses
and for a show make lengthy prayers. Such men will be
punished most severely.' (Mark 12:35–40).

We have seen Jesus exposed to wave upon wave of attack from his enemies as they acted in unison to try to destroy his ministry. Over and over again, throughout this Gospel, we have noticed the supreme mastery which he displayed. Now, at the end of all the questioning, he shows himself again to be in complete command of the situation. The religious and political leaders could not trap him. Now it was Jesus' turn to ask them a question!

JESUS' QUESTION

Jesus believed that the Old Testament was inspired by God. He knew that his detractors shared that view, so he posed this question: 'The scribes say that the Christ is the son of David. How can that be when the Scripture tells us that David himself called the Messiah "Lord"?' Jesus' question depends not only on the scribes believing that the Old Testament was divinely inspired; but also on the fact that they believed Psalm 110 (which Jesus here cites) referred to the promised Messiah. Jesus here was exercising his ministry as the true prophet of God by doing two things.

(i) *Expounding the Scriptures.* The scribes were correct to say that the Messiah (Christ) would be the son of David, born into his family line (as, in fact, Jesus was: *Matt.* 1:1–17; *Luke* 3:23–32; *Rom.* 1:3). They were also correct in thinking that Psalm 110 described the Messiah. But could they answer the question which arose from those twin convictions? How could the great King David speak of his 'son' as his 'Lord'? No wonder 'the large crowd listened to him with delight' (v. 37)! In the battle of difficult questions, Jesus had not only answered questions his opponents regarded as unanswerable; he asked them a question they found unanswerable!!

But our Lord's response was not simply a smart, trick question. It was a deeply serious one. It held a vital clue to the identity of the Messiah. David's son could only be his Lord if he existed before him *and* after him. Jesus did not tell the teachers of the law the answer. It would remain veiled from them so long as they stubbornly resisted Jesus' ministry. But Jesus knew the answer: David's Lord was the eternal Son of God; David's Lord became his 'son' when he was conceived in the womb of Mary and was born in Bethlehem, the city of David. That was the answer to the biblical question which baffled the lawyers.

Notice, however, that in his exposition of the Scriptures, Jesus was doing something else, which all true biblical exposition does:

(ii) *Exposing false teachers.* As he continued his teaching (v. 38), he warned the people against the teachers who were leading them astray. No doubt there were some among the people who were sufficiently spiritually minded to feel a deep unease about the influence of the scribes. But perhaps they were too respectful, or too timid to raise their voices. In any case, they doubtless found it almost impossible to put their finger on exactly what made them feel so uneasy. But when Jesus spoke, it all became crystal clear.

THREE CHARGES

Jesus brought three specific charges against the teachers of the law – which will, in varying degrees, always be true of false teachers:

(i) *They were ambitious men.* They looked for the honour men can give rather than the honour God alone gives. They were attracted by the trappings of power ('flowing robes' v. 38), and the adulation of man ('greeted in the market-places' v. 38). Instead of helping those they taught to know, trust and serve God, they used their position to further their own self-centred ambitions and their desire for a reputation.

(ii) *They were proud men.* They loved to have the best seats and sit at the table with the 'top' people (v. 39) in both secular and religious life. All this was in stark contrast to what one of their number had just heard from the lips of Jesus: love for God and neighbour marked obedience to the law which they professed to teach. Instead they had put love for self at the top of their list, however much they disguised the fact.

(iii) *They were greedy men.* They made wealthy widows their prey (v. 40), and perhaps poor ones too. These were women whose husbands had, during their lifetime, made all the major decisions for them. Now, lacking that experienced guidance and companionship, they fell prey to these wicked men masquerading as servants of God. Without saying any more, Jesus exposed their despicable lifestyle and their polluted hearts.

PUBLIC MINISTRY ENDED

These solemn words signal the end of Jesus' public teaching in the Gospel of Mark. Throughout the entire period of his ministry, as we have seen, he found himself under constant attack by these religious leaders. He had dealt with them graciously, faithfully, patiently. Now, it seems, they had hardened their hearts irreversibly against him. All that remained for him to do was to unmask their deceit. This he did. His last words to the teachers of the law warned them that they would be 'punished most severely' (v. 40).

There is a message here which applies to teachers of God's word today: By their fruits we know whether they are really true to Jesus Christ, or not.

56

A Widow's Mite

Jesus sat down opposite the place where the offerings were put and watched the crowd putting their money into the temple treasury. Many rich people threw in large amounts. But a poor widow came and put in two very small copper coins, worth only a fraction of a penny. Calling his disciples to him, Jesus said, 'I tell you the truth, this poor widow has put more into the treasury than all the others. They all gave out of their wealth; but she, out of her poverty, put in everything – all she had to live on' (Mark 12:41–44).

Jesus was a great observer of human experience in general. But he also had an eye for the individual. This wonderful little story illustrates both of these qualities. It describes a woman whose devotion to the Lord stands in marked contrast to that of the educated theologians who had proved to be such a thorn in Jesus' side.

Having finished his teaching in the temple courts (*Mark* 12:35), our Lord sat down near the area (in the Court of Women) where visitors to the temple placed their offerings. It was soon to be Passover. Doubtless Jerusalem was already being flooded with pilgrims from all over the world. Its normal population of 50,000 was increased by some 200,000 pilgrims. Some, like the Ethiopian eunuch described in Acts 8:27, were certainly people of considerable devotion, influence and wealth. Doubtless some of them were making very substantial contributions indeed.

When you remember two things, this scene is all the more dramatic. On the wall of the Court of Women stood thirteen brass receptacles, in the shape of trumpets. In Jesus' time, of course,

there were no banknotes, cheque books or credit cards! Every
offering deposited in the receptacles could be 'heard' even if it was
not 'seen'! The seats where Jesus sat down and 'watched the crowd
putting their money into the temple treasury' (v. 41) must have
been a popular spot for local people to sit, and perhaps day-dream
a little! No doubt there were those around Jesus who were just
'dying to know' what he thought of some of these fabulously rich
people and their enormous gifts to God's house!

TWO COINS IN A TRUMPET

Was there a lull in the excitement after several wealthy pilgrims in
succession had put in their gifts, when Jesus saw this poor widow
woman come forward to the receptacles? Did nobody else take any
real notice of her? Did the crowd – like ourselves sometimes – turn
and look elsewhere in case their gaze should embarrass this dear
soul who clearly would contribute next to nothing to the Lord's
work?

There is something magnificent in Jesus' response here. Did he
smile as he heard the almost inaudible tinkle of the widow's two
coins fall into the treasury? 'Peter, James, John, Andrew' he called
out, 'Over here! Look!' Did he actually go over to the widow, now
astonished at the attention she was receiving? We do not know. But
we do know what he said: 'This woman has given more than any of
the others' (v. 43). What a reversal of the disciples' point of view!
What a riddle for the crowd to puzzle over! What an unexpected
encouragement for the widow, that this should be the Lord's
assessment of her giving!

NOT WORTH TWOPENCE?

So emphatic about this is Jesus that he prefaces his remarks with
the solemn 'I tell you the truth' (the 'amen' which appears some
thirteen times in Mark's Gospel, and is really equivalent to the
Old Testament's 'As I live, says the Lord'). But, how can this be?
Surely a thousand pounds is worth far more than one pound, in
anybody's arithmetic? Can God not do more with large amounts
than with small?

Jesus explains that the divine accountancy works on different principles from the human, and in doing so teaches us several important lessons about Christian giving.

God does not need your money. He requires no benefactors to help him establish his kingdom. Nothing you can do or give will add to his riches. He owns the entire universe, and can employ everything in it for his own holy purposes. Furthermore, he owns your money too! He is able to give it to you and withdraw it from you at a moment's notice. You are simply his steward. Anything you give to him he has first given to you, like a father giving pocket money to his children to help them buy his birthday present!

God chooses to use whatever gifts he wants to further his kingdom. He can use a small gift for a great purpose and a great gift for a small purpose! With a great gift, a massive organisation may be set up which is in constant financial difficulties and eventually goes bankrupt; with a small gift, a Gospel, or New Testament may be purchased which leads to the conversion of someone who wins many others to Christ, or is the instrument of a great revival – or, for that matter, points a millionaire to Christ! Jesus is underlining this in what he says. If we grasped it, we would never be proud of the amount we give.

HOW TO GIVE

But there are three further lessons underlined here:

(i) *Our giving is to be measured by proportion, not by addition.* The woman gave more because she gave everything she had (v. 44). Two pence out of two pence is a factor of one; one thousand out of ten thousand is a factor of one tenth!

(ii) *Our giving is not measured by amount, but by sacrifice.* This is why Jesus commended the widow. It cost her to give; others might not notice the difference in their bank balances.

(iii) *Our giving is always in the sight of Jesus Christ.* It is his estimate that really matters, not the estimate of men.

In most Christian fellowships prayer precedes or follows the offering. That is no formality. For it is not the amount of money given which produces the Lord's blessing on our gifts. We give out of privilege; we need to pray that it will please the Lord to use our gifts as he pleases, and to help us to give in a way that pleases him.

57

Future Events

*As he was leaving the temple, one of his disciples said to him,
'Look, Teacher! What massive stones! What magnificent
buildings!' 'Do you see all these great buildings?' replied
Jesus. 'Not one stone here will be left on another; every one
will be thrown down.' As Jesus was sitting on the Mount of
Olives opposite the temple, Peter, James, John and Andrew
asked him privately, 'Tell us, when will these things
happen? And what will be the sign that they are all about to
be fulfilled?' Jesus said to them: 'Watch out that no-one
deceives you. Many will come in my name, claiming "I am
he," and will deceive many. When you hear of wars and
rumours of wars, do not be alarmed. Such things must
happen, but the end is still to come. Nation will rise against
nation, and kingdom against kingdom. There will be earthquakes in various places, and famines. These are the
beginning of birth-pains. You must be on your guard. You
will be handed over to the local councils and flogged in the
synagogues. On account of me you will stand before governors
and kings as witnesses to them. And the gospel must first be
preached to all nations. Whenever you are arrested and
brought to trial, do not worry beforehand about what to say.
Just say whatever is given you at the time, for it is not you
speaking, but the Holy Spirit'* (Mark 13:1–11).

Jesus had been teaching in the temple in Jerusalem. It was the
focal point of faith for his contemporaries, as it had been for
their forefathers. In a literal sense it was, for them 'the house
of God'. He had promised to dwell there, among his people and

show them his glory. But in many ways 'Ichabod' (the glory has departed, *1 Sam.* 4:21) seemed to be written across it. Externally, it was still able to draw out the deepest emotions of those who worshipped there. It reminded them of earlier days when its courts had rung with praise, and when their forefathers had met with God. It was the symbol of God's restoring of his people from bondage and exile. Yet, when Jesus had come to the temple of God, he had found it degraded into the centre of commercial enterprise. It had been turned into a 'den of robbers' (*Mark* 11:17). The only thing Jesus had found in its precincts to commend was the whole-hearted devotion of a poor and insignificant widow!

There was no denying that the temple was impressive. As the disciple band left it, one of them commented on its grandeur (v. 1). Immediately Jesus counselled him to see beyond the façade to the reality, and beyond the present to the future: within a generation (see v. 30) these buildings would all be destroyed!

The disciples must have been stunned, but they said nothing until they had sat down together on the Mount of Olives, opposite the temple (v. 3). Then three of them raised the question which was on all of their minds. Had they heard him correctly? Had he really prophesied the destruction of God's sacred temple? For the disciples that could mean only one thing: the end of the world. That is made clear in Matthew's fuller record of the series of questions the disciples asked Jesus: 'When will this happen, and what will be the sign of your coming and of the end of the age?' (*Matt.* 24:3).

Inevitably the disciples associated all these events with one another. When we read through the various accounts in the Gospels of Jesus' teaching, however, we see that he clearly distinguished them from each other.

Significantly, Mark does not even mention the third question about the end of the age. He mentions only the question about the destruction of Jerusalem. In doing so, he helps us to grasp that it is this – the destruction of the temple and the city – which is the centrepiece of Jesus' discussion in the verses which follow.

Jesus' first word is one of wise counsel, which the church has too often ignored: Do not be deceived (v. 5)! What does he mean?

Our Lord knew that many of his followers could easily fall prey to false teachers who would make capital (in more ways than one, alas) out of the distinctively Christian conviction that human history is heading towards a conclusion at the return of Christ. Some people would actually claim to be Christ; others would point to the 'signs of the times' – wars and rumours of wars (v. 7), and insist that these events, coupled with natural disasters like earthquakes and famine, are signs that the end of the world is just months away.

BIRTH-PAINS

It is vital to grasp the significance of Jesus' response to this. These events are simply 'the beginning of birth-pains' (v. 8). His illustration is apt. Labour pains certainly indicate that a birth is about to take place. But who knows how long a woman's labour may be? The birth-pains indicate that childbirth has begun, they do not serve as a prophecy of the exact moment of delivery. This 'beginning of birth-pains' does not tell us whether the end will be tomorrow or next century. Events may be drawn out by God in his patience (*2 Pet.* 3:9) or they may accelerate rapidly. We must always live in readiness and expectation. But we must not allow ourselves to be led into panic by a wrong diagnosis of the 'contractions' in the universe.

TO SUFFER AND TO WITNESS

Why is this important? Notice Jesus' comments.

(i) *We may have to endure suffering* (v. 9a). There may be persecution to be endured (v. 13a). We need to face that realistically. We cannot afford to be blinded to the realities by a false hope (or wish) that the end will come before the Christian life becomes 'too hot to handle' for us.

(ii) *We are to be witnesses to Christ.* His purpose is that the gospel must be preached to all people groups (v. 10). It is a sad commentary on the church's misunderstanding of this passage that at times Christians have virtually abandoned the task of evangelism because 'the times are evil'. Those are the very times when evangelism is most crucial (see *2 Tim.* 3:1–4:5).

Yes, the destruction of the temple would take place within a matter of decades. It would be an event of such magnitude that the disciples could certainly be forgiven for thinking it would mark the end of everything. But Jesus was teaching them that instead it would mark only the dawning of a new era. Jerusalem could no longer keep the covenant mercy of God within its walls. If it did not recognise the Christ and proclaim him to the nations, its divine purpose would be brought to an end. It would be destroyed. Instead these ordinary men would take the gospel to the four corners of the earth. They would be the dwelling place of God's Spirit; they would be his temple; they would show forth his glory among the peoples (*1 Pet.* 2:5–9)!

Jesus will come 'soon'. But when Scripture speaks about him coming 'soon', it is measuring time on God's clock, not man's. It means that the return of the Lord is now the next great event on the divine calendar. He has the date marked in red, although no one else has seen either the page of the calendar, or the date he has ringed (see v. 32)! In the meantime, he is working patiently for the salvation of men. Jesus says we should do the same.

58

The Son of Man Comes

'Brother will betray brother to death, and a father his child.
Children will rebel against their parents and have them put to
death. All men will hate you because of me, but he who stands
firm to the end will be saved. When you see "the abomination
that causes desolation" standing where it does not belong – let
the reader understand – then let those who are in Judea flee to
the mountains. Let no-one on the roof of his house go down or
enter the house to take anything out. Let no-one in the field
go back to get his cloak. How dreadful it will be in those days
for pregnant women and nursing mothers! Pray that this will
not take place in winter, because those will be days of distress
unequalled from the beginning, when God created the world,
until now – and never to be equalled again. If the Lord had
not cut short those days, no-one would survive. But for the
sake of the elect, whom he has chosen, he has shortened them.
At that time if anyone says to you, "Look, here is the
Christ!" or, "Look, there he is!" do not believe it. For false
Christs and false prophets will appear and perform signs and
miracles to deceive the elect – if that were possible. So be on
your guard; I have told you everything ahead of time.

But in those days, following that distress, "the sun will be
darkened, and the moon will not give its light; the stars will
fall from the sky, and the heavenly bodies will be shaken." At
that time men will see the Son of Man coming in clouds with
great power and glory. And he will send his angels and gather
his elect from the four winds, from the ends of the earth to the
ends of the heavens.

Now learn this lesson from the fig-tree: As soon as its twigs *get tender and its leaves come out, you know that summer is near. Even so, when you see these things happening, you know that it is near, right at the door. I tell you the truth, this generation will certainly not pass away until all these things have happened. Heaven and earth will pass away, but my words will never pass away'* (Mark 13:12–31).

Jesus often used the questions he was asked as opportunities to give instruction to his disciples. He had just prophesied the destruction of the Jerusalem temple. His disciples associated that with the end of the world. Now he was patiently counselling them not to confuse these two events, lest they be led astray by false teachers. They must recognise the possibility that they might have to face prolonged suffering for the sake of the gospel. In particular, Jesus was concerned to teach the disciples that it would be their responsibility to bring the gospel to all peoples. The end would not come before that purpose had been fulfilled (vv. 10–11).

The interpretation of this section is critical for understanding the whole chapter. For Jesus speaks of 'the end' (v. 13) and the 'abomination of desolation' (v. 14). He describes events of cosmic magnitude taking place: 'the sun will be darkened and the moon will not give its light' (v. 24). He speaks of 'the Son of Man coming in clouds with great power and glory' to gather his elect (vv. 26-27). What is he talking about?

THE ABOMINATION OF DESOLATION

At first sight, it might seem obvious that Jesus is speaking here about the second coming. But we ought not to jump to that conclusion without asking what some of these statements (drawn from the language of the Old Testament) would have meant to his hearers. When we do that, it seems more likely that a good deal of what Jesus says here has specific reference to the destruction of Jerusalem, which took place in A.D. 70.

'The abomination of desolation' was an expression first used by Daniel (*Dan.* 9:27; 11:31; 12:11). It clearly refers to some gross act of sacrilege committed against the Lord. The Jewish people had seen at least one illustration of its meaning when Antiochus Epiphanes had erected an altar to the pagan god Zeus over the altar of burnt offering and, to underline his blasphemy, had sacrificed pigs on it (in 168 B.C.).

Within the lifetime of some of those who heard Jesus speak, similar actions had been perpetrated within the temple. Within a few years of Jesus' prophecy, the Roman Emperor Caligula had planned to build a statue of himself on the same altar; then, two years before the temple was actually destroyed, Jewish zealots committed various atrocities in the temple, and a clown named Phanni was installed as high priest. The fact that Jesus gives instructions that any disciples in Jerusalem at that time should flee suggests that he is thinking of events within their lifetime. The historian Josephus records that when Titus besieged Jerusalem in A.D. 70, somewhere in the region of one million Jews died at that time by crucifixion, famine and other horrors. Our Lord's words were to be literally fulfilled.

Jesus expected his followers to be courageous in their discipleship; but he warned them to avoid the rashness of fanaticism. They were not to think that Jerusalem was so crucial to the purposes of God that they must stay there at all costs. No; more important to them even than the beloved city of Jerusalem was their calling to preach the gospel. They should flee (v. 14ff). They should be careful not to be deceived by false 'saviours' who would appear and even work miracles in their sight.

THE SON OF MAN COMES!

It is difficult to know whether verses 24–27 refer to those events in A.D. 70 or to the end of the age. The language Jesus uses reflects the way in which the Old Testament described the Day of the Lord (*Isa.* 13:10; 33:4). But those words may refer to extraordinary political upheavals. And the coming of the Son of Man may refer to his establishing of his kingdom, rather than his coming again. Certainly, in Daniel 7:14 (the source of this idea) the coming of the Son of Man refers to his enthronement at the right hand of God, not to his coming from the right hand of God. In this case, the sending of the 'angels' (literally, 'messengers') would refer to the world-wide proclamation of the gospel which followed the destruction of Jerusalem.

In verses 28–31, Jesus does seem to refer specifically to the destruction of Jerusalem. Just as leaves on the fig tree are normally the sign of the approach of summer, so these events should be a sign to the people (v. 29). Notice how he emphasises that these things will happen within the lifetime of that generation (v. 30). While this has sometimes been taken to refer to the Jewish people, that is not the most natural interpretation. Jesus probably never spoke with greater feeling and solemnity. One day even heaven and earth will pass away, he said – but these words would stand for ever!

LESSONS

What are we meant to learn from a passage such as this, which seems to be open to such various interpretations?

First, we are urged to listen to what Jesus says, not to what others say. Otherwise we will be easily deceived. We are to be on our guard, since Jesus has spoken to us (v. 23).

Secondly, we are not to be taken by surprise by the sufferings of God's people, nor by the catastrophes of history. These are the birthpangs which herald the dawning of a new age.

Thirdly, we require a good dose of common sense in living the Christian life – Jesus warns his disciples not to invite suffering unnecessarily (vv. 14–20). Yes, God will guard his people; but he guards them through their obedience to Jesus' commands.

We see here, again, that when Jesus speaks about the future, his words are meant to change the way we live in the present. That is a recurring theme in all biblical teaching about the time to come.

59

Be Prepared!

'No-one knows about that day or hour, not even the angels in heaven, nor the Son, but only the Father. Be on guard! Be alert! You do not know when that time will come. It's like a man going away: He leaves his house and puts his servants in charge, each with his assigned task, and tells the one at the door to keep watch. Therefore keep watch because you do not know when the owner of the house will come back – whether in the evening, or at midnight, or when the cock crows, or at dawn. If he comes suddenly, do not let him find you sleeping. What I say to you, I say to everyone: "Watch!"' (Mark 13:32–37).

In reading the New Testament, one of the features we should always look out for is the connection between the truth and its practical application. Often that application is very clearly spelled out, since it flows inevitably from the teaching of the gospel. We find exactly the same here. Jesus has been teaching his disciples about the destruction of the temple, and distinguishing that event from the great event of his personal return. But one thing binds both events together: the response the disciples are to make in their lives.

This is characteristic of the apostles' teaching about the future. In the light of what is going to happen, we are to live lives which bring honour to Christ. We are to respond appropriately to God's activity in human history. In this closing section of Mark 13, Jesus spells out what this implies.

Jesus tells a parable about a man who goes away from home

leaving his servants in charge. They are to live in the consciousness that the master may return at any time. They are to look after his affairs faithfully in the meantime.

THE MASTER'S HOUSE

What does Jesus mean? He reminds us that the 'house' in which we have been left in charge is not ours, but his. How often we act as though we had forgotten this! Frequently, when there is division among the people of God, it is because this 'family rule' has been forgotten. We act as though we owned the church, and as if what we found acceptable was the principle on which it should be structured. We need to remember that we live in the Master's house, not our own. We have a responsibility to him.

APPOINTED TASKS

But Jesus also stresses that each individual in his household has an appointed task (v. 24). There is, for example 'one at the door' (v. 34); others have different roles to play. But all of the servants in a well-ordered household know what their role is, and attend to it. Only when each individual fulfils his or her own task does the household run smoothly (cf. *Eph.* 4:11–16). There is an element of responsibility; there is also an element of individuality.

All of the servants are to share one attitude to their work and ministry: they are to labour in the consciousness that the owner of the house will return. The date is unknown (v. 32). We should therefore be alert, keeping awake, doing our duty, as we wait for him to return (vv. 33-36).

WAITING FOR THE RETURNING LORD

This is one of the cardinal principles of true Christian living: to live every day in the light of Christ's certain return; to do everything – yes, everything – for his inspection. Christians do not necessarily have better skills than others who make no Christian profession; but they do have stronger motives to use their skills properly, in readiness for their heavenly Master's comments. That is why everything we do should in some way reflect the grace and glory of Christ and be part of our witness to him.

The early Christians did not always understand Jesus' teaching. In Thessalonica, for example, some members of the church seem to have abandoned their daily work because they believed that Christ would return soon (*2 Thess.* 3:6–15). In the light of that event (so they mistakenly thought) work was far too unspiritual. But the true fruit of anticipation in the life of a Christian is the quality of his daily work and the glory which surrounds his fulfilment of his daily duty. That is what our Lord expects us to be doing when he returns.

FAITHFULNESS

How would you spend tomorrow if you knew Jesus was going to return in the evening? John Wesley was once asked that question as he made his way from one preaching engagement to another. He took out his diary, read the list of engagements he had for the following day, and said, 'These are the things I would do tomorrow if I knew the Lord was returning then.' That is the way Jesus challenges all of us to live.

How sad it is that instead of seeing this teaching about the future as the spur to new obedience and faithfulness, it has often been the excuse for either controversy or laziness in the Christian church. That has been true from the days of the first churches until now (as the New Testament letters show). We must remember to read such passages as Mark 13 with great humility of mind. But we must also remember that they summon us to rigorous, practical obedience to the Lord. If what we have learned in this chapter does not make us more watchful as Christians, then we have not yet allowed Jesus to have the last word in our lives. For his last word here is precisely that: 'What I say to you, I say to everyone: "Watch"' (v. 37).

Since you do not know when your Master will return (vv. 32, 33, 35), are you awake, and watching?

60

Love for Jesus

Now the Passover and the Feast of Unleavened Bread were only two days away, and the chief priests and the teachers of the law were looking for some sly way to arrest Jesus and kill him. 'But not during the Feast,' they said, 'or the people may riot.' While he was in Bethany, reclining at the table in the home of a man known as Simon the Leper, a woman came with an alabaster jar of very expensive perfume, made of pure nard. She broke the jar and poured the perfume on his head. Some of those present were saying indignantly to one another, 'Why this waste of perfume? It could have been sold for more than a year's wages and the money given to the poor.' And they rebuked her harshly. 'Leave her alone,' said Jesus. 'Why are you bothering her? She has done a beautiful thing to me. The poor you will always have with you, and you can help them any time you want. But you will not always have me. She did what she could. She poured perfume on my body beforehand to prepare for my burial. I tell you the truth, wherever the gospel is preached throughout the world, what she has done will also be told, in memory of her.' Then Judas Iscariot, one of the Twelve, went to the chief priests to betray Jesus to them. They were delighted to hear this and promised to give him money. So he watched for an opportunity to hand him over (Mark 14:1–11).

W hen you read Mark 13 with its vivid record of Jesus' teaching, it is not difficult to imagine yourself on the Mount of Olives, looking across to the temple – transported for a moment beyond the present world into the great vision of the future which

Jesus portrayed. But now Mark brings us back from the future into the harsh realities which faced Jesus in the present.

When Jesus was in the temple, among his enemies, his one source of encouragement lay in the wholehearted sacrificial life-style of a widow woman who had put all she had into the offering. That must have been a remarkable thing for Mark's first readers to discover in such a male-dominated society. It is not insignificant that, in this scene, set apparently among Jesus' friends, it is once again the action of a woman which stands out as a source of blessing to our Lord.

We are here entering the closing section of the Gospel. From now on, Mark's record describes the events which lead up to the cross with the careful precision of a diarist. He notes the day (and sometimes even the time of day) of one event after another. Here he begins by telling us that as the Passover drew near, the religious leaders were committed to arresting and killing Jesus. They wanted to find some 'sly way' (v. 1) to do it. They also wanted to avoid killing him during Passover, in case riots broke out in the overcrowded city. By verse 11, their 'prayers' have been answered in the way they least expected: Judas, the treasurer of the disciple band had agreed to betray his Master!

A WOMAN'S ACTION

Just at this point, Mark introduces a story which seems like a 'pause' in the narrative, but in fact partly explains what follows. He describes an event which stands (again) in marked contrast to the conniving hatred of the religious leaders.

Jesus was in Bethany, some two miles from Jerusalem, dining with a man known as Simon the Leper (perhaps because Jesus had cured him). A woman broke open a jar of expensive ointment and poured its contents over Jesus' head, in an act of anointing.

Three elements in what followed are important:

(i) *Action.* This woman brought with her a jar of perfume which the disciples valued at more than an average man's wages for an entire year. Presumably this was a family heirloom, passed on from generation to generation; it was an investment for a 'rainy day' in this woman's life. But, at this moment in this woman's spiritual pilgrimage she had a reason to be grateful to Jesus. In a moment of quiet commitment she had resolved that he should receive her most precious possession. Quietly she had taken it from its place, and carried it to Simon's house, where Jesus was. In gratitude for the past, she poured her 'future' and her 'security' on Jesus. No wonder he described her action as 'beautiful'!

(ii) *Reaction.* Some of the spectators were indignant (v. 4). They knew that if the perfume had been sold and the proceeds given to the poor, it could have done so much good. And so they harshly rebuked the woman (v. 5).

The harshness of their response underlines the remaining hardness in their hearts, and perhaps also the poverty of their own devotion to the Lord. It is significant that this particular event seemed to act as the catalyst to bring Judas and the chief priests together (vv. 10–11). The one thing he could not tolerate, apparently, was such wholehearted devotion to Jesus which had no other motive than love for him. Judas was one of those religious people who rarely see that their interest in Christ lies more in what he can do to further their goals than in what he wants to do to change their lives. He, with others, could not tell the difference between grace and waste. Their attitude indicated that they understood all too little of the outpouring of love in Jesus' heart towards sinners!

(iii) *Commendation.* Jesus responded to the woman with joyful appreciation. Yes, the money could have been given to the poor. But it had been given to the poor – to Jesus himself, who for our sake had become poor so that we might become rich (*2 Cor.* 8:9). Unlike the others, this woman had some inkling that Jesus would not be with them much longer, while the 'other' poor would always be present. In this sense, she had anointed Jesus for his burial. 'She did what she could' (v. 8). Her critics had done nothing. For that reason her deed is a perpetual memorial of the true response to the one who became poor that we might become rich.

The presence of a grudging spirit towards Christ and his work in the world is always a sinister sign. Here were men who were more interested in their service than in their Master! How sad that so many of Jesus' disciples seem to live so much of their lives grudgingly. The lesson Jesus pointed out to his disciples from this woman was: in the Christian life there should be neither holding back nor turning back.

Are those lessons we have learned?

61

The Traitor

On the first day of the Feast of Unleavened Bread, when it was customary to sacrifice the Passover lamb, Jesus' disciples asked him, 'Where do you want us to go and make preparations for you to eat the Passover?' So he sent two of his disciples, telling them, 'Go into the city, and a man carrying a jar of water will meet you. Follow him. Say to the owner of the house he enters, "The Teacher asks: Where is my guest room, where I may eat the Passover with my disciples?" He will show you a large upper room furnished and ready. Make preparations for us there.' The disciples left, went into the city and found things just as Jesus had told them. So they prepared the Passover. When evening came, Jesus arrived with the Twelve. While they were reclining at the table eating, he said, 'I tell you the truth, one of you will betray me – one who is eating with me.' They were saddened, and one by one they said to him, 'Surely not I?' 'It is one of the Twelve,' he replied, 'one who dips bread into the bowl with me. The Son of Man will go just as it is written about him. But woe to that man who betrays the Son of Man! It would be better for him if he had not been born' (Mark 14:12–21).

It was now the time of the Passover. As thousands of pilgrims crowded into Jerusalem for the feast, the disciples' minds turned to the obvious question: What were they going to do about the Passover meal? Where should they go to make preparations (v. 12)?

There was force in such a question. Where could they go if Jesus was to be secure? There was a price on his head, as John's Gospel indicates: 'the chief priests and Pharisees had given orders

that if anyone found out where Jesus was, he should report it so
that they might arrest him' (*John* 11:57). We also know, now, that
Judas had agreed to betray him. Jesus' life was in grave danger.

SECRECY WITHOUT FEAR

The first thing to notice, in this connection, is the secrecy of Jesus'
arrangements. Two of the disciples are told to go into the city.
There they will see a man carrying a water jar on his head. That
was an unusual sight. Normally only the women carried these jars;
men carried wineskins. Perhaps this was a prearranged signal. This
man would be their 'contact' and would lead them to the room
where they could prepare for the Passover.

Jesus did not make such arrangements out of fear. When we
read the 'Upper Room Discourse' in John 14–17, or listen in this
Gospel to the institution of the Lord's Supper, we realise how
burdened he must have been to have a few hours of complete
privacy with his followers. He wanted to lead them further in their
knowledge of God's purposes. His secrecy was the part of wisdom,
not fear. The fact that he knew he was to die did not mean that he
should simply abandon himself to his foes. That in itself is an
important lesson for us to learn.

SURELY NOT I?

In this context, a further revelation takes place. Jesus tells the
disciples that the betrayal he had prophesied earlier (*Mark* 10:33)
would arise within their own group. His earlier use of the word
'betray' had hinted at this. But doubtless none of them had really
taken in what that implied. Even now they could not believe it.
One by one they asked, 'Is it I?'

Judas too, apparently, used these words. Perhaps that was the
reason Jesus spoke so sternly about the terrible responsibility he
would bear. It would have been better that he had never been born
(v. 21). Judas' later suicide indicates that he realised this – too late.
His eyes were opened to the terrible crime he had committed, and
he died in utter despair. But, as Jesus' last pleadings and warnings
were issued, Judas was both blind and deaf to his overtures. Even

though our Lord warned him of the terrible consequences of his sin, his heart seems to have remained unmoved.

SIN'S DOMINION

Judas is the example *par excellence* of the man who believes that he can never sin his way out of the grace of God. We should remember him if we ever think we can decide the point at which we will stop sinning. Sin deceives as well as hardens. It leads us to that hardness of heart and blindness of understanding which ignores the last amber light. Ultimately even the warnings of the Son of God through his word are silenced. If we yield to sin (as Judas had done in his heart, for whatever reason) it masters us (*John* 8:34). We are no longer free or able to choose the moment when we will engage in a mutiny of grace and overthrow its influence on us. Judas realised that when it was too late. At first he would not repent; eventually he could not repent.

SCRIPTURE FULFILLED

But these important considerations should not make us ignore the remarkable poise and dignity which Jesus himself shows in the midst of this great crisis in his life. He knows that all of these things will take place 'just as it had been written' (v. 21). His life is completely submitted to his Father's will. That will has been revealed in Scripture, and he bows to it. Because his life is governed by the teaching of Scripture, his death will be neither accident nor tragedy.

At no point in Jesus' ministry is his submission to Scripture more frequently mentioned than in these last hours of his life. This is one of the clearest indications that he recognised it to be God's living word. That, in turn, is one of the most important reasons why Christians should believe Scripture. But, notice, Jesus did not believe Scripture in a merely hypothetical or theoretical way. He believed it and obeyed it without compromise. In this, too, he is the 'pioneer of our salvation' (*Heb.* 12:2). When he calls us to obey God's Word, he summons us to follow him, not to go over uncharted ground. He has gone before, and proved that God's Word can be relied on in the darkest hours of life and death.

Of course, our lives do not fulfil prophecy as Jesus did. Yet the same Spirit who inspired Scripture, and strengthened Jesus to understand and obey it, has been given to us. The sign that I truly follow Christ and am filled with his Spirit will therefore be this: submission to God's Word!

62

The Last Supper

While they were eating, Jesus took bread, gave thanks and broke it, and gave it to his disciples, saying, 'Take it; this is my body.' Then he took the cup, gave thanks and offered it to them, and they all drank from it. 'This is my blood of the covenant, which is poured out for many,' he said to them. 'I tell you the truth, I will not drink again of the fruit of the vine until that day when I drink it anew in the kingdom of God.' When they had sung a hymn, they went out to the Mount of Olives (Mark 14:22–26).

The preparations had all been made for Jesus and his disciples to share the Passover together. They were reclining at table, in the middle of the meal. It was an event to which Jesus had looked forward with special eagerness (*Luke* 22:15) – eagerness to do what he had to do, and, doubtless, eagerness that the darkest hours of his life should be faced in obedience to his Father. Now, after years of patient preparation, the time had come. No more waiting would be required, only the endurance of the terrible agony of the cross, and his separation from fellowship with God and man. Yet, even this he would endure, encouraged by 'the joy that was set before him' (*Heb.* 12:2).

THE PASSOVER

The Passover meal was a beautiful and moving ritual. It was conducted by the head of the house (in this instance, Jesus himself as the leader of the disciple band). Several cups of wine were drunk during the course of the evening. The first was brought in and drunk before the arrival of the traditional Passover food (unleavened bread, bitter herbs, stewed fruit, greens and roast lamb). When the food was brought in, the youngest person would ask the traditional question: 'Why do we eat these foods on this night?'

In reply the father would recount the story of God's grace in the Exodus. The company would respond with songs of praise and sing Psalms 113–115. Then the second cup would be passed round. Just before the meal itself was eaten, the plate of unleavened bread was lifted up, with the words: 'This is the bread of affliction which our fathers ate in the land of Egypt. Let everyone who hungers come and eat; let everyone who is needy come and eat the Passover meal'. The father would give thanks for the bread, and break off a piece for each person present. It would then be passed round from one to another.

NEW BREAD AND WINE

The bread was normally eaten in the silence which followed. But on this occasion Jesus spoke: 'I myself am the Passover Bread'. His life would be given as a substitute for his people!

The meal then began, and when it was completed, the father took the third cup of wine, blessed it and passed it round. Psalms 116–118 were then sung and the Passover celebration concluded with the drinking of a fourth cup.

It was as the third cup of wine was about to be drunk that Jesus interjected a further 'new' note into the celebration. This cup was the cup of the new covenant sealed in his blood! Just as blood had been shed in the Passover, his blood would be shed 'for many'. They were to drink from this cup as an expression of their communion with him, and their share in all that he would do for them in forging that covenant with God.

The final 'difference' in this Passover celebration now followed. Jesus announced that he would not drink the fourth cup: 'I will not drink again of the fruit of the vine' (v. 25). But, rather than abbreviating their fellowship, he was indicating to them that he planned to extend it, and so he added 'until that day when I drink it anew in the kingdom of God'. The cup which usually brought the Passover to an end he would now drink at the beginning of the time of endless fellowship in God's kingdom!

With these words ringing in their ears, and Christ's teaching vividly and visually presented to them, they sang the traditional closing praises from Psalms 116–118, and made their way to the Mount of Olives (v. 26). In this simple way, Jesus inaugurated the Lord's Supper.

THE LORD'S SUPPER

This Christian sacrament has been a focal point for some of the most painful disagreements in the history of Christianity. Is there any way we can relearn what Jesus was teaching his disciples so that when we share in the Lord's Supper together we can 'follow his example in word and in deed'?

There are four key elements in Mark's account of the Last Supper:

(i) *It celebrates the 'new covenant' which God makes with us through Christ.* He is the Passover lamb, sacrificed for us (*1 Cor.* 5 :7). His death accomplishes the new Exodus (cf. *Luke* 9.31 where, as we have already noticed, the Greek word 'exodus' is used to describe what Jesus accomplished on the cross).

What is so important about this? Jesus' sacrifice is the means by which God binds sinners to himself and brings them deliverance from bondage in sin.

(ii) *It focuses our attention on Jesus himself.* He inaugurated the Lord's Supper while he was still with his disciples so that they would not be confused about what he meant when he said 'this is my body, this is my blood' (vv. 22, 24). The fact that he was present with them made it unmistakably clear that these elements were symbols of Jesus himself – they were not magically transformed into something else. That is a vital lesson to learn: in the Lord's Supper our attention is not focused on the bread and the wine, but on the Lord Jesus who gives them to us.

(iii) *It underlines the importance of communion with Jesus.* The sharing of the bread and the wine was a sign of sharing in the blessings of the Passover; the eating and drinking of the 'new' bread and wine is a symbol of our fellowship with Jesus in all he has done for us. Taking the bread and drinking the wine symbolises taking him as Saviour and Lord!

(iv) *It reminds us of the incompleteness of the Christian life.* The Last Supper was an unfinished meal; the last cup remained on the table, untouched. In the same way, the Communion service in our churches is an 'unfinished meal'. We are proclaiming the Lord's death 'until he comes' (*1 Cor.* 11:26). Like the first disciples, we should rise from the table eagerly looking forward to the day when we will drink with Jesus in his Father's kingdom!

63

Jesus' Clear Sightedness

'You will all fall away,' Jesus told them, 'for it is written: "I will strike the shepherd, and the sheep will be scattered." But after I have risen, I will go ahead of you into Galilee.' Peter declared, 'Even if all fall away, I will not.' 'I tell you the truth,' Jesus answered, 'today – yes, tonight – before the cock crows twice you yourself will disown me three times.' But Peter insisted emphatically, 'Even if I have to die with you, I will never disown you.' And all the others said the same (Mark 14:27–31).

One of the outstanding features of Mark's Gospel is the poise and authority of Jesus. Now that we are in the closing scenes of his life, that becomes all the clearer. Jesus, who is the victim, the One who is about to enter the darkness of Gethsemane and the deep darkness of Calvary, is the only one who is really in control of himself and the situation. In this short section, Mark indicates several things about Jesus which help us to understand the reasons for his dignity. In essence they may be summed up like this: Jesus saw in his situation what no one else had eyes to see.

SCRIPTURE FULFILLED

Jesus saw that Scripture was being fulfilled. He knew that his friends would abandon him as they were overcome with fear, for Scripture foretold that when God's Shepherd was smitten, the sheep would be scattered (*Zech.* 13:7, quoted here in v. 27). He knew himself to be the Shepherd of whom the prophet had spoken. He knew that the smiting was his death, foretold in Isaiah 53:4. It was because this teaching of Scripture had saturated his heart and mind that nothing could ultimately surprise him and unbalance him.

This was true in a unique sense of Jesus. But Peter recognised that in his suffering Jesus was also giving his disciples 'an example that you should follow in his steps' (*1 Pet.* 2:21). The word he uses for 'example' would have been used of a teacher showing a child to write by writing a letter and asking the child to copy it down. This is exactly what Jesus does. 'Look how my life was marked by a poise which came from my submission to my Father's word. Now, you copy that.'

THE HAND OF GOD

Jesus also saw the hand of God in his experience. One of the reasons for the disciples' failure was that they saw only the terrible circumstances they were in. Their vision was filled with the sight of opposition and danger. Jesus saw that too. But he could see beyond it, to the hand of God. That was why he placed special emphasis on the identity of the One who would smite and bruise him. It would be 'I' – The Great I Am of the Old Testament – God his Father! However painful that thought was to him, he also recognised that he could trust his Father implicitly. Not one blow would fall upon him that was unnecessary for the salvation of men. It was because of this implicit trust that Jesus endured so faithfully.

FAILURE AMONG DISCIPLES

Jesus saw into his disciples' hearts and knew that they would fail. 'You will all fall away', he said (v. 27). That included Peter, despite his protests to the contrary. That is why, although he must have been deeply pained by his disciples' failures, he was not really taken by surprise. He was safeguarded from a disappointment which leads to bitterness because he saw the real state of human nature.

The marvel is that Jesus did not love Peter any less. Even although he would deny him three times, Jesus loved him. Later, when Jesus' threefold questioning by the morning fire on the shore of Galilee must have reminded him of his denial, Peter at last confessed. 'Lord you know all things . . . you know that for all my failures, I really do love you' (*John* 21:15–17).

This is something we need to remember about Jesus when we fail. Our sins can easily harden our hearts against him and blind us to his grace. Do not think that he is ever taken by surprise when you fail him. Go to him immediately, and confess your sin, and the weakness of your love for him.

FUTURE JOY

Jesus knew that the resurrection lay ahead of him. Notice what he says in verse 28 (words which the disciples were too preoccupied to take in until later – *Mark* 16:7): 'After I have risen'. He knew that he would triumph over darkness and death and rise again. That did not lessen the heaviness of Gethsemane or the darkness of Calvary. But it did enable him to 'endure the cross and despise the shame', because he could see beyond it to 'the joy that was set before him' (*Heb.* 12:2).

PRINCIPLES FOR LIVING

Here, then, are four principles by which every Christian should live:

(i) *Submit the whole of your life to Scripture.* It is the rock on which all spiritual stability will be built.

(ii) *Focus on what God is doing in your circumstances.* Do not become obsessed about what either man or nature may be doing. You may not at first recognise God's footprints (cf. *Psa.* 77:19), but believe that they are there, and be assured that he is working out his perfect purpose in the midst of the chaos around you.

(iii) *Trust your fellow Christians.* However, do not forget that they are saints, not angels. We ourselves fail; others fail us; Christ alone is unfailing. Put your trust first in him, and learn to live within the fellowship of failures knowing that he will never fail you.

(iv) *Remember that all the enigmas of life will never be resolved until the final resurrection.* When the darkness of your present experience seems to make God's hand utterly invisible, look beyond the darkness to the dawning of that morning when the shadows will flee away and 'God will wipe away every tear' from your eyes (*Rev.* 7:17).

64

The Sacred Heart of Christ

They went to a place called Gethsemane, and Jesus said to his disciples, 'Sit here while I pray.' He took Peter, James and John along with him, and he began to be deeply distressed and troubled. 'My soul is overwhelmed with sorrow to the point of death,' he said to them. 'Stay here and keep watch.' Going a little farther, he fell to the ground and prayed that if possible the hour might pass from him. 'Abba, Father,' he said, 'everything is possible for you. Take this cup from me. Yet not what I will, but what you will.' Then he returned to his disciples and found them sleeping. 'Simon,' he said to Peter, 'are you asleep? Could you not keep watch for one hour? Watch and pray so that you will not fall into temptation. The spirit is willing, but the body is weak.' Once more he went away and prayed the same thing. When he came back, he again found them sleeping, because their eyes were heavy. They did not know what to say to him. Returning the third time, he said to them, 'Are you still sleeping and resting? Enough! The hour has come. Look, the Son of Man is betrayed into the hands of sinners. Rise! Let us go! Here comes my betrayer!' (Mark 14:32–42).

The Garden of Gethsemane is one of the most sacred and solemn scenes in the entire Bible. Such was the intensity of Jesus' experience there that Luke, the physician, recorded that Jesus' sweat was like globules of blood. At the end of the experience, 'an angel from heaven appeared to him and strengthened him' (*Luke* 22:43). Alexander Whyte, a famous Scottish minister in the nineteenth century once said, with insight, that in heaven, after he had seen Christ himself, he would like his first conversation to be with this angel. Who knows what depths of suffering he came to witness?

Mark's account includes three special elements in Jesus' agony in the Garden.

JESUS' FEELINGS

The first element is that of our Lord's mental condition. Only rarely in the Gospels are we told about Jesus' inner attitude to his experiences. But here we learn that he was 'deeply distressed and troubled' (v. 33). The language used here is very strong indeed; it conveys the idea of a man who is far away from home and feels abandoned, longing for companionship but finding none. It is clear that Jesus' whole being was profoundly shaken as he began to feel the weight of his coming suffering. Nor did he hide this from his dearest friends: 'My soul is overwhelmed with sorrow to the point of death' he told them (v. 34).

Jesus was about to be exposed to the one thing in life he really feared: not the cruel death which would end it (he knew he would rise again), but the indescribable experience of feeling himself to be God-forsaken. He felt he could not live – indeed, that life was not worth living – without the consciousness of his Father's love for him.

Yet the fact that he entered that darkness and experienced such grief is the source of all our comfort. It assures us that he understands our darkest hours. But more, it means that he has drawn the sting from our darkest hour for he has entered our God-forsaken condition so that we might share his God-accepted relationship to the Father!

JESUS' SUBMISSION

The second element in this story focuses on Jesus' submission to the Father.

He prayed that the cup the Father was giving him might be taken away. (This, incidentally, teaches us that it is not necessarily wrong to ask for something which God does not intend to do, so long as our hearts are prepared to submit to his will, whatever that is.) This 'cup' was something he had spoken about before (see *Mark* 10:38). It had been employed by the Old Testament prophets as a symbol of the outpoured judgment of God (*Isa.* 51:17, 22; *Jer.* 25:15,17; *Ezek.* 23:31-33; *Hab.* 2:16). Drinking it meant shame before men and alienation from God. Jesus knew that, and in his perfect humanity shrank from it. Had he not done so, we could never have believed him to be fully, as well as truly human. Yet his Father's will was that he should drink it, and to his purpose our Lord submitted.

Everything in Jesus longed to escape from this terrible experience, seen in its own light; yet everything in Jesus also longed to be obedient to the Father – and in that light he bowed before him, praying 'Not my will, but your will, be done, Father'. So he took the cup. Never in the Gospels does the humanity of Jesus shine through more clearly; never in the Gospels does his holiness appear more forcibly.

JESUS' DISAPPOINTMENT

The third element in Jesus' consciousness here is his tremendous sense of disappointment in his disciples. He had already prophesied that they would desert him (v. 27). But it would be a mistake to conclude from this that Jesus did not feel their failure keenly. He had asked them to watch and pray. He needed them as guards at his final time of prayer in the garden. He urged them to pray with him lest they find themselves exposed and powerless in the testing time which was about to come. But they failed him miserably. Time and again they heard him urge them to watch and pray; time and again they could not summon the resources to stay awake with their Master. In the light of that it is no surprise to read later in the chapter that 'everyone deserted him and fled' (v. 50).

Jesus remained faithful when his heart was breaking, when the cup was bitter and when his companions were weak. In the light of this Peter's words are all the more challenging – when we remember that he was there, with Jesus in Gethsemane: 'Christ suffered for you, leaving an example, that you should follow in his steps' (*1 Pet.* 2:21).

The implication is clear. Without his faithfulness in Gethsemane, he would not have been faithful 'unto death' on Calvary. This test was a prelude and preparation for that test. It is always the case. We need to learn to 'watch and pray' in our current situation, or we will never be able to do so when the 'evil day' comes.

Gethsemane was unique. We do not go through our own Gethsemane. Jesus has done that for us. But we must learn to place our feet in the footsteps of faithfulness which he planted there, if we are to be his disciples.

65

Left Alone

Just as he was speaking, Judas, one of the Twelve, appeared.
With him was a crowd armed with swords and clubs, sent
from the chief priests, the teachers of the law, and the elders.
Now the betrayer had arranged a signal with them: 'The one
I kiss is the man; arrest him and lead him away under
guard.' Going at once to Jesus, Judas said, 'Rabbi!' and
kissed him. The men seized Jesus and arrested him. Then one
of those standing near drew his sword and struck the servant
of the high priest, cutting off his ear. 'Am I leading a
rebellion,' said Jesus, 'that you have come out with swords
and clubs to capture me? Every day I was with you, teaching
in the temple courts, and you did not arrest me. But the
Scriptures must be fulfilled.' Then everyone deserted him and
fled. A young man, wearing nothing but a linen garment, was
following Jesus. When they seized him, he fled naked, leaving
his garment behind (Mark 14:43–52).

This fourteenth chapter in Mark's Gospel began with an
intimation of what was taking place 'behind the scenes' as
Jesus and his disciples were together in the Upper Room sharing in
the Passover meal, and then in the Garden of Gethsemane. The
religious leaders were plotting to kill Jesus. Now their plot had
been activated.

Judas Iscariot had been present in the Upper Room, but had left
during the evening (see *John* 13:30). Having already arranged to
betray Jesus (*Mark* 14:10–11), he now went to make the last-
minute arrangements. He knew that Jesus would go to the Garden
of Gethsemane, and so he led an armed crowd there to capture

him. In the narrative describing what followed, several things stand out for comment.

INTIMIDATED BY JESUS?

The fear in the hearts of Jesus' enemies stands out. They came to arrest him 'armed to the teeth', (v. 43). Jesus immediately pointed out how sinister this was (v. 48). He was no revolutionary! Words of violence had never crossed his lips. He had never used any of his gifts for destructive purposes – yet religious leaders were sending this gang of armed men to hound him down!

Inherent in Jesus' words is a moral appeal to those who had come with Judas. Our Lord knew they did not bear the ultimate guilt. They were acting thoughtlessly, under instruction from their seniors. He knew that they would carry out their orders. But he wanted to speak to their consciences in a way that might be used later to convict them of their own sin and of his own righteousness. For all we know some of them may have been convicted when Peter preached on the Day of Pentecost (see *Acts* 2:36ff).

It is clear that our Lord's enemies were intimidated by him, and by the holiness of his life. Those who are religious but antagonistic to Christ always are intimidated by him, and seek to silence him by force and by numbers. This should have been a solemn warning to the Christian church throughout the ages. How tragic that sometimes those who have had authority in the church have sought to silence the voice of Christ by force!

THE TRAITOR

The second sad feature of this narrative is the dishonesty of Judas the traitor. He gave the prearranged signal – the one he kissed was the one who should be arrested. With a sign of devotion he betrayed the Lord (vv. 44–45).

The fact that a sign was even needed underlines the fact that those who came to arrest Jesus came by night. In the dim light, only someone who knew Jesus well would have been able to distinguish him from the others. If the arrest had been legitimate, they would have made it during the day – as Jesus indicates (v. 49).

Was this an appeal to Judas? Or was his conscience so seared now that he could not see the illegal actions in which he had involved himself? Months before this event took place, when Judas was the well-respected treasurer of the disciple band, he would probably have been incapable of believing that any of the disciples could do such a thing. But he had begun to steal from the disciples' fund. He had taken what belonged to his fellows. He had taken what belonged to Jesus! Was it the case with Judas, as with others, that he was driven to hide those 'small' sins, until he would choose to have Jesus murdered rather than himself discovered? At the end of the day, betraying Christ came more easily to him than confessing his sin. His tragedy has often been repeated. He stands as a warning to us when we fall into sin: openly confess it to Christ, and be cleansed, or the darkness in your heart may one day engulf your whole soul.

PANIC

Mark also records the panic of the disciples (v. 50). Their failure was clearly not of the same magnitude as Judas'. It displayed their weakness rather than their callousness. But it was not the weakness of a moment, as we have seen. It was the result of failing to build a solid foundation in watching and praying earlier in the evening. They had been more conscious of their tiredness than of their frailty. They were not the last of whom that was true. Like Judas, they stand before us as memorials of what can take place when we give in to weakness which we regard as 'justifiable' until we taste its consequences.

SERENITY

Finally, we should notice once again the serenity of Jesus in the midst of this injustice. He is in complete control. It is he who explains the underlying significance of what is taking place. It is because 'the Scriptures must be fulfilled' (v. 50). The Man who knows that God will always keep his word is the One whose 'ordered life' confesses the 'beauty of God's peace'.

A STRANGE FOOTNOTE

Mark's record of the arrest concludes with what at first sight is a strange footnote. A young man was following Jesus. He was seized and, in his panic to escape, fled naked, leaving his linen garment behind. Such garments were expensive, indicating that this young man came from a wealthy family – as Mark himself seems to have done. Perhaps it was Mark himself. Whether it was or not, the event is reminiscent of Amos' description of the time of God's judgment when even the bravest of men would 'flee naked on that day' (*Amos* 2:16).

What to other observers was the beginning of the trial and last judgment of Jesus was, also, the trial and last judgment of the Jewish leaders. Jesus was being left entirely alone. In what he was about to do no one would stand with him. No one could. He would stand alone as Saviour because he alone was fit to bear the judgment of God in our place.

66

Witnessing a Good Confession

They took Jesus to the high priest, and all the chief priests, elders and teachers of the law came together. Peter followed him at a distance, right into the courtyard of the high priest. There he sat with the guards and warmed himself at the fire. The chief priests and the whole Sanhedrin were looking for evidence against Jesus so that they could put him to death, but they did not find any. Many testified falsely against him, but their statements did not agree. Then some stood up and gave this false testimony against him, 'We heard him say, "I will destroy this man-made temple and in three days will build another, not made by man."' Yet even then their testimony did not agree. Then the high priest stood up before them and asked Jesus, 'Are you not going to answer? What is this testimony that these men are bringing against you?' But Jesus remained silent and gave no answer. Again the high priest asked him, 'Are you the Christ, the Son of the Blessed One?' 'I am,' said Jesus. 'And you will see the Son of Man sitting at the right hand of the Mighty One and coming on the clouds of heaven.' The high priest tore his clothes, 'Why do we need any more witnesses?' he asked. 'You have heard the blasphemy. What do you think?' They all condemned him as worthy of death. Then some began to spit at him; they blindfolded him, struck him with their fists and said, 'Prophesy!' And the guards took him and beat him (Mark 14:53–65).

Jesus was now brought before the Sanhedrin (v. 53). It was the highest ruling court of the Jews, and was modelled on Moses and his seventy elders. It had the strictest rules to guard against any miscarriage of justice. It also had wide powers, although during the Roman occupation of Palestine it could not normally carry out a death sentence. This is the reason why, after his condemnation by the religious court, Jesus was taken to the Roman procurator Pontius Pilate and accused of treason which was a capital offence in Roman law.

Despite its constitution, however, it is clear that a basic miscarriage of true justice took place in the case of Jesus. Mark records that – however they might follow the constitutional procedures outwardly – the Sanhedrin members were deliberately looking for a way of removing Jesus from the scene (v. 55). The court was far from impartial. In normal circumstances the rules of the Sanhedrin gave the benefit of the doubt to the accused. But it is clear that some of its members had already decided on a verdict of 'guilty' for Jesus even before the trial had begun. They wanted to put him to death (v. 55). So they brought false witnesses forward. But their testimony did not agree (a point of great importance in Jewish law, which should have stood in Jesus' favour, but simply incited his opponents all the more).

THE TRUE WITNESS

In contrast to these false witnesses, our Lord stood before the Sanhedrin as the 'faithful and true witness' (*Rev.* 1:5). When false charges were brought against him, he said nothing. Symbolically he emphasised that no genuine charge had been brought against him. There was no substantiated accusation to answer. He did not need to respond. No doubt Jesus was remembering (and was reminding those members of the court who still had some spiritual sensitivity of) Isaiah's prophecy about the Servant of the Lord: 'He was oppressed and afflicted, yet he did not open his mouth . . . as a sheep before her shearers is silent, so he did not open his mouth' (*Isa.* 53:13). Did some of them 'hear' what Jesus was saying without opening his mouth?

But later Jesus did speak, when the high priest questioned him directly (and under oath, *Matt.* 26:63): 'Are you the Christ, the Son of the Blessed One?'

I AM THE MESSIAH

Jesus now revealed the identity which he had kept veiled throughout his ministry. Yes, he was the Messiah – although not the kind expected by the Jews, as they all knew well. Indeed, he went further. He was combining several Old Testament figures to express his identity: he stood before them as the Suffering Servant; he had confessed to being the Messiah; now he revealed himself as the Son of Man, described in Daniel 7:13–14.

In his vision Daniel saw 'one like a son of man, coming with the clouds of heaven. He approached the Ancient of Days and was led into his presence. He was given authority, glory and sovereign power; all peoples, nations and men of every language worshipped him. His dominion is an everlasting dominion that will not pass away, and his kingdom is one that will never be destroyed' (*Dan.* 7:13–14). Jesus, whom the Sanhedrin proposed to judge, was claiming to be the king and judge of all the earth!

No examination of this claim needed to be made – at least in the opinion of the Sanhedrin. How could this man, deserted by his followers, standing powerless before them, possibly be the glorious Messiah of the Jewish people? The idea was – to the high priest, anyway – blasphemous. He tore his robes and called for a verdict of guilty. Jesus was condemned as worthy of death (v. 64).

UNDILUTED HATRED

The final verse of this passage tells us what religious men may become when they have rejected Jesus Christ: beasts of passion. They sought to belittle Jesus by spitting on him; they mocked him by blindfolding him, striking him and calling on him to show he was the Messiah by 'prophesying' who had hit him. Who would believe these gentleman scholars could be so vitriolic? How could they spit on the Son of God and then hand him over to their law officers for more of the same treatment?

The scene would be incredible were it not for the fact that it has been repeated down through history. Many a follower of Christ has been treated in this way, simply because of faithfulness to the

Lord. As with Jesus, so with his disciples: the light reveals much that has been hidden in the darkness.

Later in his ministry, Simon Peter wrote of Jesus as our example in suffering. He had this scene in mind (which perhaps he heard even if he did not see: verses 53–54, 66). 'When they hurled their insults at him he did not retaliate; when he suffered, he made no threats. Instead, he entrusted himself to him who judges justly' (*1 Pet.* 2:23):

> *In my place condemned he stood:*
> *Sealed my pardon with his blood:*
> *Hallelujah! What a Saviour!*

67

The Crumbling Rock

While Peter was below in the courtyard, one of the servant girls of the high priest came by. When she saw Peter warming himself, she looked closely at him. 'You also were with that Nazarene, Jesus,' she said. But he denied it. 'I don't know or understand what you're talking about,' he said, and went out into the entrance. When the servant girl saw him there, she said again to those standing around, 'This fellow is one of them.' Again he denied it. After a little while, those standing near said to Peter, 'Surely you are one of them, for you are a Galilean.' He began to call down curses on himself, and he swore to them, 'I don't know this man you're talking about.' Immediately the cock crowed the second time. Then Peter remembered the word Jesus had spoken to him: 'Before the cock crows twice you will disown me three times.' And he broke down and wept (Mark 14:66–72).

Poor Peter! He loved his Master too much to desert him absolutely, and so he had followed him 'at a distance' (v. 54), and at considerable personal risk. Yet he loved himself too much to be able to remain indifferent to the consequences of all-out faithfulness. It is instructive to realise that he is better remembered for his denial than he is for the degree of faithfulness he demonstrated. Sometimes we malign Peter. We should remember that he was the only one of the disciples who took even this risk. But his testimony underlines the fact that even the bravest and brashest of them failed on that night.

PETER TESTED

Mark here records the progress of Peter's testing. First, the servant girl thinks she has seen Peter somewhere before. Perhaps she had seen the disciple band when they had been together in the temple earlier in that week. In the flickering night lights she needed to peer through the gloom to be absolutely sure (v. 67). Yes, it was the same man – and she said so!

Peter denied the girl's statements in the most general of terms. He did a 'typical cover-up'. But his actions spoke for themselves. With a guilty conscience he went out into the entry way, perhaps hoping that distanced from the light he could remain unrecognised. But the servant girl was not to be outdone. Passing by the entry she spoke again, only this time she appealed to those around her. 'You are one of them', she insisted (v. 70). But again Peter denied it.

As the moments passed, perhaps Peter gradually made his way back into the courtyard proper. He was certainly anxious for his Master. Did he fall into conversation with those around him? Now his accent betrayed him. So they pressed him: 'You are a Galilean! You must be one of his disciples' (v. 70). The flood-gates of self-control were broken open; in the most solemn terms Peter denied his Lord. Calling down curses on himself if he were telling a lie, he insisted he did not know Jesus!

At that moment, three things happened, almost simultaneously: a rooster crowed; the sound was mingled in Peter's memory with something else – Jesus' voice saying 'Before the rooster crows twice, you will disown me three times' (v. 72). You can almost hear Peter telling this story in his preaching, and adding, 'I broke down and wept' (v. 72).

WEAKNESS YIELDS EASILY

This moving part of the Gospel of Mark is intended to teach us some important lessons. One of them is that our personal weaknesses need only the least pressure from temptation to bring us to our knees. There was something admirable about the way Peter had followed Jesus. But there was also something tragic about it: he still did not take seriously his Master's searching analysis of his moral failures. The enquiries of a servant girl were enough to draw out from him the horrible realities of his own heart. He put himself first, before his Lord. He would disown his Lord rather than deny himself.

JESUS' EYES

Peter was without excuse, and in the mercy of Christ he realised it. We know from Luke 22:61 that at the very moment of his denial, he looked across the courtyard and met the eyes of Jesus. That was to be his salvation, for he saw in those eyes not condemnation but compassion. That was the turning point in his life. Jesus had tried to 'break him down' many times before. Now, in this most painful and memorable of ways, Peter saw himself as he really was, repented, and was remade into the great apostle.

JUDAS AND PETER

In the closing section of the Gospel, Peter and Judas are placed side by side. Both fail. But while one was lost, the other was saved. Where did the difference lie?

We can answer that question on several levels. We could delve into the mystery of God's sovereign working in men's lives, and try to answer it. But Scripture tends to answer it on a different level altogether: Peter remembered the Lord's word, wept bitterly, and turned to Jesus for forgiveness. He placed his hope in the promise of restoration Christ had given to him ('When you have turned back, strengthen your brothers', *Luke* 22:31–32).

By stark contrast, Judas had no hope, only regret. Both men knew despair; but Judas despaired of God and of grace; Peter despaired of self, and found hope in Christ and his word.

Of all men, perhaps, Peter is the clearest New Testament example of the experience of Psalm 130: 'If you, O Lord, kept a record of sins, O Lord, who could stand? But with you there is forgiveness; therefore you are feared. I wait for the Lord, my soul waits, and in his word I put my hope' (*Psa.* 130:3–5).

We often associate the strength and power of Simon Peter's

ministry with the resurrection, or Pentecost. He was a witness to Christ who was filled with the Spirit and preached with boldness. All that is true. But here Mark takes us down into the foundations of Peter's spiritual leadership. He was emptied first of all, that he might be filled; he was broken down, that he might be made strong; he wept, that he might know the joy of true forgiveness.

Your experience will not be quite the same as his. But God has not discarded that pattern for moulding men and women into the Christians he wants them to be, has he?

68

Suffered Under Pontius Pilate

Very early in the morning, the chief priests, with the elders, the teachers of the law and the whole Sanhedrin, reached a decision. They bound Jesus, led him away and turned him over to Pilate. 'Are you the king of the Jews?' asked Pilate. 'Yes, it is as you say,' Jesus replied. The chief priests accused him of many things. So again Pilate asked him, 'Aren't you going to answer? See how many things they are accusing you of.' But Jesus still made no reply, and Pilate was amazed. Now it was the custom at the Feast to release a prisoner whom the people requested. A man called Barabbas was in prison with the insurrectionists who had committed murder in the uprising. The crowd came up and asked Pilate to do for them what he usually did. 'Do you want me to release to you the king of the Jews?' asked Pilate, knowing it was out of envy that the chief priests had handed Jesus over to him. But the chief priests stirred up the crowd to have Pilate release Barabbas instead. 'What shall I do, then, with the one you call the king of the Jews?' Pilate asked them. 'Crucify him!' they shouted. 'Why? What crime has he committed?' asked Pilate. But they shouted all the louder, 'Crucify him!' Wanting to satisfy the crowd, Pilate released Barabbas to them. He had Jesus flogged, and handed him over to be crucified (Mark 15:1–15).

One by one, all those who came into contact with Jesus revealed their moral inadequacies and failure. We have already seen the evil of the religious leaders come to a head in their plot to kill Jesus. We have watched Simon Peter's bravado collapse in the face of testing. It is now early in the morning. The Sanhedrin has found Jesus guilty of blasphemy (14:64). But its members knew that such a charge would not be recognised by a Roman court – and in their current political subservience, it required the condemnation of Roman as well as Jewish law if Jesus were to be put to death 'legally'.

We may well imagine that there were members of the Sanhedrin who were not present. Perhaps there were some members present who secretly felt great misgivings about the proceedings. But the fact of the matter was that all who were present consented to the verdict of guilty and to the fact that Jesus was 'worthy of death' (14:64). But further discussion was needed if his death was to take place. They would need to persuade Pilate – known to be a despiser of the Jews – to let them have their way. In the eyes of his enemies, the death of Jesus was not yet a certainty. It would need to be accomplished by careful political manoeuvring. And so it was.

PONTIUS PILATE

Our Lord was bound (v. 1) and led to Pontius Pilate, a man whom history would have well-nigh forgotten were it not for his part in this drama. He was the Roman governor. The power of life and death lay with him. This story gives us some insight into his character. He was shrewd enough to realise why Jesus had been brought to him; he saw through the envy of the priests (v. 10). But he was too weak to do anything about it. When faced with the cries of the people: he 'wanted to satisfy the crowd' (v. 15). Only Jesus stands with his dignity intact as he takes another step forward to his terrible, yet divinely ordained, destiny. He is presented to us in this passage from three perspectives.

THE KING REJECTED

Jesus is the King of the Jews who is rejected by them. He was accused by the priests of high treason. He had confessed to being the Messiah (14:62). His accusers 'translated' that for Pilate. It meant he had claimed to be a king. Anyone who professed to be 'king' was by definition rebelling against the emperor, and was guilty of treason. This explains Pilate's question: 'Are you the king of the Jews?' (v. 2). It also explains Jesus' answer, which is more fully given in John's Gospel (*John* 18:28–37). His words 'It is as you say' (v. 2) are an affirmative answer, but they also display a certain reserve. Yes, Jesus is king, but he is not the kind of 'king' his accusers want Pilate to believe he is. His kingdom belongs to another world.

Pilate seems to have understood this. He did all he felt he reasonably could to have Jesus released. He did not see him as a threat to his own position or to that of the emperor. What amazed him was that these Jews (whom he so despised) were determined to reject Jesus. It did not seem to make sense to him. What had Jesus done to make the religious leaders so envious of him? Why should they reject someone who claimed to be their king? Pilate must have realised there was something beyond human explanation in what was taking place before his very eyes. But, alas, he never clearly saw what it was.

THE SHEEP BEFORE THE SHEARERS

Jesus was like a sheep who is dumb before its shearers. As the chief priests hurled their accusations at the prisoner, he said nothing. He seemed to be resigned to receiving a death sentence. Pilate would not have known the Scriptures well enough to understand what was happening. But could no member of the Sanhedrin interpret Scripture clearly enough to see that the prophecy of the Suffering Servant was being fulfilled before them? Jesus was the One of whom Isaiah had spoken: 'He was oppressed and afflicted, yet he did not open his mouth; he was led like a lamb to the slaughter, and as a sheep before her shearers is silent, so he did not open his mouth' (*Isa.* 53:7). All the time Jesus was unveiling his true identity. But they did not have eyes to see it. Or, if they did see it, they were heaping guilt upon themselves moment by moment as they turned away from the clear revelation of the Messiah.

THE INNOCENT CONDEMNED

Supremely, in these verses, Jesus is the innocent One who is found guilty. Pilate was able to challenge the crowd's cry for Jesus' crucifixion with his question: 'What crime has he committed?'

[256]

(v. 14). The crowd had no answer. They knew he was innocent. Pilate knew he was innocent. Why then was he found guilty?

The answer lies in the interpretation of these events which Jesus had already given to his disciples. Why 'must' the Son of Man suffer (*Mark* 8:31)? It was, as Peter later explained, so that the just would die for the unjust, to bring us to God (*1 Pet.* 3:18). He was innocent, but declared to be guilty. Another man (Barabbas) was guilty, but was treated as though innocent (vv. 11–15). Jesus died in his place.

Without knowing it, the religious leaders and Pilate and Barabbas were all part of a tapestry of grace which God was weaving for sinners. Their actions spoke louder than their words, louder than the cries of the crowds for Jesus' blood. Jesus was not dying for his own crimes, but for the crimes of others; not for his own sins, but the sins of others. He did not die for himself, he died for us!

Have you ever seen what they were all too blind to notice?

69

Behold Your King!

The soldiers led Jesus away into the palace (that is, the Praetorium) and called together the whole company of soldiers. They put a purple robe on him, then twisted together a crown of thorns and set it on him. And they began to call out to him, 'Hail, king of the Jews!' Again and again they struck him on the head with a staff and spat on him. Falling on their knees, they paid homage to him. And when they had mocked him, they took off the purple robe and put his own clothes on him. Then they led him out to crucify him. A certain man from Cyrene, Simon the father of Alexander and Rufus, was passing by on his way in from the country, and they forced him to carry the cross. They brought Jesus to the place called Golgotha (which means The Place of the Skull). Then they offered him wine mixed with myrrh, but he did not take it. And they crucified him. Dividing up his clothes, they cast lots to see what each would get. It was the third hour when they crucified him. The written notice of the charge against him read: THE KING OF THE JEWS. They crucified two robbers with him, one on his right and one on his left. Those who passed by hurled insults at him, shaking their heads and saying, 'So! You who are going to destroy the temple and build it in three days, come down from the cross and save yourself!' In the same way the chief priests and the teachers of the law mocked him among themselves. 'He saved others,' they said, 'but he can't save himself! Let this Christ, this King of Israel, come down now from the cross, that we may see and believe.' Those crucified with him also heaped insults on him (Mark 15:16–32).

J esus had come to be the Messiah – the anointed prophet, king
and priest of God's people. But throughout his public ministry
his identity had been veiled. Conscious of how easily the claim
to be Messiah would be misunderstood, Jesus had sought to
inform his hearers what kind of Messiah he really was, before
publicly acknowledging that this was his identity.

Now, however, he had confessed his messianic character. He was
'The Christ, the Son of the Blessed One' (14:61). He publicly confronted Jews and Gentiles alike with his messianic identity, and
challenged them to respond. Only two responses were possible:
acceptance or rejection. In Mark's account of Jesus' rejection he
points out just how thoroughgoing this rejection was.

THE PROPHET BLINDFOLDED

The religious leaders specifically rejected his claim to be the
prophet of God, and derided him for it. They blindfolded him,
struck him with their fists, and then mocked him, 'Prophesy! Go
on, Messiah, tell us who hit you!' (14:65). We have to look twice at
this statement and its context – yes, later, the temple guards took
Jesus and beat him; but that was only after the Sanhedrin itself had
collectively shown its true colours and the perverted hearts of its
individual members.

THE KING MOCKED

When Jesus was handed over to the secular authorities, his claim to
be the Messiah was equally rejected, but this time the focus of the
rejection is his claim to be king.

Having been cruelly flogged (a punishment so horrifying that
many prisoners actually died), Jesus was now led away to be held
by the Roman soldiers.

These men displayed one of the most frightening traits in the
human personality: discipline of an unusual degree in one area,
and gross moral indiscipline in another. They were neither the
first nor the last to act in this fashion. But there is something
particularly grotesque about their little 'game'. They had called
their fellow-soldiers together for an hour of entertainment with

Jesus. Utterly alone, humiliated and virtually naked, Jesus was set in front of them in mock-regal dress – a crown of thorns and a purple robe. They called him 'king of the Jews' while spitting on him and striking him on the head. 'They mocked him', says Mark (v. 20) until the time had come to lead him to the place where he would be crucified. They would show Jesus what they really thought of his claims. They did not have the eyes to see that the only thing they were doing was fulfilling to the letter the manifesto he had earlier published among his disciples (*Mark* 9:31). Even in the hour of his deepest humiliation, he was reigning as king.

REIGNING IN WEAKNESS

At this stage in the proceedings leading finally to crucifixion, a man might be too weakened to carry the beam of the cross on which he would be impaled. The soldiers therefore press-ganged a man by the name of Simon, from Cyrene, to carry the plank. Mark mentions his sons, Alexander and Rufus, which seems to indicate that they were known to the first readers of this Gospel – and if so had presumably become Christians. The story of their conversion was perhaps so well known that Mark did not need to say any more! If so, he could have given no clearer hint of the power of God's kingdom than this – in his weakest hour, Jesus began his reign of grace in one home and family!

The king must remain in control of all his faculties, and so Jesus refused the wine mixed with myrrh and given as a drug to relieve the terrible pain of crucifixion. Even now messianic prophecies continued to be fulfilled: as the crowds watched, the soldiers cast lots for his clothing (*Psa.* 22:18).

Earlier in the Gospel, Mark had recorded the request of James and John to be at his right hand and his left. They had not under-stood the cup he would drink and the baptism he would experience. Now two others were at his right hand and his left. These men, along with those who passed by and the religious leaders, poured similar contempt on him. They despised him as prophet ('You who are going to destroy the temple and build it in three days . . .' v. 29); they mocked him as priest ('He saved others, he cannot save himself'); they humiliated him as king ('If he is the king, let him prove it by coming down from the cross . . .' v. 32). How blind they were to what was actually happening. Only if he refused to save himself could he save others. The very words they spoke could have brought them to the heart of the gospel. But they could not understand God's ways, or recognise his Messiah, even when above him were the words: 'The king of the Jews' (v. 26).

We are here present at a scene which Jesus must often have contemplated. As early as Mark 2:20, he had spoken of how he would be 'taken' from his disciples. As he had come nearer to that event he had explained its significance to the disciples: he would be rejected, would suffer and die in a cruel and humiliating fashion. None of this was unexpected; all of it was under his control. Crucified as king, he was king still. He made the cross his first throne.

70

The Priest Sacrificed

*At the sixth hour darkness came over the whole land until the
ninth hour. And at the ninth hour Jesus cried out in a loud
voice, 'Eloi, Eloi, lama sabachthani?' – which means, 'My
God, my God, why have you forsaken me?' When some of
those standing near heard this, they said, 'Listen, he's calling
Elijah.' One man ran, filled a sponge with wine vinegar, put
it on a stick, and offered it to Jesus to drink. 'Now leave him
alone. Let's see if Elijah comes to take him down,' he said.
With a loud cry, Jesus breathed his last. The curtain of the
temple was torn in two from top to bottom. And when the
centurion, who stood there in front of Jesus, heard his cry and
saw how he died, he said, 'Surely this man was the Son of
God!' Some women were watching from a distance. Among
them were Mary Magdalene, Mary the mother of James the
younger and of Joses, and Salome. In Galilee these women
had followed him and cared for his needs. Many other women
who had come up with him to Jerusalem were also there*
(Mark 15:33–41).

As the messianic prophet, Jesus had been despised and abused;
as the messianic king, he had been mocked and enthroned on
a Roman gibbet. Now Mark shows us that as the messianic priest
he became the sacrificial victim for the sins of his people.

As Jesus hung on the cross a strange darkness came over the
land. Mark does not explain its significance to us. Perhaps he
assumed that as his readers had followed the course of events
they would make a connection between this darkness and the
celebration of the Passover.

In the Exodus from Egypt, the plague of darkness had been God's last word to Pharaoh before the angel of death visited the land. Thereafter only those who were protected by the shed blood of the Passover lamb would be delivered from the visitation of God's wrath. Now the Exodus was finding its ultimate fulfilment in the exodus which Jesus was accomplishing at Jerusalem (*Luke* 9:31). There was a plague of darkness preceding the sacrifice of Christ as the Passover lamb (*1 Cor.* 5:7). But this time, it was God's own firstborn who was to die.

This is why the terrible cry of dereliction issued from Christ's lips: 'My God, why have you forsaken me?' (v. 34). He was experiencing what was involved in being the sin-bearer in the presence of the sinless God. As he came before God as the high priest of his people, he carried no substitutionary sacrifice for them. He brought only himself. And thus as priest he also became the victim.

Mark notices several things about this dark experience.

MISUNDERSTOOD

It was misunderstood by many of those who watched the crucifixion. They assumed that Jesus must be calling for Elijah ('Eloi, Eloi . . .', v. 34). There seems to have been a popular religious belief in Palestine that Elijah acted as a kind of patron saint of sufferers. And so someone offered Jesus a drink – presumably in the hope of keeping him sufficiently alert to see what else he might say, or indeed what might happen. In the face of the most momentous event in their lives, indeed in human history, some of the crowd were incapable of understanding what was happening and what Jesus meant, because their minds were clouded with superstition. Had they known Scripture as well as they knew folk religion, their minds would have been drawn to Psalm 22 which Jesus was quoting. There they would have learned the true meaning of Jesus' death.

SYMBOLISED

But the meaning of Jesus' experience was also symbolised by the tearing of the temple curtain, from top to bottom. Mark does not specify whether this curtain was the one which stood between the Holy Place and the Holy of Holies (*Exod.* 26:31–35) or over the entrance to the Holy Place (*Exod.* 26:37). But in either case the significance of the tear is the same: the old established priestly ritual for entrance into the presence of God had now been abolished. The temple now stood desecrated – by God himself. Jesus' death had created a new way into God's presence.

COMMUNICATED

Some element of the significance of Jesus' death was also communicated to the Roman centurion who was responsible for carrying out Pilate's orders. As he stood by, he heard something which was probably unique in his experience: a crucified man crying out with a loud voice, and dying (v. 37).

Why was that so significant? Because crucified men often took two days or even longer to die. It was a death of prolonged agony and increasing weakness. Crucified men simply did not cry out with loud voices. They had no strength left to do so.

Exactly what the centurion meant by his words we do not really know. But Mark at least invites his readers to make his words their own. Throughout the Gospel, as we have seen, he brings us back time and again to face the question: Who is Jesus? Here, in his weakness and rejection, Jesus is seen to be none other than the Son of God.

WITNESSED

Mark also tells us that Jesus' death was witnessed, from a distance, by the group of women who had ministered to him and the disciples in Galilee (vv. 40–41), as well as by others. These same women reappear in Mark's narrative at Jesus' burial and then as witnesses of the empty tomb. They saw him die; they saw the tomb where he was laid (v. 47); and they saw the stone rolled away on the first Easter morning.

Why should Mark include them here? Because they were eye-witnesses of the central facts of the Christian gospel which were to be enshrined in the great creeds and hymns of the Christian church, as well as in the rest of the New Testament. Jesus 'suffered under Pontius Pilate, was crucified, dead and buried . . . on the third day he rose again from the dead' (The Apostles' Creed). The true priest had entered into the presence of God on our behalf, bearing the sacrifice for our sins – himself. Soon he would emerge, in full view of his people, his work completed, his sacrifice accepted, and communion with God restored!

71

The Grave of a Rich Man

It was Preparation Day (that is, the day before the Sabbath). So as evening approached, Joseph of Arimathea, a prominent member of the Council, who was himself waiting for the kingdom of God, went boldly to Pilate and asked for Jesus' body. Pilate was surprised to hear that he was already dead. Summoning the centurion, he asked him if Jesus had already died. When he learned from the centurion that it was so, he gave the body to Joseph. So Joseph bought some linen cloth, took down the body, wrapped it in the linen, and placed it in a tomb cut out of rock. Then he rolled a stone against the entrance of the tomb. Mary Magdalene and Mary the mother of Joses saw where he was laid (Mark 15:42–47).

Jesus was dead. Throughout his Gospel Mark has often described how people responded to Jesus at different stages in his ministry. He continues to do so here. In the lives of at least two men, the death of Christ confirmed attitudes which had been germinating in their hearts for some time.

It was mid-afternoon on the Friday of Passover week when Jesus died. Only a short time remained before sundown and the traditional beginning of the Jewish Sabbath. If Jesus were to be buried, it would need to be hurriedly.

JOSEPH OF ARIMATHEA

The body of an executed criminal was handed over to his family or friends only when special request was made to the Roman authorities. It is at this point that Joseph of Arimathea steps on to the stage of the Gospel history. We learn a great deal about him here. He was a rich man. He was also a man who had searched the Scriptures with a genuine longing for the coming of the kingdom of God (v. 43). He had heard Jesus, and had believed in him, secretly, frightened of the possible consequences of open disciple-ship (see *John* 19:38). In his case, those consequences would have been considerable, because he was a member of the Sanhedrin – in fact Mark says he was a prominent member (v. 43). For reasons we are not told, he was probably absent from the meeting of the Sanhedrin which had condemned Jesus to death (*Luke* 23:51).

Perhaps that fatal decision of the Council had been the deciding factor for Joseph. Whatever else he understood about the death of Jesus, he knew he could no longer side silently with those who had so viciously sought his death. He must now come into the open. Even though Jesus was dead, Joseph was determined to follow and honour him in whatever way was left open to him. He came to the Roman governor and asked for Jesus' body to be released so that he could make provision for its proper burial. Quickly he (and doubt-less his servants) made the arrangements, and Jesus was buried in Joseph's rock tomb. A stone was rolled across the entrance, as Mary Magdalene and Mary, mother of Joses watched (vv. 46–47).

CROSSROADS

Joseph realised that no one can remain a secret disciple of Jesus indefinitely. There invariably comes a point at which we must burn our boats and cross our bridges. It may be when his real significance dawns on us with special power. It may be when others publicly reject Jesus, and we must confess that we will stand with him, whatever the cost. It may be both, as it seems to have been for this man. But in any event, every disciple must stand up to be counted. In the case of Joseph, he risked everything by doing so. We do not know what the actual repercussions were. We do know that 'it is with your heart that you believe and are justified, and it is with your mouth that you confess and are saved. As the Scripture says, "Anyone who trusts in him will never be put to shame"' (*Rom.* 10:10–11).

CONTRAST

Joseph's boldness (v. 43) is contrasted with Pilate's hesitation. Surely this interview was one of the great ironies of history. Here was the Roman governor who had had the privilege of interviewing Jesus, and on whose shoulders lay the responsibility for his life or death, humanly speaking – yet who, in his acting, was the instrument of God's purposes, all unknowingly. Here too was the respected member of the Sanhedrin which had voted the death sentence on Jesus. He was now an open disciple of the rejected and humiliated Nazarene. All Pilate could do was to confess his surprise that Jesus had died so quickly. He went through a formal investigation procedure, questioning the centurion in charge and then allowing Joseph to bury the body. It was tantamount to admitting that Jesus had never been a serious threat to the *Pax Romana* in the first place. Pilate knew that all too well. Yet his conscience seems already to have been deadened by the passage of time.

THE ONE THING THAT REALLY MATTERS

The same twenty-four hours rendered the names of these two men immortal in human history. That is why Mark mentions them. But the one thing which gave both of their lives the ultimate significance they have was . . . what? It was their reaction to Jesus. Both of them seemed to think at one time that they could delay their final response to him, perhaps indefinitely. But events overtook them. The decision which Pilate faced, 'What shall I do with the one you call the king of the Jews?' (*Mark* 15:12), was thrust upon them both when they least expected it.

It is often the same for us. We cannot pick and choose the timing of our decision to follow or to reject Jesus Christ, as though the issue could be delayed. God thrusts us into circumstances which confirm once and for all time the decisions and directions of our hearts.

As we come to the closing chapter of the Gospel it is time for us to ask ourselves: Where do I stand? With Pilate? Or with Joseph?

72

Resurrection!

When the Sabbath was over, Mary Magdalene, Mary the mother of James, and Salome bought spices so that they might go to anoint Jesus' body. Very early on the first day of the week, just after sunrise, they were on their way to the tomb and they asked each other, 'Who will roll the stone away from the entrance of the tomb?' But when they looked up, they saw that the stone, which was very large, had been rolled away. As they entered the tomb, they saw a young man dressed in a white robe sitting on the right side, and they were alarmed. 'Don't be alarmed,' he said, 'You are looking for Jesus the Nazarene who was crucified. He has risen! He is not here. See the place where they laid him. But go, tell his disciples and Peter, "He is going ahead of you into Galilee. There you will see him, just as he told you."' Trembling and bewildered, the women went out and fled from the tomb. They said nothing to anyone, because they were afraid (Mark 16:1–8).

Mark's account of the discovery of the resurrection of Jesus bears all the characteristics of an authentic report. It is a psychological as well as a moral impossibility that the early church manufactured these verses. Several features of the narrative demonstrate this.

AUTHENTIC ACCOUNT

(i) *The women's role.* Mark tells us that it was the women who first discovered the empty tomb and who heard the first announcement of the resurrection. To our twentieth-century western minds that

may seem unremarkable. But in the context of first-century
Palestine it was highly significant, for women were often treated as
second-class citizens. Their testimony would be inadmissible in
a court of law. As witnesses they had no standing! No one who
wanted to fabricate a convincing account of the resurrection in
first-century Palestine would have dreamed of doing it in this way.

(ii) *The story breathes authenticity.* In going to the tomb these
women were following their hearts rather than their heads. Jesus
had been dead for two days in a climate where bodies were subject
to rapid decay. Further, these very women had seen the stone
rolled across the grave. It was only as they walked together to the
tomb that it seems to have dawned on them that they would be
incapable of moving it themselves.

(iii) *They clearly did not expect a resurrection.* In spite of the fact
that Jesus had told his disciples that he would rise again, the
discovery alarmed them and filled them with fear (vv. 5, 8).

As they arrived at the tomb, they encountered a figure in white –
an angelic young man – who told them what had happened. Jesus
had died as they knew. He had been buried, as they had seen. Now
he was risen: they need only look in the tomb where he was buried.
He was no longer there. He had risen!

TRUE OR FALSE?

Since the days of the infant church men have tried to 'disprove' the
resurrection of Jesus. They have argued that the disciples stole
the body, or the Jews stole the body, or Jesus did not really die on
the cross and was resuscitated. But when we read the testimony
of the Gospels, all of these arguments fall to the ground, and the
testimony of this messenger remains. Had the disciples stolen
the body, none of the marks of authentic reporting in this passage
would be there. Nor would the marks of new power have been
present in their own lives, had they known that the message they
preached was pure fiction. Had the Jews stolen the body, the
preaching of the early church would have quickly called forth his
earthly remains. Pilate had carefully checked Jesus' death. But

even if he had not done so, the idea of his resuscitation in the cool of the tomb remains ludicrous. For it involves the disciples preaching Christ as the truth but making the central element in their proclamation something they knew to be a lie.

... AND PETER

Yet, while this defence of the historical fact of the resurrection can be gleaned from the Gospels, we should notice that the burden of the message the women received was rather different. The disciples were to go to Galilee. There they would meet Jesus. And Peter in particular was to be given this message (v. 7).

Why Peter? As we have seen, this was Peter's Gospel. But there is more to the message. This was Jesus' first word to his disciples since he had been torn from them in Gethsemane. His eyes had gazed on Peter's in the courtyard, but no words had passed between them (*Luke* 22:61). His Lord understood all that Peter must have been going through – the sense of shame and despair he had known as he wept bitterly. There were special reasons why Peter must meet with Jesus in Galilee. He needed to face up to his failure, be forgiven and restored to useful service. There, in Galilee, he would begin again to follow his Lord.

But perhaps the most interesting thing about these verses (with which Mark's Gospel probably originally ended) is their conclusion. The women were bewildered. They left the empty tomb trembling. They fled home silently, saying nothing to anyone they met, 'because they were afraid' (v. 8).

Should they not have returned home rejoicing in the news they had heard? Is there not something unexpected about this response? That in itself is a mark of its authenticity (if we were to invent the story we would not end it in this way). But it is more. In Mark's Gospel, this fear is always man's response to the breaking in of the power of God. It is the fear the disciples experienced when Jesus stilled the storm; the fear of the Gerasenes when Jesus delivered Legion; the fear of the disciples as they saw Jesus setting his face to Jerusalem to die on the cross. This fear is the response of men and women to Jesus as he shows his power and majesty as the Son of God.

Mark began his Gospel by telling us who Jesus is. He wrote his Gospel to make us ask the question: Who is Jesus? and answer it accurately. Now he shows us the nature of a true response to Jesus. It is to be moved with a sense of awe and wonder that the Son of God came among men, and lived and died and rose again for our salvation. That sense of awe is the beginning of a new life of fellowship with a risen Lord.

Has Mark's Gospel brought us to know that, yet?

73

A Later Postscript

When Jesus rose early on the first day of the week, he appeared first to Mary Magdalene, out of whom he had driven seven demons. She went and told those who had been with him and who were mourning and weeping. When they heard that Jesus was alive and that she had seen him, they did not believe it. Afterwards Jesus appeared in a different form to two of them while they were walking in the country. These returned and reported it to the rest; but they did not believe them either. Later Jesus appeared to the Eleven as they were eating; he rebuked them for their lack of faith and their stubborn refusal to believe those who had seen him after he had risen. He said to them, 'Go into all the world and preach the good news to all creation. Whoever believes and is baptised will be saved, but whoever does not believe will be condemned. And these signs will accompany those who believe: In my name they will drive out demons; they will speak in new tongues; they will pick up snakes with their hands; and when they drink deadly poison, it will not hurt them at all; they will place their hands on sick people, and they will get well.' After the Lord Jesus had spoken to them, he was taken up into heaven and he sat at the right hand of God. Then the disciples went out and preached everywhere, and the Lord worked with them and confirmed his word by the signs that accompanied it (Mark 16:9–20).

The Christian church does not possess the original manuscript of the Gospel which John Mark wrote. We have only copies. Sometimes those copies contain slight differences from one another. A word may be different, occasionally even an entire verse, as modern translations sometimes indicate. Here, in Mark 16:9–20, however, we encounter an unusual problem, as the *New International Version* text indicates. The oldest reliable manuscripts of Mark's Gospel do not contain these verses!

HAND-WRITTEN GOSPELS

How could such differences occur? We need to remember that the Gospels were written long before the invention of printing. Mark was not able to take his manuscript along to the local printing press, ask them to typeset it, then read the proofs and have thousands of copies all exactly the same printed for distribution. If anyone wanted a 'Mark's Gospel' they had to sit down with what Mark had written and laboriously copy it out by hand. If, by any chance, they copied a word wrongly, or missed something out, then that mistake would probably be repeated when someone else took a copy of their copy of Mark!

When we remember that for fifteen hundred years people were copying the Gospel by hand, it is not surprising to learn that many small discrepancies crept into later manuscript copies.

How then can we be sure that we have the genuine text which Mark wrote? Only by trying to trace the copies back to their originals, by placing them in 'families' as experts do, and eventually locating the earliest copies of the Gospel and trying to work out, if mistakes were made in copying, where and how they took place.

A SUMMARY OF OTHER GOSPELS

It is not difficult to see how, for example, some verses might be added to Mark's Gospel. If someone had copied out the text, and realised that it had (as Mark's Gospel does) a rather sudden ending, they might well add an appendix, summarising some of the relevant teaching of the other Gospels, or the different traditions of the church.

It seems likely that this happened in the case of Mark, since the two most reliable early manuscripts of the end of Mark's Gospel conclude at verse 8 with the words 'because they were afraid'. They do not include verses 9–20.

Of course, it is possible that the ending is missing in these manuscripts. Perhaps other manuscripts which are not so old are copies of even earlier manuscripts.

AN ADDITION

But most New Testament experts are convinced that Mark 16:9–20 did not belong to the original text of the Gospel. Why?

For one thing these verses are not written in the same style as the rest of the Gospel. For another, they read more like a summary of early church tradition than the material we have in the other Gospels. Their contents do not quite fit with the testimony of the four Gospels. For example Mark 16:12–13 seems to be a summary of Luke 24:13–34, but it does not really seem consistent with it. Again the promises given in Mark 16:17–18 read like a summary of some of the amazing things which took place in the early church. Nowhere else did Jesus seem to promise the kind of physical immunity which is spoken of here.

So, for these and other reasons (but especially because these verses do not seem to appear in our earliest copies of Mark's Gospel), it seems likely they are additional material which somehow crept in at a later date.

A STRANGE ENDING?

Why then does Mark's Gospel end on such a different note from the other Gospels?

It may be – as some have thought – that he was interrupted before he could finish his Gospel, or that the original ending of the Gospel has been lost. But these explanations seem unlikely. Certainly there is no hint in the records of the church that this is what happened.

The true answer is likely to be quite simply that Mark intended to finish his Gospel just as he did. He wanted to convey to his readers that the disciples (despite all that Jesus had taught them) had not expected the resurrection. It was no piece of wish-fulfilment. They were stunned by it. And they were stunned by the implications of the resurrection. Jesus really was the Son of God!

He really would be with them for ever! They could scarcely take it in. Mark could not have expressed this more forcefully than he did.

The closing verses of Mark's Gospel leave us with some fundamental questions about Jesus and our relationship to him. That is exactly what the Gospel was intended to do!

Group Study Guide

SCHEME FOR GROUP BIBLE STUDY
(Covering 13 Weeks)

	Study Passage	Chapters
1.	Mark 1:1–13	1–2
2.	Mark 1:14–3:6	3–10
3.	Mark 3:7–5:20	11–19
4.	Mark 5:21–6:29	20–24
5.	Mark 6:30–7:23	25–29
6.	Mark 7:24–8:38	30–36
7.	Mark 9:1–50	37–42
8.	Mark 10:1–52	43–48
9.	Mark 11:1–33	49–50
10.	Mark 12:1–44	51–56
11.	Mark 13:1–37	57–59
12.	Mark 14:1–52	60–65
13.	Mark 14:53–16:8 [20]	66–73

This Study Guide has been prepared for group Bible study, but it can also be used individually. Those who use it on their own may find it helpful to keep a notebook of their responses.

The way in which group Bible studies are led can greatly enhance their value. A well-conducted study will appear as though it has been easy to lead, but that is usually because the leader has worked hard and planned well. Clear aims are essential.

AIMS

In all Bible study, individual or corporate, we have several aims:

1. To gain an understanding of the original meaning of the particular passage of Scripture.

2. To apply this to ourselves and our own situation.

3. To develop some specific ways of putting the biblical teaching into practice.

2 Timothy 3:16–17 provides a helpful structure. Paul says that Scripture is useful for:

(i) teaching us;

(ii) rebuking us;

(iii) correcting, or changing us;

(iv) training us in righteousness.

Consequently, in studying any passage of Scripture, we should always have in mind these questions:

What does this passage teach us (about God, ourselves, etc.)?

Does it rebuke us in some way?

How can its teaching transform us?

What equipment does it give us for serving Christ?

In fact these four questions alone would provide a safe guide in any Bible study.

PRINCIPLES

In group Bible study we meet in order to learn about God's word and ways 'together with all the saints' (*Eph.* 3:18). But our own experience, as well as Scripture, tells us that the saints are not always what they are called to be in every situation – including group Bible study! Leaders ordinarily have to work hard and prepare well if the work of the group is to be spiritually profitable. The following guidelines for leaders may help to make this a reality.

Preparation:

1. Study and understand the passage yourself. The better prepared and more sure of the direction of the study you are, the more likely it is that the group will have a beneficial and enjoyable study.

Ask: What are the main things this passage is saying? How can this be made clear? This is not the same question as the more common 'What does this passage "say to you"?' which expects a reaction rather than an exposition of the passage. Be clear about that distinction yourself and work at making it clear in the group study.

2. On the basis of your own study form a clear idea *before* the group meets of (i) the main theme(s) of the passage which should be opened out for discussion, and (ii) some general conclusions the group ought to reach as a result of the study. Here the questions which arise from 2 Timothy 3:16–17 should act as our guide.

3. The guidelines and questions which follow may help to provide a general framework for each discussion; leaders should use them as starting places which can be further developed. It is usually helpful to have a specific goal or theme in mind for group discussion, and one is suggested for each study. But even more important than tracing a single theme is understanding the teaching and the implications of the passage.

Leading the Group:

1. Announce the passage and theme for the study and begin with prayer. In group studies it may be helpful to invite a different person to lead in prayer each time you meet.

2. Introduce the passage and theme, briefly reminding people of its outline, and highlighting the content of each subsidiary section.

3. Lead the group through the discussion questions. Use your own if you are comfortable in doing so; those provided may be used, developing them with your own points. As discussion proceeds, continue to encourage the group first of all to discuss the significance of the passage (teaching) and only then its application

(meaning for us). It may be helpful to write important points and applications on a board by way of summary as well as visual aid.

4. At the end of each meeting remind members of the group of its assignments for the next meeting and encourage them to come prepared. Be sufficiently prepared as the leader to give specific assignments to individuals or even couples or groups to come with specific contributions ('John, would you try to find out something about the scribes and Pharisees for the next meeting?' 'Betty, would you see what you can find out about the different ways in which Mark 10:1–12 has been interpreted?').

5. Remember that you are the leader of the group! Encourage clear contributions and do not be embarrassed to ask someone to explain what they have said more fully, or to help them to do so ('Do you mean . . . ?').

Most groups include the 'over-talkative', the 'over-silent' and the 'red-herring raisers'! Leaders must control the first, encourage the second and redirect the third! Each leader will develop his or her own most natural way of doing that; but it will be helpful to think out what that is before the occasion arises! The first two groups can be helped by some judicious direction of questions to specific individuals or even groups (e.g., 'How do those who are not working outside of the home apply this?' 'Jane, you know something about this from personal experience . . .'); the third by redirecting the discussion to the passage itself ('That is an interesting point, but isn't it true that this passage really concentrates on . . . ?'). It may be helpful to break the group up into smaller groups sometimes, giving each sub-group specific points to discuss and to report back on. A wise arranging of these smaller groups may also help each member to participate.

More important than any techniques we may develop is the help of the Spirit enabling us to understand and to apply the Scriptures. Have and encourage a humble, prayerful spirit.

6. Keep faith with the schedule; it is better that some of the group wished the study could have been longer than that others are inconvenienced by it stretching beyond the time limits set.

7. Close in prayer. As time permits, spend the closing minutes in corporate prayer, encouraging the group to apply what they have learned in praise and thanks, intercession and petition.

STUDY 1: Mark 1:1–13

AIM: to recognise the kind of book Mark's Gospel is, and to see the ways in which Jesus Christ is its central message.

1.   What points from the introduction to Mark (pp. xiii–xvii) do you consider most important?

Why is it important to see that Mark's Gospel is more than a series of stories recorded in chronological order?

2.   Three exercises should be completed:

(i) look up the key question in Mark 4:41; 8:27 and 14:61;

(ii) discuss why so much of the Gospel is devoted to only one week of Jesus' life;

(iii) read over Acts 10:36–43 and discuss the similarities in the basic pattern of Peter's sermon and Mark's Gospel. When we witness to Christ should our testimony be basically the same as Peter's?

3.   If the Gospel is 'about Jesus Christ', what does Mark underline in these introductory sections:

(i) In the ministry of John the Baptist as Jesus' forerunner (1:1–8)?

(ii) In the way in which Jesus is identified at his baptism and the conflict experience in the wilderness (1:9–13)?

4.   Important applications of this section involve the following:

(i) In a minor sense, we are all 'forerunners' of Jesus to others. How is John the Baptist a model in this?

(ii) Basic to Mark's presentation of Christ is the fact that all Jesus does is *for us*. Notice the way in which Jesus' work is described as 'baptism' (1:8; 10:38–39). We tend to think of our baptism as a sign of our response to Christ. Discuss how his baptism reminds us that our baptism points us to what he has done for us (cf. *Rom.* 6:1–4).

5.   Mark mentions the temptations only briefly, but emphasises four things: the role of the Spirit, the inhospitability of the environment, the strategy of Satan and the supernatural ministry Jesus received from angels. Relate this to your Christian experience in the light of Eph. 6:10–20; 1 Pet. 5:8–9; Heb. 2:14–18; 4:14–16.

FOR STUDY 2:

(i) Read Mark 1:14–3:6 and chapters 3–10 of the text.

(ii) What do Heb. 2:18; 4:15; 1 Cor. 10:13 and James 1:13–15 teach about temptation?

STUDY 2: Mark 1:14–3:6

AIM: to see the relationship between the message of the kingdom and the events of Jesus' ministry.

1. What do the following mean?
 (i) there is 'good news';
 (ii) 'the time has come';
 (iii) 'the kingdom . . . is near';
 (iv) 'repent and believe'.

2. The kingdom of God is a central theme in Jesus' preaching. Notice how his parables are kingdom-orientated (*Mark* 4:11–12) and how discipleship is understood in terms of it (*Mark* 10:15–25). The kingdom, the sphere in which God's reign is expressed, has a present aspect (it is 'near') but in another sense awaits its consummation.

   How can we define the kingdom of God? How do we enter it? In what sense do the four features listed above determine the nature of kingdom life?

3. What do we learn about the nature of the kingdom's presence in the activity of Jesus its king in:
 (i) His authority in calling the disciples (1:14–20);
 (ii) The authority of his preaching (1:21–28);
 (iii) The restorative power of the presence of the kingdom in a fallen world (1:29–34; 40–41);
 (iv) The 'secret' of the kingdom which Jesus appears to safeguard (1:25; 34; 44). Why did he do this when it is 'good news'?
 (v) The conflict which the presence of the kingdom creates in the supernatural world (1:24–26) and the religious community (2:6ff; 16ff; 18ff; 24ff). Are the two related in any way (*Eph.* 6:10ff)?

4. In 2:13–3:6 it becomes clear that the old order cannot tolerate the presence of the new (see especially 2:21). What are these two orders? What are their most important characteristics?

   Ferguson later (p. 38) says that 'The great error of the Pharisees was twofold. They had a wrong view of God, and consequently an inadequate view of sin.' Is this true, and if so, are there ways in which this also applies to our resistance to the kingdom?

5.   How does the presence of the kingdom affect:
 (i) fasting;
 (ii) the Sabbath? (2:18–28).

6.   When we pray 'your kingdom come' we are asking for the new order to invade the old not simply in the future, but also in the present. What conflicts does that prayer create in your own life and its context? In what ways do you need to continue to pray for the kingdom to be fully realised in your life?

FOR STUDY 3:
 (i) Read Mark 3:7–5:20 and chapters 11–19 of the text.
 (ii) Pray specifically about the ways in which the kingdom of Jesus Christ must be allowed to destroy the old order of things in your own life.

STUDY 3: Mark 3:7–5:20

AIM: to recognise that the coming of Christ's kingdom creates a conflict between itself and the various manifestations of the powers of darkness.

1.   The conflict motif we have already noted in Mark continues throughout chapter 3 and that theme can be traced through into chapter5.

It is in this context that Jesus chooses his twelve apostles (3:13–19). Notice their three functions (3:14–15). What are they? In one sense these apostles ('sent ones') have unique qualifications for a unique role; in another sense, we too are called to fellowship with Christ (*1 Cor.* 1:9; *Phil.* 3:10–14), to be witnesses to him (*Phil.* 2:15) and possess his authority (*John* 15:7–8). How should this threefold calling give structure to our lives?

What are some of the ways this works out in practice?

2.   In proving that he is not in league with the devil, Jesus gives the disciples a general spiritual principle (3:27); how does it apply to our witness as Christians today?

3.   Jesus suggests that in the course of their hostility to him some of the teachers of the law have come close to committing an unforgivable sin – blasphemy against the Holy Spirit (3:28–30).

It has been said that in giving counsel to people who believe they have committed this sin we should say: 'Let us talk first about your sins which can be forgiven.' What do you think can be of help in that approach?

4.   The coming of the kingdom may create a conflict in our priorities: kingdom or family (3:31–35). What biblical principles help us here? (See *Exod.* 20:12; *1 Cor.* 7:25–38; *Eph.* 5:21–6:4; *Col.* 3:18–21; *1 Pet.* 3:1–7.)

5.   Parables are more than 'earthly stories with a heavenly meaning'. The parable of the sower and the soils in Mark 4:1–20 in fact continues the theme of conflict and opposition. In it Jesus reveals the nature of heart–opposition to the message of the kingdom. Explore his analysis in terms of his four categories of

hearers (vv. 4, 15; vv. 5–6, 16; vv. 7, 18–19; vv. 8, 20) and apply what he says to your own life in the contemporary world.

How, then, should we apply the parable of the light and the two parables about the seeds?

6. Mark 4:35–5:13 brings this section to an end with two stories which demonstrate Jesus' authority in conflict situations; over the disorders in nature and in an individual human life. Yet neither story has the 'happy ending' we might expect (see 4:41a and 5:19) – at least at first glance. But a comparison of Acts 12:6 with Mark 4:38 and Mark 5:20 with 8:31 may suggest a different story. How?

FOR STUDY 4:

(i) Read Mark 5:21–6:29 and chapters 20–24 of the text.
(ii) Pray for and take an opportunity to tell someone about the great things the Lord has done for you.

STUDY 4: Mark 5:21–6:29

AIM: To see that the power of Christ and his kingdom is accompanied by deep humility, compassion and grace and that this is part of the offence of the kingdom.

1.   In this series of events in Jesus' ministry the continuing echo of opposition and rejection may be heard (note particularly 5:40; 6:3–5; 6:11). But against that dark background the power and grace of the kingdom emerges.

   The 'split-screen' technique Mark uses in 5:21–43 highlights the contrast as well as the similarities between the needy woman and the young girl. It also sheds light on several important things about Jesus: his care for women, his love for both young and old; his ability to meet every need; his poise and his patience.

   Consider him as an example for Christians in each of these respects.

   In what ways do you fall short of his example? List the kind of things you need to pray that his Spirit will work into your life too.

2.   Paul says that the cross and the humility and suffering of Christ are an offence to people (*1 Cor.* 1:18). That principle is relevant in Mark 6:2–3. What is it about Christ, or about his disciples that proves to be a particular stumbling block today? Is there anything about Christ or the way he leads us that we are in danger of finding an offence?

3.   John the Baptist was at one time in danger of taking offence at Jesus (see *Luke* 7:18–23). Instead it is clear that he grew increasingly like Christ, so that Herod superstitiously feared that Jesus was John raised from the dead! From the narrative of John's faithfulness in 6:14–29, identify John's Christ-like qualities and the reactions they evoked (for example, in vv. 19, 20).

   How, if at all, should John's example in 6:18 be applied in our relationships with others today?

4.   Is Herod's ambivalent attitude to John repeated in the attitude of non-Christians to believers today?

FOR STUDY 5:
  (i) Read Mark 6:30–7:23 and chapters 25–29 of the text.
  (ii) Commit yourself to growing more like Christ in one specific detail of your life. Notice what you discover as a result.

[286]

STUDY 5: Mark 6:30–7:23

AIM: To see the continuing advance of the kingdom in Jesus' ministry of power and compassion, and to consider the hardness of heart that remains both in believers and unbelievers.

1. In this section of Mark (extending to 8:30), Jesus regularly withdraws outside of the region of Galilee. A striking feature of the narrative is the frequent reference to 'bread', 'loaves' or 'food' (as in 6:37; 6:52; 7:2; 7:19; 7:27; 8:5; 8:14). Jesus himself is the Bread of Life and meets all of the needs of his people (see *John* 6:32–35).

Notice our Lord's concern that his disciples should 'get some rest' (6:31) following the exertions of their mission in 6:12. Why was this important? (Compare the example of God's dealings with Elijah in 1 Kings 19:1–9.) What do you think are some of the wider implications of the fact that Christ is concerned for the physical well-being of his servants? Can we apply this to our own ministry to e.g. returning missionaries, serving pastors and others?

2. Miracles such as the feeding of the five thousand are works of power. But at least two other elements are involved: they are expressions of compassion and signs of the kingdom's presence. In what ways are these characteristics seen in this miracle? Is there any significance in the fact that the miracle of feeding is incidental to Jesus' teaching, and not vice-versa?

3. A further characteristic of miracles in Scripture is that they often preserve and deliver God's people in times of great pressure or severe opposition. Apart from that context some miracles might appear to trivialise God's power. Mark 6:45ff is a case in point. Trace this pattern in other miracles in the Old and New Testaments.

4. How is it possible to witness Christ's power as the disciples did and yet have hearts that are hardened (*Mark* 6:52)? In what ways do you think this happens in your own life?

5. In 7:1–23, Jesus deals with 'the traditions of the elders' (7:5). How would you define these in Jesus' time, and in our own? For what does Jesus criticise them (7:6–15)?

How can we apply Jesus' teaching in 7:17–23?

FOR STUDY 6:
(i) Read Mark 7:24–8:38 and chapters 30–36 of the text.
(ii) List the specific ways in which you have a tendency to hardness of heart, and provide a biblical remedy for each.

STUDY 6: Mark 7:24–8:38

AIM: To see in Jesus and the events of his ministry examples for the Christian witness to imitate.

1.   Wherever Jesus goes (and in this section of the Gospel he seems to be on the move almost constantly) the presence and power of the kingdom is illustrated.

Jesus' conversation with the Syro-phoenician woman is sometimes misread. Notice that his purpose in his words in 7:27 seems to be to test for and to evoke the very faith which is expressed in 7:28. Is there a lesson here to help us in our witness to and conversation with people?

2.   The significance of the healing of the deaf mute (7:31–37) is given to us in 7:37 with its echo of Isaiah 35:5–6. The 'deep sigh' of v. 34 is of special interest as an expression of profound emotion on Jesus' part, reminiscent of 8:12 (see also *John* 11:35, 38). Clearly Jesus' emotional experience was rich and varied.

If the coming of the kingdom does not stifle emotion, but cleanses it, what impact does that have on our own lives?

3.   It is often claimed that the feeding of the four thousand in 8:1–13 is simply a crude repetition of the earlier feeding miracle in 6:30ff. This, it is sometimes said, is an 'assured result of modern scholarship'. In fact, however, that position is held by those who do not believe the first miracle of feeding took place. What details in the text indicate that in Mark's mind this was a distinct miracle?

4.   From time to time in church history there have been those who have insisted that 'miracles' are major evangelistic tools. Notice, however, that in the wake of both feeding miracles the disciples give expression to their spiritual frailty (6:52; 7:15). What did they 'still not understand' (8:21)?

Are there important lessons here?

5.   Jesus' actions in giving sight to the blind man at Bethsaida (8:22ff) seem to carry parabolic significance for the disciples (they too need a 'second touch').

The opening of the disciples' eyes involves the confession of

Christ's identity (8:27–30), but also an understanding of his ministry as suffering servant and discipleship as a life of cross-bearing. Is there some sense in which the same may be true for us as contemporary Christians?

6.   (i) In an age when we are constantly told the importance of 'loving ourselves', how are we to respond to Jesus' teaching that we must deny ourselves and lose our lives (8:34–35)?

(ii) Are there any ways in which you are in danger of being ashamed of Christ (8:38)

(iii) If this section is the 'turning point' in the Gospel (Ferguson, pp. 127, 146), how can its teaching be a 'turning point' in our Christian lives?

FOR STUDY 7:

(i)   Read Mark 9:1–50 and chapters 37–42 of the text.

(ii)   Make a list of several people you know (or have contact with, however slight) who are disadvantaged in some way. Pray for each of them and plan a specific way of being an instrument of Christ's blessing to each of them.

STUDY 7: Mark 9:1–50

AIM: To see illustrated in the Gospel narrative the New Testament principle that while the kingdom of Christ has already been inaugurated in the world and in his disciples, it is not yet fully realised.

1. Mark 9:1 is one of the most enigmatic statements in the Gospel. It may refer to (i) the resurrection and Pentecost and the consequent expansion of the kingdom; or (ii) the transfiguration. In fact we see the power of the kingdom in both. Mark 9 therefore presents us with a stark contrast: the power of the king and the sinful weakness of the disciples; the presence of the kingdom *already* and the fact that it has *not yet* come fully.

This is a key to the New Testament's teaching on the basic structure of the Christian life. We live between the 'already' and the 'not yet' (cf., for example, *1 John* 3:1–2).

Read Rom. 6:1–14, Eph. 4:17–5:21 and Col. 3:1–16 in the light of this pattern, and state their teaching in terms of it.

2. The transfiguration of Jesus illustrates the tremendous transforming power of the kingdom of God. That transformation takes place now (*2 Cor.* 3:18) and will be consummated in the future. Read Phil. 3:20–21 and 1 Cor. 15:42–49 and consider the application of this in the light of 1 John 3:1–3 and Rom. 12:1–2.

3. This further display of glory by Jesus created fear in the hearts of the disciples (9:6, cf. 4:41; *Rev.* 1:17). Why should this be the case? Why does this 'fear' reappear in 9:32?

4. Again Peter is the spokesman for the disciple band (cf. 8:29), but stumbles spiritually and says the wrong thing (cf. 8:32; 14:27–31, 66–72). How would you analyse Peter's failure?

Read through 1 Peter and note down the verses in it which help us to avoid stumbling.

5. The story of the demon-possessed boy underlines the necessity of faith ('unbelieving', v. 19; 'him who believes', v. 23; 'I do believe', v. 24). Later Jesus seems to relate this to prayer (v. 29). What is the relationship between faith and prayer and how does faith operate in prayer? (See *James* 5:13–18; *John* 15:7).

6.   The pride of the disciples emerges in what follows (9:33–50).
What remedy for it does Jesus prescribe? Compare the analysis of
James in James 4:1–12.

FOR STUDY 8:
 (i) Read Mark 10:1–52 and chapters 43–48 of the text.
(ii) Use 1 Peter as an additional Bible reading this week.

STUDY 8: Mark 10:1–52

AIM: To see how life in the kingdom of God contrasts with all this-worldly perspectives.

1.   It is probably significant that Jesus is in the territory ruled by Herod when the Pharisees test his 'views' on divorce (10:2, cf. 6:14–29). His answer is a model for us whenever we are 'tested' intellectually about the Christian faith.

Jesus: (i) appeals to Scripture. So too did the Pharisees (v. 4). By contrast with them, however, Jesus appeals to the design of God; the Pharisees distorted God's legal restrictions on man's sinfulness into licence;

(ii) refuses to take our sinful condition as normative; God's design is normative.

Ferguson comments on the extent to which the disciples had been influenced in their thinking by their environment. To what extent is that true of the church today in this area? How can we put Rom. 12:1–2 into practice here?

Ferguson also refers to the exception clause in Matthew's version of this narrative (*Matt.* 19:9) and to 1 Cor. 7:15ff. How are these passages to be understood and applied?

2.   Even the disciples were guilty of having their thoughts conformed to a this-worldly pattern and are rebuked. Why?

Jesus says, 'The kingdom of God belongs to such as these [children]' (10:14). Who are these children, and in what sense is the kingdom theirs? What are the practical implications of these words in terms of the privileges and responsibilities of both parents and children in a believing home?

3.   The rich ruler is not an isolated case of riches which bring spiritual poverty. The New Testament often sees addiction to wealth or possessions as a major spiritual stumbling block. See such passages as: Mark 4:19; Luke 6:24ff; 12:21; Col. 3:5; 1 Tim. 6:9–10; James 5:1–6. But what principle does Jesus give us (in 10:29–31) to help avoid this snare?

4.   Martin Luther used to distinguish what he called 'the theology of glory' (the church in its pomp and ritual, riches and power)

from 'the theology of the cross'. How are these two theologies illustrated in Mark 10:35–45 and also in the experience of Bartimaeus in 10:46–52?

FOR STUDY 9:
 (i) Read Mark 11:1–33 and chapters 49–50 of the text.
(ii) Note down the ways in which you are personally tempted to 'let the world squeeze you into its mould' (*Rom.* 12:2, J. B. Phillips' translation). How can your mind be renewed and your life transformed in these areas?

STUDY 9: Mark 11:1-33

AIM: To see the way in which Jesus' majesty and grace as the promised Messiah are revealed and to see the implications of this for the Christian life.

1.   Mark 11 is an extended description of Jesus' regal presence as he enters Jerusalem at the beginning of the Passion Week, the record of which dominates Mark's Gospel. Here again the underlying question of 4:41; 8:29 and 14:61 is being answered in terms of Jesus' fulfilment of prophecy, his personal humility and his messianic authority.

Ferguson describes Jesus' riding into Jerusalem as his 'crossing the Rubicon'. In what sense was this true?

2.   Elements about the triumphal entry prophesied in Zechariah 9:9 suggest messianic humility (cf. *Matt.* 11:28–30). In what ways were these characteristics displayed by Jesus throughout his ministry, and especially in this last week?

Other elements are reminiscent of the transfiguration in the way in which Jesus' majesty is revealed (9:2ff). In what ways does his triumphal entry give hints of his ascension and his final glory (cf. *Psa.* 24:1ff)?

3.   Mark 11:11 portrays a very natural human act on Jesus' part. What would have been in his mind as he 'looked around at everything'?

4.   In the light of 1 Peter 4:17, how would you apply 11:15–17 today to (i) the church in general; (ii) your church; (iii) yourself?

Is the meaning of cursing of the fig tree still applicable to the Christian church? See Rev. 2:5; 3:16.

5.   11:22–25 seems to suggest we can ask for what we like, but the rest of Jesus' teaching suggests that the faith which receives answers to prayer always operates in the context of God's Word and promises (*John* 15:5–8). Hence the exhortation in v. 22. Notice, too, the moral qualifications for true prayer in v. 25. How does all this fit together?

Since the Dead Sea is visible from the Mount of Olives it is possible that v. 23 should be read as a specific reference to the dramatic events described in Zech. 14:1ff, especially v. 4.

Several allusions to Zechariah occur in the Passion narrative (cf. also *Zech.* 9:9 with *Mark* 11:1–10; *Zech.* 13:7 with *Mark* 14:27).

6.   Commenting on Mark 11:27–33, Ferguson says that 'We would do well to learn from him [Jesus] how to respond to cynical opponents of the gospel.' What does he mean? Can you think of some practical illustrations?

FOR STUDY 10:
 (i) Read Mark 12:1–44 and chapters 51–56 of the text.
 (ii) If meekness and humility were the only personal characteristics in himself to which Jesus drew attention, in what specific areas of your life does that present a challenge to grow in Christlikeness?

STUDY 10: Mark 12:1–44

AIM: To study the kingdom authority of Jesus and to see its implications in the lives of those who serve him.

1.   Mark further develops his portrait of the authority of Jesus in establishing his kingdom in chapter 12. At no point is Jesus a tragic and passive victim of events. Rather Mark portrays his complete control over his circumstances. His death results from the timing of his actions, not those of his enemies (Mark 14:2 indicates the extent to which this is so).

What were the 'signals' Jesus gave in the parable in 12:1–11 that it was being told 'against' the religious leaders (v. 12).

2.   Jesus' teaching unites against him those who would otherwise be hostile to each other (for example, Pharisees, v. 13, and Sadducees, v. 18. See also *Luke* 23:12). Is this still true, in your experience? How did he respond?

3.   Ferguson applies Jesus' words in 12:17 as follows: 'The man who is devoted to God does not make the issue of his political freedom the number one priority in his life. He knows that he can serve God, freely in his heart, under the most oppressive of regimes' (p. 193).

Is this true? Does it mean that Christians will always accept the status quo?

4.   The error of the Sadducees was that they did not 'know the Scriptures or the power of God' (12:24). How does Jesus show up their ignorance?

What does it mean in practical terms for you to know the Scriptures and the power of God?

5.   Jesus recognised that the teacher of the law mentioned in 12:28 expressed a different spirit in his question. But what did Jesus mean by saying that he was 'not far from the kingdom of God'? Why did this reply bring all questioning of Jesus to an end? How did it intimate what Jesus would spell out clearly in vv. 38–40?

6.   Mark 12:41–44 is clearly intended to draw a further contrast between the 'theology of glory' and the 'theology of the cross'.

The religious leaders are dismissed; the impoverished widow is commended and welcomed. What is there about her action which illustrates the principles of the life of the kingdom?

Ferguson's application of this passage to the Christian's giving reflects the influence of 2 Cor. 8. How does that passage work out in detail the principles of this woman's giving?

FOR STUDY 11:
(i) Read Mark 13:1–37 and chapters 57–59 of the text.
(ii) Examine your personal finances. Are you being a faithful steward of them?

STUDY 11: Mark 13:1–37

AIM: To learn some of the practical implications for the first disciples and for ourselves of Jesus' teaching about the future.

1. Mark 13 is widely recognised as the most difficult chapter in the Gospel to interpret with any degree of certainty. Unfortunately that fact does not prevent some Christians regarding their interpretation as the *only* tenable one. Ferguson suggests that the context of Jesus' teaching is an important clue to its content. He says that it is 'the destruction of the temple and the city [of Jerusalem] – which is the centrepiece of Jesus' discussion'. He takes the view that the disciples assumed this implied the end of the age, and that Jesus is helping them to distinguish these two events – the first is only a forerunner of the second.

Trace Ferguson's view through 13:1–31 to make sure you follow it. Does it make good sense of the passage?

2. Notice Jesus' exhortations: 'Watch out that no one deceives you' (v. 5); 'do not be alarmed' (v. 7); 'be on your guard' (vv. 9, 23); 'do not worry' (v. 11); 'flee to the mountains' (v. 14); 'pray' (v. 18); 'if anyone says "Look, here is Christ". . . do not believe it' (v. 21); 'learn this lesson from the fig tree' (v. 28); 'Watch' (v. 37). What is the basis for these exhortations?

3. Why do you think Jesus told the disciples what he did in v. 32? Why, despite this, have people so often tried to predict the time of the Lord's return?

4. Jesus tells his disciples both (i) not to be surprised by suffering and (ii) not to invite it unnecessarily. What are the implications of that for the way we live as Christians in our society?

5. When Christ returns people will be either 'sleeping' or 'watching' (vv. 36–37). These two verbs summarise the two attitudes to Christ's return described elsewhere in the New Testament. Make a list of the characteristics you find in the following passages: Rom. 13:11–14; 1 Cor. 15:50–58; 2 Cor. 5:1–11; Phil. 3:20–4:1; Col. 3:4–11, 23–24; 1 Thess 5:1–11; 1 Pet. 1:3–9; 2 Pet. 3:11–15; 1 John 3:1–3.
What can you do to be ready for the Lord's return?

FOR STUDY 12:
 (i) Read Mark 14:1–52 and chapters 60–65 in the text.
 (ii) Use as additional Bible readings this week the passages in point 5 (above).

STUDY 12: Mark 14:1–52

AIM: To see the love of Christ and to learn to love him more.

1. Apparently the only bodies which could not be anointed in preparation for burial after death were those of executed criminals. The anointing of Jesus by the anonymous woman in this passage therefore anticipates his impending Passion.

Her action displayed her unreserved commitment to and love for Christ. In addition her deed pointed to the meaning of Jesus' ministry. The reactions to it similarly revealed what was in the hearts of the observers. Is it true that all expressions of our love for Christ have this effect? Can you illustrate this from your own experience?

How can we distinguish between an unreserved and commendable love for Jesus and an action that is actually foolish? Does this passage teach us how to respond to some actions of other Christians that seem to us to be a foolish waste?

What is the last thing you would ever give to Jesus?

2. Why do you think it seems that this action had a significant effect on Judas Iscariot (14:10–11)? Does Satan still use evidences of grace in others to stir up a sinful response in either unbelievers or believers (*John* 13:2, 27–30)? How would we recognise and guard against his activity in our own lives (see *Eph.* 6:10–18; *1 Pet.* 5:8–9; *Rev.* 12:7–11)?

3. It is not stated in Mark's Gospel that at the Last Supper Jesus was inaugurating the Lord's Supper, perhaps because those who read the Gospel were expected to know this (cf. *1 Cor.* 11:23–26).

Note down what you think of when you take the Lord's Supper.

Ferguson states that if we follow Mark's account, there are four key elements in the Supper: (i) the new covenant; (ii) Christ himself; (iii) communion with Christ; (iv) the incompleteness of our present experience, until Christ returns. How do these show us the love of Christ and call forth our love for him? Are these central in your own thoughts? What helps us to make them so?

4. Responding to Jesus' prophecy of the failure of the disciples' failure to love him as he deserved, Peter again emerges as their spokesman (14:27–31). His words underline how little he really knew himself. How can we learn from Peter's mistakes to be more sensitive to our spiritual weakness, and what precautions can we take against it?

5. Ferguson notes that the 'cup' to which Jesus refers in Gethsemane is identified in the Old Testament prophets. Look up the references he gives (*Isa.* 51:17, 22; *Jer.* 25:15, 17; *Ezek.* 23:31–33; *Hab.* 2:16). List the effects of drinking the cup, and then read through the Passion narratives in the Gospels taking note of the ways in which these Old Testament descriptions are fulfilled in Jesus' experience. This is what Paul means when he says that God 'did not spare' Christ (*Rom.* 8:32).

    Why should this account lead to unreserved devotion to Christ?

FOR STUDY 13:
 (i) Read Mark 14:53–16:8 [20] and chapters 66–73 in the text.
(ii) Richard of Chichester prayed 'to see thee more clearly, follow thee more nearly, and love thee more dearly'. How does this passage of Scripture encourage us to new devotion to Christ?

STUDY 13: Mark 14:53–16:8[20]

AIM: To understand the meaning of Christ's death on the cross and to appreciate the strength of the testimony to his resurrection.

1.   Under oath (*Matt.* 27:63) Jesus revealed his identity and thus answers the question which underlies the whole of Mark's Gospel. The three titles used in 14:61–62 are understood to be claims to divine identity, hence the death sentence of 14:63–64 which God himself would later reverse.

Each title (Messiah, Son of Man, Son of God) carries its own significance which can be studied with the aid of a Bible dictionary or traced in a concordance. Briefly state what each title means and why it is important for a full understanding of Jesus and his ministry.

2.   In Mark 14, both Judas and Peter sin. Is it significant that the other disciples did not know the truth about Judas? In the light of this, Ferguson asks what the difference is between them. Does Scripture shed any light on that question?

What is the difference, if any, between backsliding and apostasy?

3.   The early Christians saw in the Passion narrative the fulfilment of Isaiah 52:13–53:12. Read over that passage and make a list of the ways in which it appears to be fulfilled in the events of Jesus' suffering.

In 15:16–41 Ferguson sees Christ revealed as Prophet, Priest and King. How do these three (messianic) roles help us to understand the significance of his work?

4.   The reference to Alexander and Rufus in Mark 15:21 seems to suggest that they were known to the author or first readers of this Gospel and suggests that these sons of Simon who took up the cross and followed Christ were later converted. Reflect on this as an illustration of what Paul says about his ministry in 2 Cor. 4:7–12.

5.   From this passage, how would you answer the question: What does the Gospel of Mark tell us about the significance of the

cross?

6. The Gospel concludes with the resurrection of Jesus. With what arguments against the resurrection are you familiar? Work through Mark 15:42–16:8 and note from Mark's account of the Gospel reasons why the resurrection is well-attested.

REVIEW:

(i) Read through Mark's Gospel at one sitting.

(ii) Write down the chief lessons you have learned from your study of Mark's Gospel.

FOR FURTHER READING

L. A. Cole: *Mark*, Tyndale New Testament Commentary, Leicester, IVP, 1989

W. L. Lane, *The Gospel According to Mark*, New International Commentary on the New Testament, Grand Rapids, Mich., Eerdmans, 1974